Thinking Rugby

Thinking Rugby

TRAINING YOUR MIND FOR PEAK PERFORMANCE

Ken Hodge, Ph.D. & Alex McKenzie, Ph.D.

School of Physical Education, University of Otago

REED

Published by Reed Books, a division of Reed Publishing (New Zealand) Ltd,
39 Rawene Road, Birkenhead, Auckland 10. Associated branches, companies
and representatives throughout the world.

ISBN 0 7900 0666 9

Edited by Peter Dowling
Designed by Michele Stutton; typeset by Graeme Leather
Cover photo: Neil Mackenzie/Photosport
Photos courtesy of the *Otago Daily Times*, except page 52 (Farah Palmer) and
page 84 (Monique Hirovanaa).

First published 1999

Printed in New Zealand

Contents

Preface

> Be quick in your decision, and be quick to act upon it.
>
> To be caught in two minds is fatal. The hesitating player is a danger to his side . . .
>
> Always discuss the plan of action very thoroughly with your colleagues just
> before going on the field, so that there shall be a very complete understanding
> all round as to what is to be attempted and how . . .
>
> Think over all the incidents of the last match in your leisure hours, and particularly
> try to recall some of the most successful and the most unsuccessful tactics,
> and draw the morals from them to the best of your ability. This private study is very
> beneficial, and tends to make a player use his head more when he plays the game . . . [1]

These quotes seem like the latest offering from an elite player or coach of the 1990s. Remarkably, they were in fact written by the Dave Gallaher and Billy Stead, captain and vice-captain respectively of the legendary 1905 All Black team. As you can see, 'thinking rugby' is not a new idea: mental skills have been a key part of successful rugby performance since the game began!

As an interactive team game that demands complex tactical decision-making, rugby has long been regarded by coaches as the ultimate thinking game. Rugby challenges us to be strong, fit, skilful, and smart; but most of all it challenges us to be *mentally tough*! To be a consistent player, and be part of a consistent team, every player needs to develop excellent thinking skills. Combining these skills and psychological factors such as motivation, commitment, and concentration are vital for the mentally tough rugby player. But how do you develop or train these thinking skills?

In this book we provide you, as a player or coach, with practical psychological skills ('thinking skills') that you can use to improve your performance and enjoyment in rugby. *Thinking Rugby* targets the 'serious' rugby player or coach; but you don't have to be an elite player or coach to use these skills and methods. Psychological skills are applicable to any level of rugby and just like physical, technical, and tactical skills they should be modified for your age and level of rugby development. A coach teaching physical or technical skills to Small Blacks rather than the All Blacks would teach them at a simplified level, and these thinking skills should be tailored in the same way: we have taught them to players as young as eleven or twelve as well as to seasoned representative players.

The emphasis that mental toughness places on thinking skills and psychological factors sometimes prompts players and coaches to talk of using a 'shrink' — a psychologist who attempts to 'shrink' mental problems. But rather than focusing on shrinking problems, we regard the focus of mental toughness as being on stretching capabilities — so rather than being called 'shrinks' we prefer to be called 'stretches'! And as stretches we believe in the old rugby cliche that the game is played in the 'top six inches'. Consequently the goal of mental toughness training is to 'put an old head on young shoulders', so that all players can make good use of that 'top six inches'!

Between the two of us we have 52 years' rugby-playing experience and 18 years' rugby-coaching experience in New Zealand, the U.S., and Canada. In addition, between us we have 16 years' experience teaching thinking skills and mental toughness training to rugby coaches and players. Through that collective experience we feel that we have accumulated considerable knowledge about psychological needs, thinking skills, and mental toughness training relevant to rugby.

While we both work as sport psychology consultants and lecturers in sport and exercise psychology, we have not written this book with those roles in mind. Also, while we have completed research on psych skills in rugby, we have not written this book as a research book either. *We have written this book because we love rugby and want to put something practical and useful back into our great game.*

How to use this book

Thinking Rugby is a practical resource book that draws on the programme of Psych Skills Training (PST) developed in Ken's book *Sport Motivation*. It is designed to take you step-by-step through the process of developing a PST programme tailored to your needs. This programme incorporates the development of appropriate PST skills, and includes many practical methods and evaluation techniques. It provides you with the basic sportpsych information for designing a new PST programme or evaluating your current programme, with the help of worksheets, examples, and case studies.

Start with Part I for an introduction to key terms and concepts, and planning your PST programme. After completing your Peak Performance Profile and identifying your psych skill needs you may wish to go directly to the relevant PST skill chapters in Part II and complete the specific skill worksheets before you choose the methods you will use to train each skill. On the other hand, you may choose to skim read all of Parts II and III before you begin to put together your PST programme. The choice is yours.

The Psych Skills Training programme is not designed to over-complicate your rugby or your training. Not all of the information in this book will be necessary for your personal PST needs. If it ain't broke, don't fix it — only change or try to fix your psych skills training if it isn't working.

Acknowledgements

Thanks to the following people who offered excellent feedback and suggestions for improvement on drafts of this book.

Rugby:
Anton Oliver (All Black, 1995–)
Josh Kronfeld (All Black, 1995–)
Farah Palmer (Captain, Black Ferns, 1997–)
Steve Martin (Rugby Manager, Otago Rugby Union)
Murray Roulston (Coaching Coordinator, Otago Rugby Union)

SportPsych:
Jeremy Dugdale (University of Otago / University of Western Australia)
Kylie Wilson (University of Otago / University of Wales, Bangor)
Dave Hadfield (Massey University)

Thanks are also due to the *Otago Daily Times* for the generous help of their staff in sourcing photographs.

Finally, we are very grateful for the excellent advice and help received from Peter Janssen, Peter Dowling and Alison Southby of Reed Publishing.

Part I

What is 'Thinking Rugby'?

The whole game is thought, gone is the day of brute strength and ignorance. Rugby is a game of thought. Play the game at pace and be a thinker.

— JACK GLEESON (ALL BLACK COACH 1977–78)

1. The basis of 'Thinking Rugby'

SCENARIO 1: Jack

Jack plays number eight for a senior club team. He has been on the edge of selection for the provincial rep team for the past four years but until this season has only managed a few games for the B team — mainly because he was an inconsistent player. His form fluctuated from week to week and he was guilty of losing concentration, not following the game plan, and making key mistakes in most games. However, this season he has been selected for the rep team after an outstanding club season in which he has been very consistent and has reduced his error rate considerably. He seems to have the golden touch. He invariably makes 5 metres-plus off the back of the scrum, his option-taking for backrow moves has been superb, he has barely missed a tackle all season, and his support play has been brilliant. Jack's fitness and skill levels are no different to other seasons: the difference is in the way that he mentally prepares for each game. In the past Jack used to rely on the coach and captain to get him psyched-up and focused for the game, but this season he has taken charge of his own mental preparation and commitment, and as a result he has developed the key characteristic that all top players must have — mental toughness.

SCENARIO 2: Bob

Bob is the first five-eighth for the same provincial rep team as Jack. He has been a regular in the team for the past three years and in that time has played some pretty good rugby without ever being brilliant. His major strengths have been his calm decision-making, his option-taking and his superb goal kicking. This year, however, he is struggling to keep his place in the rep team after a poor club season (by his standards). On top of that, in the pre-season rep team matches he has struggled badly with his goal kicking and his general play has suffered as his confidence in his goal kicking has slipped. Previously Bob hadn't needed to practise his goal kicking much — he reckoned he was a natural — but now he is at a loss as to how to fix his kicking game.

And, since he is so worried about his goal kicking, his confidence in decision-making and option-taking is also low and he has become a nervous and tentative player, letting his teammates make the 'calls'. The game he loves, which has come naturally to him up until now, is fast becoming a personal hell. To make matters worse, he was heavily late-tackled in the first game for the rep team and is now very worried about being injured in another late tackle. Opposing teams are now 'targeting' him, his teammates don't seem to have any confidence in him, and he is under enormous pressure from his coach to 'sort himself out' or be dropped from the team.

What would you do to fix things if you were Bob?

Why do you think Jack was able to improve his game so easily?
As this book progresses, these two questions will be answered. After completing psych skills assessments for Jack and Bob (see the Peak Performance Profiles for each player on pages 40–41), we will design PST programmes for them (pages 42–43), and then we will use these two players as examples for the psych skills or methods explained in the chapters that follow.

At the start of this season Jack needed to commit himself to his rugby and his training, take control of his own pre-game psych-up, sharpen up his concentration, and be a more cohesive team player, following the team's game plan. On the other hand, Bob now needs to gain some self-confidence, learn how to cope with pressure, regain his concentration, improve his decision-making, and pick up his on-field communication.

How are you going to help Bob? What did Jack do to turn things around?
Using the example of Jack's training programme and the skills and methods outlined in this book, you will be able to design a training plan for Bob — and identify your own training needs.

What sort of training plans are we talking about here? We prefer the label of Psych Skills Training (PST), but we also call it Mental Toughness Training and some players and coaches like to label it Mental Skills Training. The name doesn't matter, as long as you understand the principles of psych training and feel motivated to put the effort into improving your own mental toughness.

Who needs psych training?

Some players and coaches dismiss psych training as unnecessary for tough rugby players, or claim that such skills can't be trained ('you've either got them or you don't!') But like many other sport scientists, players, coaches and refs,[1] we think psych skills are a lot like physical skills: some people do have natural abilities (but still need to fine-tune them), while most of us need to work hard through planned practice and consistent training.

The difference between international rugby and provincial rugby is a mental difference. Physically, most provincial players are prepared well enough to play international rugby. However, there is a certain mental adjustment required to foot it at the international level. The game is faster and harder. One mistake can cost a match at test level. Decision-making needs to be more accurate. These facets are either reproduced correctly or incorrectly through mental preparation, application, and confidence.

– MIKE BREWER (ALL BLACK 1986–95)

There are those who reckon that, while psych training does have a place for age-group players and development squads, it is unnecessary for senior and elite rugby players because such players already have a high level of mental toughness.[2] Such a belief has some superficial logic to it, but players at the top level still need a coach and most now have specialised fitness trainers as well. If you need specialised coaching and fitness advice, why wouldn't you also use a 'mental coach'? If you want to be the best player you can be, you should train *all* aspects of your rugby skill needs.

Mental Toughness

Coaches often refer to 'mental strength' and 'mental toughness' when attempting to describe that elusive quality that distinguishes the great players from the good ones at any level of rugby. Players who consistently handle pressure well are often called 'mentally hard' players, while those not so consistent are often told to 'get hard'. Indeed, this book follows the theme of 'get hard or go home' — if you are not prepared to put the effort into psych skills training there is little point in reading this book or expecting to reach your potential. However, if you are willing to put considerable effort into the mental side of your game then read on.

> Toughness to me isn't an aggressive, over-the-top attitude. . . . Some people are physically tough, but they might not be emotionally or mentally tough. Some people have it all, but others are mentally babies. They can go and smash someone, but if they get smashed, they back down. I think toughness is really a mindset where you react in a game situation without even having to think about it, question it. . . . If you're not prepared to believe in yourself and have a go, you may as well pack your bags and go home.
>
> — Zinzan Brooke (All Black 1987–97)

Typically we focus on the 'horsepower' aspect of rugby performance and train hard to improve our fitness, speed and strength to go alongside our rugby skills such as passing and kicking. However, we often neglect the 'willpower' aspect of rugby performance — our psych skills and mental toughness. Jack (our number eight on page 12) is a classic example of a player who trained hard, had good skills, but wasn't mentally tough enough.

$$Rugby\ performance = horsepower + willpower$$

This basic formula is used by some coaches to describe the fundamental aspects of rugby performance. However, just increasing the training focus on 'willpower' will *not* turn a draughthorse player into a thoroughbred — in the first place you must have the necessary 'horsepower' for your playing position. But if you have the necessary horsepower, psych skills will help you to perform *consistently* to the best of your ability, whether that be at the thoroughbred or draughthorse level! Mental toughness or willpower is a skill; it can be trained and enhanced like the horsepower and technical skill aspects of performance.

In this book we define mental toughness in terms of achieving high skill level in each of eight areas; these are Commitment, Confidence, Controlling activation, Coping with pressure, Concentration, team Cohesion, Captaincy and Communication. These *8 C's of Peak Performance*, which will be described in Part II, can be trained to help each player and the team gain what players often refer to as the 'mental edge'.

The mental edge

Since they won the 1987 World Cup the All Blacks have focused on developing a team quality they refer to simply as 'the edge'.[3] They believe that they had the edge in 1987 when they won the inaugural World Cup, but that they failed to achieve it when they lost in the semi-finals of the 1991 World Cup. During the preparations for the 1995 World Cup the All Black team placed a lot of emphasis on achieving the edge. History shows that they lost the 1995 final in overtime, but that they were the form team at the tournament in terms of playing style and performance — in 1995

they had the edge. Indeed, in 1996–97 the All Blacks clearly demonstrated that they had the edge over their international opponents.

So what is 'the edge'? It is both a physical and mental 'edge', but primarily it boils down to *confidence* and *self-belief*. At the 1987 World Cup the All Blacks believed that they were much fitter and better prepared physically than their opponents, and in 1995 coach Laurie Mains and captain Sean Fitzpatrick were determined that the team would again have the edge. Laurie Mains designed 'brutal' training camps before the 1995 World Cup Squad was selected — specifically designed to sort out the players who had the mental toughness required to play the new high-intensity style that he had planned for the team. He knew that the confidence the players would gain from surviving the harsh physical nature of the pre-season camps would be invaluable for their mental toughness in the heat of the World Cup test matches.[4]

Why work on mental toughness?

The 3 P's = Possession, Position, Pace[5]

Charlie Saxton is famous in New Zealand rugby as a player (1938 All Blacks; 1945 Kiwi Team), selector (Otago 1948–57), manager (1967 All Black team to the UK), and administrator (New Zealand Rugby Union Council 1956–71; President 1974). He's also famous for his contribution to the playing style of New Zealand rugby. In 1960 he wrote *The ABC of Rugby*, a short coaching book in which he extolled the virtues of three key aspects of successful rugby: the 3 P's of Possession, Position and Pace. His coaching philosophy has had a significant influence on the New Zealand approach to the game over the last 35 years.[6]

However, we believe that in the 1990s, with developments in the game wrought by law changes and professionalism, we need to expand Saxton's 3 P's to the 7 P's of

Possession, Position, Pace, Physical fitness, Physical skills, Pressure and *Psych skills*. In fact, psych skills and mental toughness are a vital part of each of the other six aspects of rugby performance.

Possession: A player needs commitment and concentration in order to execute the technical ball-winning skills. You also need psych skills to help you make good tactical decisions about how to win possession — and what to do with possession when you have it.

Position: Each player needs to make smart decisions in order to gain a tactical advantage and establish field position. You also need psych skills to execute proper body-positioning and maintain the discipline to stick to the roles of your position.

Pace: As the game has sped up with the new laws, the time available for thinking and decision-making has sharply decreased. In modern, fast-paced rugby it is vital to maintain concentration, cope with pressure, and make smart decisions.

Physical fitness: The modern game is played at a very fast pace for the full 80 minutes, and the tackles and hits are harder. The increased demand for fitness, speed and strength highlights the need for psych skills such as training motivation and commitment.

Physical skills: The game has become an interesting paradox of very specialised skills for each position, as well as every player needing a set of multi-skills for catching, passing, tackling, mauling, and running (from prop all the way through to fullback). Commitment, self-confidence and concentration are required for players to develop their sets of physical skills.

> Don't accept a weakness without trying to fix it, and always work on multi-skilling yourself. The All Blacks focus on multi-skills in our training, and it's just so important for all players to achieve.
> — MARTIN TOOMEY (ALL BLACK FITNESS TRAINER 1992–)

Pressure: Physical contact pressure is part of rugby, but the mental pressure of relentless attack from the opposition and the tactical decision-making required can combine to make the game a pressure-filled, potentially stressful experience. The ability both to apply and absorb pressure characterises New Zealand rugby.[7] Bob (our first five) is currently under extreme pressure for his place in the team; he needs to be mentally tough to cope with that pressure.

Psych skills: Commitment, self-confidence, coping with pressure, concentration and decision-making — these and other psych skills are important if you are to execute the physical rugby skills successfully. To improve your psych skills and mental toughness you need to work on psych skills training.

> Rugby is a game you learn on your feet. Every game throws up a new circumstance, a new challenge. You must work out how best to overcome an awkward opponent, how you may 'think' him out of the game . . . The street-smart player, the player who thinks better and longer than his opponent, will overcome and survive.
>
> — BRIAN LOCHORE (ALL BLACK 1963–71, ALL BLACK COACH 1985–87)

From a coaching and training viewpoint it is easiest to think of these 7 P's as being jigsaw pieces that fit together to form the 'big picture' of peak performance in rugby. The development of psych skills is not a 'quick fix' or an effortless process. Developing your mental toughness will take considerable time and effort on your part. To ensure that you train 'smart', rather than just hard, take the time now to study the Thinking Rugby Jigsaw Puzzle on this page and the Peak Performance Profile in chapter 2 to help you make some decisions about what psych skills you need to work on, and the likely methods that you should practice to improve those skills.

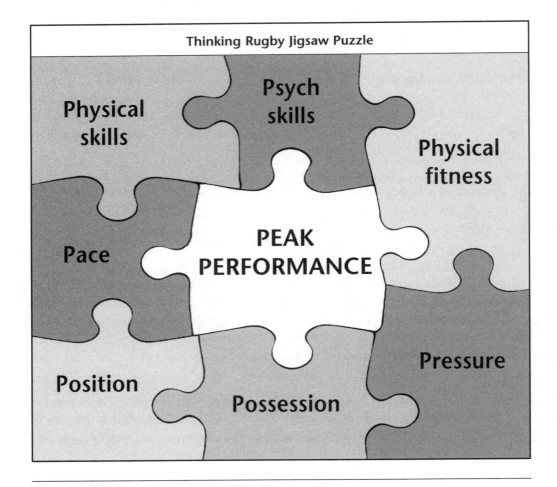

Thinking Rugby Jigsaw Puzzle

Physical skills · Psych skills · Physical fitness · Pace · PEAK PERFORMANCE · Position · Possession · Pressure

> People have told me you need to be strong, so I've got to get into the gym and do the work. If I didn't I'd have probably broken a few bones by now the way I play. It's always good to beat the forwards in the weight room. They don't like it.
>
> — CHRISTIAN CULLEN (ALL BLACK 1996–)
> ON TRAINING

Psych skills training takes time and effort

Psychological skills greatly influence performance. At the elite level there may be only 5–10 percent difference between winning and losing, between the successful and unsuccessful player — and mental toughness may account for that 5–10 percent difference! Few players develop their psych skills to the full, so there is considerable potential for improvement in psych skills when the physical and technical skills are already at their peak. Psych skills are like physical skills in that they are developed by basic skill learning, then fine-tuning, and then practice, practice, practice, which takes determination and discipline. Many successful players already possess psych skills such as motivation and self-confidence to some extent, but often they have learned them through a lengthy, haphazard trial-and-error process. Psych skills training (PST) is designed to shorten this learning process, and help you to reach your Ideal Performance State.

Ideal Performance State

The Ideal Performance State is that mood or state in which you feel totally focused, both mentally and physically, on your rugby performance and are confident that you will perform to your best; like being on 'automatic pilot'. Unfortunately the Ideal Performance State usually proves an elusive state for most players — it doesn't happen often enough!

People were a bit sceptical about a 19-year-old playing international football in the front row, but I think it was just a mental thing. If you're mentally there, and I'm already physically there, then why can't you [play international rugby]?

— Anton Oliver (All Black 1995–) after sitting on the All Blacks bench in 1995

We played ourselves to exhaustion. The backs ran and ran . . . and ran again. The endless movement as well as the physical contest drained the forwards. The boys who had not played came yahooing down from the grandstand to celebrate another win and were met with a torrent of silence. Heads were between knees or flung back with closed eyes against concrete walls; bodies draped on bodies. Nothing was said for 20 minutes. That's the most peaceful feeling you can ever have in your life — to prepare mentally and physically for a test, to take preparation onto the field, to score tries, to create the positions from which tries are scored, to see a new plan unfold and bewilder the opposition, to win thousands of miles from home in front of a marvellously partisan crowd. And, at the end of it, to be hopelessly, gloriously exhausted. That is perfect peace. That is utter fulfilment. That is why we play rugby.

— Brian Lochore commenting on the Ideal Performance State in rugby reached by the 1967 All Blacks vs France

Research has identified the Ideal Performance State as requiring the following skills:[8]

★ Mental preparation, mental readiness — control of activation.

★ Complete concentration on task at hand — concentration.

★ High degree of self-confidence — confidence.

★ High motivation and determination to do well in your sport — commitment.

★ Ability to cope with stress and anxiety — coping with pressure.

The focus of all these skills is on attaining 'the edge'. However, the Ideal Performance State is not just for elite players — it can be achieved by all players performing to their full potential.

Psych skills training is designed to help you reach your Ideal Performance State on a regular basis. To reach it, you first need to know what it is, so the PST pro-gramme outlined in this book is directed at identifying your particular Ideal Performance State, and then helping you reach it more often — to help you get into 'automatic pilot' regularly.

Peak performance

One of the most positive experiences in rugby or any sport is the feeling of peak performance.[9] Peak performance results in personal bests and outstanding achievements — the edge — and is a consequence of you achieving your Ideal Performance State.[10]

> Your mind detaches from your body a little and you go with the flow.
> — IEUAN EVANS (WELSH INTERNATIONAL 1988–96)

Peak performance occurs when there is a balance between the perceived challenges of the situation and your perceived abilities to meet the challenge.[11] Your interpretation of a challenging situation is critical — perception of your own ability and perception of the task challenge are essential. The diagram below illustrates the importance of getting a balance between the perceived challenges and your perceived abilities to meet them.

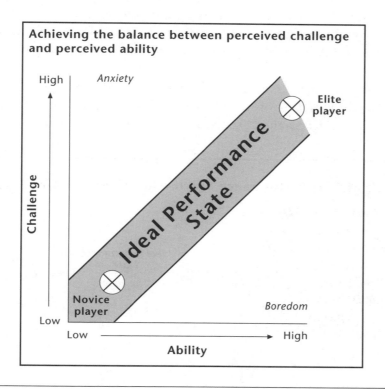

No doubt you have played with or against players who have all the ability required for playing rugby at your current level, but who are unable to perform consistently to their potential. They perform the required skills perfectly at practice or in minor games, but in big games they seldom play as well as they are capable. These players usually perceive the challenge of the big game to be beyond their abilities, and are not able to switch on their Ideal Performance State because they perceive the big game situation inaccurately. PST is designed to help players like this develop a more accurate perception of the situation and of their capability to meet the challenge of that situation.

Sport science research has revealed that players from a range of sports tended to perceive the challenge of the task as high in both their best and worst performances, but it was the perception of the necessary skills to cope with the challenge that differed markedly.[12] Skills were perceived to match the challenge in the best performance, but to be much lower than the challenge when performance was poor. To be an achiever, you have believe in yourself. *You have to believe that you have the skills to meet the challenge.*

The Ideal Performance State is related to a focus on task goals, or on 'how' to win.[13] While a task goal helps you achieve peak performance, too much of a focus on outcome goals (such as winning, or scoring a certain number of points) can hinder you from achieving peak performance.[14] If you focus exclusively on an outcome goal you may be distracted by how well you are performing compared to your opponents, or you may focus too much on the score rather than on the immediate tasks. In other words, you would be focused on winning instead of on how to win. Research has shown that nearly 88 percent of players reported an outcome focus during their worst performance.[15]

In contrast, the focus during best performances should be on skill mastery and be process-centered. This focus of attention will also be discussed later when we look at the psych skill of 'concentration' (see chapter 7). However, the bottom line is that if

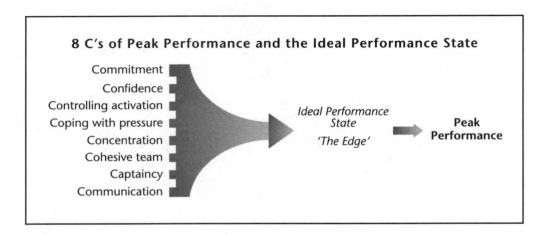

8 C's of Peak Performance and the Ideal Performance State

Commitment
Confidence
Controlling activation
Coping with pressure
Concentration
Cohesive team
Captaincy
Communication

Ideal Performance State 'The Edge'

Peak Performance

I was totally focused on everything I did. My mind didn't wander. It was one of those games where for 80 minutes . . . I thought totally on what I was doing at hand. I was real clear in what I was doing and what my job was. I knew exactly what I was trying to do.

— ARRAN PENE (ALL BLACK 1992–95)
DESCRIBING HIS 'BEST-EVER' GAME

In a case study of peak performance in rugby, All Black number eight Arran Pene identified a number of psychological characteristics that were present before and during his best and worst performances.[15] Pene indicated that before his all-time best game he was in an Ideal Performance State that included a feeling of complete confidence, a peak level of activation, and a total focus on the upcoming performance. During this game he reported a feeling of being totally concentrated on the tasks at hand and he also experienced feelings of complete confidence and control. On the other hand, before and during his worst game Pene commented that he deviated from his normal mental preparation, was not totally focused on his tasks, and experienced a number of negative thoughts and feelings, especially a lack of confidence. During this match he tended to either dwell on past events (e.g., an injury he was carrying) or spend time thinking about future ones, rather than keeping a 'right now, in-the-present' concentration focus.

The psych skill of 'focused attention' or 'peak concentration' appeared to be the key aspect of peak performance for Arran Pene. Indeed, Pene reported that the systematic use of psych skills and methods such as imagery and goal setting had played a significant role in helping him achieve his all-time best performance. He also indicated that his worst game was partially a result of being distracted and unable to stick to his PST programme.

you focus on task goals and personal standards you are more likely to achieve peak performance.

Peak performance is not about playing perfect rugby. It's about playing your best rugby on a consistent basis, and to do this you need to focus on how to win, not winning itself. The best way to adopt this focus is to work on the 8 C's of Peak Performance.

Three steps to your own Ideal Performance State

1. You must understand the distinction between task goals and outcome goals, and the enormous impact that these goals have on your performance. You must work hard to focus on task goals, since these are related to the skills that you need in order to perform well, and are goals that you have control over (see chapter 3, Motivation and commitment).

2. During the actual game it is vital that you focus mainly on task goals. That does not mean that you should never be focused on an outcome goal during the game. Winning is not a dirty word! We all want to win, but during the game you should primarily focus on how to win. It is natural that you will want to compare your competitive ability with others — after all, rugby is a competitive sport. An outcome goal can provide motivation and incentive for training just as much as a task goal, and can provide motivation and psych-up before and during the game. However, to get into your Ideal Performance State and achieve peak performance you must be primarily task-focused.

3. Since it is the perception of ability and perception of the task challenge that affects the Ideal Performance State, you need to develop a high, stable level of self-confidence in your rugby ability (see chapter 4, Self-confidence).

Summary

Remember, the Ideal Performance State contributes to both success and enjoyment in rugby. However, it doesn't often occur by chance — you need to plan your PST programme to help you have the edge. When you learn how to switch on your automatic pilot, the Ideal Performance State becomes second nature.

PST is designed to help you switch on your autopilot, but it is not intended to overcomplicate your rugby performance. You should plan a PST programme to work on the psych skill areas that you need to kick-start your autopilot and the Ideal Performance State but not necessarily to increase the amount of thinking you do. On the contrary, PST is all about limiting your thinking to the bare minimum required to help you get into your Ideal Performance State, into that wonderful mental rhythm and flow when you barely need to think at all!

One size does not fit all!

PST programmes *must* be separately designed for each individual player. To individualise your psych skills training you first need to identify your mental strengths and weaknesses — your psych skill needs — by completing one or more of the following:

★ A Peak Performance Profile (filled out by you and, if possible, your coach; see pages 38–39).

★ Interview/discussion with your coach or a sportpsych consultant.

★ Match or video observation by you, your coach or a sportpsych consultant.

The next step is to identify your key psych skill strengths and weaknesses, which will then be categorised into three types: foundation skills, performance skills and facilitative skills. These three categories, and the key distinction between psych skills and the psych methods used to attain them, are explained in detail in chapter 2.

With your individualised PST programme you will then be able to practise the right psych skills and methods required for you to reach your personal Ideal Performance State.

2. Psychological Skills Training (PST)

> You can list things like fitness, skills, concentration, talent, confidence, and you have the ingredients of a great team. If you add the main ingredient, which is a hardened attitude, then you create the awesome team.
>
> — STU WILSON (ALL BLACK 1976–83)

Psychological Skills Training focuses on you learning practical psychological (psych) skills and methods so that you can develop your thinking skills or mental toughness to the same high level as your physical abilities. Indeed, the key difference between a good performance and a poor performance may be your psych skill level rather than your physical skill level. This does not mean that psych skills are more important than physical, tactical, or technical skills. Psych skills are just one aspect of performance, and like physical skills and technical skills they need to be learned correctly, fine-tuned by the player and coach, and then practised regularly.

It is important to realise that this focus on Psych Skills Training is not just for All Blacks or rep players. These skills are equally appropriate and important for players of all ages and levels of rugby and physical performance — whether a 40-year-old Golden Oldies player, a 16-year-old age-group player, an average club player or an All Black. In fact, anyone can use PST to help them perform to their potential, and to thoroughly enjoy their rugby.

Champion players are not extraordinary people — they are ordinary people who do extraordinary things.

Top rugby players have well developed physical and technical skills, and are fit and healthy, but many top players believe that what sets them apart from those who have not reached the same level of achievement is their psych skills.

Most players know that they should be calm and focused, be positive and confident, and stay in control of their emotions. However, they don't always know how to do it. When the PST skills and methods are explained to experienced players they often respond by saying: 'I wish I'd had this information when I first started playing. I do most of this stuff now but it took me years of trial and error to figure it out!'

Many players already use these psych skills in some form or another, but it is the haphazard and often lengthy learning process they had to endure that PST is designed to eliminate. The PST programme seeks to teach you basic psych skills and methods that have both an intuitive appeal and a sound scientific basis.[1]

Using the PST programme gives you experience ahead of the time when you need to call on it. This is a big help because, as the old saying goes:

Experience is something you usually don't get until just after you need it.
— Anon

The objectives of PST

The PST programme outlined in this book has three major objectives:

★ To help *you* consistently perform to the best of your ability — performance enhancement.

★ To help *you* enjoy your rugby more by reducing stress and improving performance.

★ To help *you* develop psychological skills for use in other life situations — anxiety and stress management, commitment, leadership, communication.

The PST Programme

All players have the potential to improve some aspect of their psych abilities. The challenge is for you to identify your particular PST skill needs and then design a PST programme for yourself. The aim is to have the brain and the body working together as a team.

Remember, you should only plan a PST programme to work on the psych skill areas that you need. We all make mistakes and we all have weaknesses, but players who are committed to peak performance refuse to accept these weaknesses; they actively work to turn them into strengths.

PST Skills versus PST Methods

The starting point for identifying your psych needs is understanding the key difference between psych skills and psych methods. This distinction is vitally important for a successful PST programme, but it is often overlooked by players and coaches.

PST skills. A PST skill — competency, capability, or ability level such as peak concentration — is developed through the use of a number of PST methods.[2] The key PST skills can be categorised as follows under the headings of 'Foundation', 'Performance' and 'Facilitative' skills:

FOUNDATION SKILLS

★ Motivation

★ Commitment

★ Self-confidence

PERFORMANCE SKILLS

★ Peak physical activation

★ Peak mental activation

★ Peak concentration

★ Coping with pressure

FACILITATIVE SKILLS

★ Team cohesion (teamwork, team spirit)

★ Interpersonal skills (captaincy, communication, media skills)

★ Lifestyle management (such as planning for 'retirement')

One way to make sense of these skill categories is to think of the three categories as the structure for a PST building or house — your own PST programme. The diagram shows that like all well-constructed buildings your PST house requires a firm foundation (of Foundation PST skills) for the main part of the house (the Performance PST skills) to be built upon. Like all homes, to protect you from environmental conditions your PST house needs a roof (the Facilitative PST Skills, which 'keep the lid on things'). As the name suggests, this last category of PST skills 'facilitates' the successful execution of the other skills.

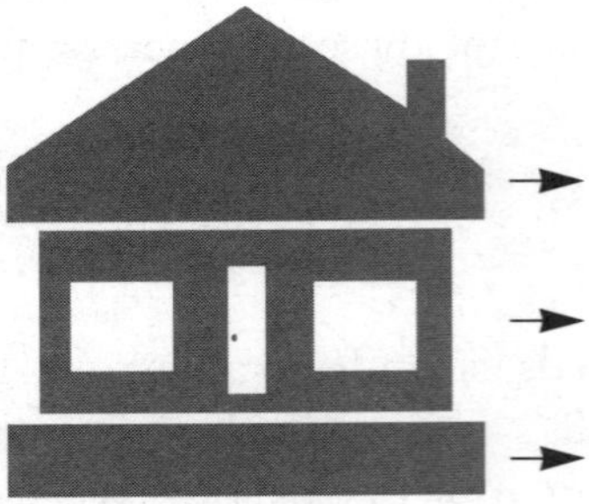

	PST Skills	Rugby example
	Facilitative PST skills	Communication of the correct 'calls'
	Performance PST skills	Backrow attacking moves Backline attacking moves
	Foundation PST skills	Stable, solid scrum

Another way of thinking about these three categories of PST skills is to use a rugby analogy (see the diagram above). Designing a PST programme is like putting together an attacking move from first-phase scrum ball. The foundation for such an attacking move is a stable scrum that goes forward. The actual performance of the move involves the accurate running of the backrow or a backline attacking move. Finally the facilitative skills required for the attacking move involve the calling and communication of the move that has been chosen — all players need to hear and understand the call or they will miss their assigned role during the attacking move (e.g., an 8-9 backrow blindside move).

PST Skills are developed through the use of a number of PST methods — just as rugby skills are developed through the use of practice drills.

PST methods. PST methods, such as imagery, goal-setting and self-talk, are techniques used to help a player develop a particular skill. A method in this sense means a procedure, technique, or drill.

FOUNDATION METHODS
★ Physical practice
★ Education (physical and psych skill requirements)
★ Peak Performance Profile

SPECIFIC PSYCH METHODS
★ Goal setting
★ Mental preparation (pre-game)
★ Imagery (visualisation)
★ Relaxation (centring)
★ Self-talk (thought control)
★ CARS plan = critical action response strategies

PST skills 'match' with PST methods. You need to select appropriate methods to practice or train in order to enhance your specific psych skill needs. For example, for the skill need of activation control (see chapter 5) a player might choose to use a number of psych methods in combination or separately:

Psych skill need = pre-game activation/psych-up

Psych methods = mental preparation, imagery, centring (short-hand relaxation), self-talk . . .

The best PST programme?
Ideally, your PST programme is an individually designed combination of PST methods selected to attain your PST skill needs. There is no 'set' or 'packaged' psych skills training programme for any one team, any one playing position, or any one type of player.

You should pick and choose and select only those PST methods needed to meet your PST skill requirements. The goal is to give yourself 'the edge' and create your Ideal Performance State. The next diagram illustrates how PST methods are matched

If you're the sort of person who likes to whistle or put on your headphones and listen to music in the changing room, you shouldn't be pressured by other people to 'act more focused' . . . Players have to try new methods and use what works for them — and it doesn't necessarily have to be what everyone else is doing. There's all sorts of different recipes for the same cake; you've just got find the right mixture for yourself.

— ZINZAN BROOKE

with PST skills and then integrated with other types of skills (such as technical skills) for enhanced performance, enjoyment and life skills.

To develop an effective PST programme for yourself, it is vital to assess your existing PST skill levels. Then your skill weaknesses can be attacked via a well planned programme of specific PST methods. Too often players and coaches focus on the teaching and learning of particular methods (such as imagery) and lose sight of the specific PST skill that the method is intended to improve (such as peak concentration). It is easy to be seduced by the method as the 'end' itself, rather than as a means to an end. The methods chosen must have a planned purpose or skill development is unlikely to occur.

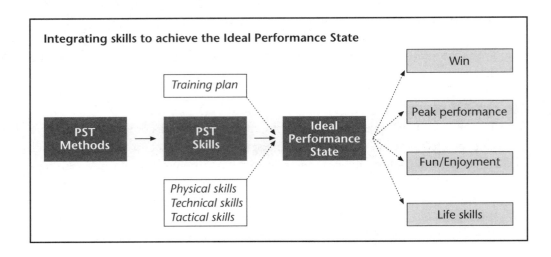

Integrating skills to achieve the Ideal Performance State

It is important to approach your PST with the same commitment to planning as you put into physical training. This requires a simple periodisation plan that takes all periods of the season into account.[3] PST skills and methods must be integrated into your training in order to simulate their use during games, and you will often need to do additional practice by yourself.

PST skills assessment: Peak Performance Profile

The Peak Performance Profile procedure is a handy way for you to put together your own peak performance 'jigsaw puzzle'. The profile will help you identify the individual pieces of your own jigsaw, give you direction, and enable you to organise a PST programme that puts the pieces together to create peak performances for yourself.

> **Sense of Direction**
> If you don't know what is important,
> then everything is important.
> When everything is important,
> then you have to do everything.
> When you have to do everything,
> you don't have time to think
> about what is really important.
> — AUTHOR UNKNOWN

Your Peak Performance Profile will help you to identify the various physical, technical, tactical, and psychological requirements for achieving peak performance in rugby. Examples of rugby qualities that might be included in each of these areas are:

PHYSICAL
- ★ Physiological requirements — strength, speed, endurance, power, flexibility.
- ★ Medical requirements (e.g., general health, injury prevention).
- ★ Nutritional requirements (e.g., training diet, pre-game meal, fluid intake).

TECHNICAL
- ★ Biomechanical requirements for rugby — techniques for successful performance of individual skills for your playing position.

TACTICAL
- ★ Strategies for each area of performance in the game — game plans for various situations.

PSYCHOLOGICAL
- ★ Mental skills — concentration, motivation, confidence, coping with pressure.

Assessments

Effective planning of a PST programme first requires assessing the sport of rugby itself. Various aspects of your playing position should be considered — aspects such as physical intensity, type of fitness required, basic physical skills, duration of basic skills, and different critical actions or moments within the game. Team aspects also need to be accounted for. This assessment should take account of the coaches, manager, administrators, leaders, captains, and the size of the squad.

The assessment of your individual skills is the most important factor in developing an effective personalised PST programme. There are a number of ways to do this, such as coaching observation, match statistics, or video analysis, but the easiest way to complete a basic assessment of your overall PST training needs is to complete a Peak Performance Profile.

Peak Performance Profile: self-assessment [4]

In identifying your PST training needs, you have to discover (or re-discover) the essential skills, qualities or themes that contribute to a successful performance in rugby — a Peak Performance Profile. Your individuality is emphasised in this process: you decide what is important for you, and you evaluate your capabilities in a very personal and individual manner.

The Peak Performance Profile invites you to develop a general jigsaw picture of yourself and your particular technical, tactical, physical and psychological needs. This picture will allow you to design an effective PST programme to improve your performance, to achieve your goals, and to get your brain and body working together as a team. The jigsaw that you create will be one that readily makes sense to you, as opposed to one that has been created for you by your coach or a sportpsych consultant.[5] (See Peak Performance Profile forms on pages 38–39.)

Peak performance profiling phases

Phase 1: Understanding the idea. Be very clear that the profile will be used to help you understand how you currently feel about your ability to achieve your peak performance. There are no right or wrong profiles. When you have developed your profile you should consider sharing it with your coach or a sportpsych consultant, and possibly with teammates that you respect, to help direct you towards the PST methods that will enhance your ability to achieve peak performance. Many players use the Peak Performance Profile assessment on a regular basis (weekly or monthly) as a detailed form of game review for fine-tuning their training.

Phase 2: Identifying themes and qualities. You need to decide on the important themes, qualities or 'performance skills' that you require to play well. It helps to discuss this with your coach or a sportpsych consultant, and/or teammates. Qualities or skills can typically be categorised as technical, tactical, physical, or psychological, although you should create labels that make sense to you. Technical qualities refer to the specific skills required for your playing position (such as passing and tackling, or scrummaging and line-outs). Tactical qualities are the strategies, tactics, and game plans used in your position (see your coach about these options). Physical qualities are the endurance, strength, power, speed, flexibility, nutritional and medical requirements of your position, while psychological qualities refer to the mental requirements of your position (such as motivation, self-confidence, and concentration). These qualities or skills collectively represent the jigsaw pieces of a peak performance in rugby.

Each player will have a slightly different set of performance skills and qualities, and a slightly different combination of psychological, technical, tactical, and physical skills. You must decide for yourself how important each skill area or performance quality is to your peak performance jigsaw picture.

You may wish to identify these performance skills through brainstorming in small groups within the team (approx. 4–5 people). If you choose this approach your task will be to select those skills or qualities that you think are appropriate for the team, taking into account your individual needs. You or your group should consider questions like 'What are the essential skills and qualities of a good rugby player?' It can also be useful to talk to a former elite player, or invite one to participate in the group discussion.

Don't be limited by the space provided on the profile form. Many players like to use the Peak Performance Skills worksheet on page 36 to write out an exhaustive list (see Jack's completed list on page 37). When you have finished the Peak Performance Skills worksheet you should then select the top three or four skills in each category of performance and transfer these to either of the Peak Performance Profile forms on pages 38–39.

There are two versions of the Peak Performance Profile for you to choose from. Peak Performance Profile (I), on page 38, is a simplified version that includes only two of the four rating assessments ('Current' and 'Best-ever'). Peak Performance Profile (II), on page 39, is the full version and includes all four rating assessments ('Current', 'Best-ever', 'Improvement' and 'Stability').

Phase 3: Assessment of the skills/qualities/themes. You now need to rate yourself on each of the skills you have identified, using the following four scales.

Current performance: Using a scale of 0–10 (0 = poor, 5 = average and 10 = excellent) rate yourself on each of the skills or qualities according to how you feel right now. You may also want your coach to rate you on these same skills or qualities of peak performance. Your coach's assessment may or may not agree with yours — this can become a basis for greater discussion and understanding between you and your coach.

Best-ever performance: Another assessment that you (and your coach) should complete is to rate your best-ever performance in relation to these skills or qualities. Most players can recall their best-ever performance, and although that performance may not have been perfect, it represents your best so far. Your best-ever profile may not necessarily have ratings of '10' for each skill, because some may be important for performance, but not absolutely vital for peak performance. Completing a best-ever rating profile helps you decide which skills or qualities require and deserve the most work to improve your ability to consistently reach peak performance.

Improvement: You should also complete ratings on the skills or qualities that need improvement, and determine how much improvement is needed (0 = huge improvement needed, 5 = moderate improvement and 10 = no improvement possible). These ratings are a bit deceptive as the scoring is the opposite of the other assessments: lower scores (such as 2 or 3) mean that the player rates him or herself as having considerable room for improvement, while high scores like 8 or 9 mean virtually no room for improvement. Elite players with well-developed skills thus often score high in 'improvement' ratings. These improvement ratings will help you to decide which skill areas have the most room for improvement, which areas you should work on immediately, and which you should leave to a later date. Clearly, the areas that have significant room for improvement and are important for your peak performance are the qualities that you should be designing a PST programme to improve!

Stability and consistency: The final rating is of the stability of your performance skills or qualities (0 = very unstable, needs control, 5 = moderate stability and 10 = very stable, maintain). Skills or qualities that are unstable or inconsistent will likely be the most important qualities to improve because their instability works against your ability to consistently produce peak performance. For example, as a hooker you may rate yourself as currently having good technical skills for line-out throwing (rating = 8), and in your best-ever performance you rated yourself highly (rating = 9), but unfortunately your line-out throwing is inconsistent from game to game and sometimes between line-outs in the same game (rating = 4). At this stage your skill at line-out throwing is inconsistent and unstable, possibly due to low levels of psych skills like concentration and coping with pressure.

Phase 4: Planning. Use your profile ratings to set goals for improving your Peak Performance Profile. For example, you may set a goal to increase a technical skill like tackling from a 'current' rating of 6 to 8; or set a goal to improve your concentration from 5 to 7. It is important to identify both strengths and weaknesses — then plan your training to maintain your strengths and to improve on your weaknesses. You should not regard weaknesses as a sign of failure or incompetence — everyone has weaknesses and the key issue is admitting them and working hard to improve them.

You can also use your profile ratings to gain a greater understanding and agreement between yourself and your coach. To work in harmony you and your coach must eliminate any major differences in assessments. Not only does the profile allow your coach to better understand you, but you gain a greater appreciation of his assessment of your performance profile. Many players also use the Peak Performance Profile assessment on a regular basis (perhaps weekly) as a detailed form of 'game review'. You may also wish to use the profiling procedure nearing the end of the season to help you assess your progress and degree of readiness of peak performance.

On page 40 you will see the Peak Performance Profile that Jack completed for himself at the start of this season, followed on page 41 by the profile that Bob completed recently. Based on these assessments we will design a PST programme for Bob to work on for the rest of this season.

The skill and the will — 30% of skill and 70% of will . . . is built into NZ rugby players.
— GRANT FOX (ALL BLACK 1985–93)

A Peak Performance Creed

If you think you are beaten you are;
If you think you dare not, you don't;
If you'd like to win, but think you can't,
it's almost a cinch you won't.

If you think you'll lose, you're lost;
For out in the world we find success begins
with a person's will;
It's all in a state of mind.

Life's battles don't always go to the stronger
or faster hand;
But sooner or later the person who wins
is the one who thinks 'I can'.
— AUTHOR UNKNOWN

Peak Performance Skills: Worksheet

Write an exhaustive list of all the performance skills / themes / qualities / characteristics of your playing position.

Name: . . . .   *Playing position:* . . . .

Technical	Tactical	Physical	Psychological

Peak Performance Skills: Worksheet

Write an exhaustive list of all the performance skills / themes / qualities / characteristics of your playing position.

Name: Jack McHugh   *Playing position:* Number eight

Technical	Tactical	Physical	Psychological
Passing in 'general' play.	'Reading' running lines on defence.	Aerobic/endurance fitness.	Pre-game psych-up — psych-up without psyching-out (activation levels).
Passing from base of scrum (e.g., '8-9').	'Reading' running lines on attack.	Anaerobic fitness — able to recover during the game.	Coping with pressure during the game.
Backrow moves; passing.	'Reading' opposition attacking moves.	Speed over 10 – 15 metres.	Motivation for skill training.
'8-ups' from scrum.	'Reading' holes in opposition defensive pattern.	Speed to breakdown or in support.	Motivation for fitness work.
Backrow moves; body position on the drive.	Options — line-out jump selection.	Upper body strength.	Confidence for each game.
Ball retention in the tackle.	Options — choosing the 'right time' for a backrow move.	Leg strength & line-out jump height.	Commitment to my goals and objectives.
Body position at second phase.	Options — choosing correct backrow moves.	Flexibility.	Team cohesion — follow game plan.
Line-out jumping.	Options — 'runner' off second phase .	Recovery from injuries.	Concentration for 80 minutes.
Supporting '5' jumper at line-out.	Options — 'pick & go' off second phase.		Ability to shift concentration — focus on the right info at the right time.
Driving on '2' jumper at line-out.			
Tackling around scrums.			
Tackling around rucks/mauls.			
Tackling: Cover 'D'.			

Peak Performance Profile (I)

List and rate the performance skills / themes / qualities / characteristics of your **best** or **peak** rugby performance. Rate yourself on each of the skills / themes / qualities using the following scale:

	0	1	2	3	4	5	6	7	8	9	10
Current + Best:	Poor					Average					Excellent

Name: . . . .   Playing position: . . . .

	CURRENT (RIGHT NOW)	BEST-EVER
TECHNICAL:		
. . . .	| . . . . . . |	| . . . . . . |
. . . .	| . . . . . . |	| . . . . . . |
. . . .	| . . . . . . |	| . . . . . . |
TACTICAL:		
. . . .	| . . . . . |	| . . . . . . |
. . . .	| . . . . . |	| . . . . . . |
. . . .	| . . . . . |	| . . . . . . |
PHYSICAL:		
. . . .	| . . . . . |	| . . . . . . |
. . . .	| . . . . . |	| . . . . . . |
. . . .	| . . . . . |	| . . . . . . |
. . . .	| . . . . . |	| . . . . . . |
PSYCHOLOGICAL:		
. . . .	| . . . . . |	| . . . . . |
. . . .	| . . . . . |	| . . . . . |
. . . .	| . . . . . |	| . . . . . |
. . . .	| . . . . . |	| . . . . . |

Peak Performance Profile (II)

List and rate the performance skills / themes / qualities / characteristics of your **best** or **peak** rugby performance. Rate yourself on each of the skills / themes / qualities using the following scale:

	0	1	2	3	4	5	6	7	8	9	10
Current + Best:	Poor					Average					Excellent
Improvement:	Huge improvement needed						No improvement possible				
Stable:	Unstable, needs control							Very stable, maintain			

Name: . . . .   *Playing position:* . . . .

	CURRENT	BEST	IMPROVEMENT	STABILITY
TECHNICAL:				
. . . .	|. . . . .|	|. . . . . .|	|. . . . . .|	|. . . . . .|
. . . .	|. . . . .|	|. . . . . .|	|. . . . .|	|. . . . . .|
. . . .	|. . . . .|	|. . . . . .|	|. . . . . .|	|. . . . . .|
TACTICAL:				
. . . .	|. . . . .|	|. . . . . .|	|. . . . . .|	|. . . . . .|
. . . .	|. . . . .|	|. . . . . .|	|. . . . . .|	|. . . . . .|
. . . .	|. . . . .|	|. . . . . .|	|. . . . . .|	|. . . . . .|
PHYSICAL:				
. . . .	|. . . . . .|	|. . . . . .|	|. . . . . .|	|. . . . . .|
. . . .	|. . . . . .|	|. . . . . .|	|. . . . . .|	|. . . . . .|
. . . .	|. . . . . .|	|. . . . . .|	|. . . . . .|	|. . . . . .|
. . . .	|. . . . . .|	|. . . . . .|	|. . . . . .|	|. . . . . .|
PSYCHOLOGICAL:				
. . . .	|. . . . . .|	|. . . . . .|	|. . . . . .|	|. . . . . .|
. . . .	|. . . . . .|	|. . . . . .|	|. . . . . .|	|. . . . . .|
. . . .	|. . . . . .|	|. . . . . .|	|. . . . . .|	|. . . . . .|
. . . .	|. . . . . .|	|. . . . . .|	|. . . . . .|	|. . . . . .|

Peak Performance Profile (II)

List and rate the performance skills / themes / qualities / characteristics of your **best** or **peak** rugby performance. Rate yourself on each of the skills / themes / qualities using the following scale:

	0	1	2	3	4	5	6	7	8	9	10

Current + Best: Poor .... Average .... Excellent

Improvement: Huge improvement needed .... No improvement possible

Stable: Unstable, needs control .... Very stable, maintain

Name: Jack McHugh . . . . **Playing position:** Number eight . . . .

	CURRENT	BEST	IMPROVEMENT	STABILITY
TECHNICAL:				
Body position at breakdown	7	8	5	7
'8-Up' from scrum	8	9	8	9
Tackling around rucks/mauls	6	7	5	7
TACTICAL:				
'Reading' running lines on attack	7	9	7	8
Line-out jump selection	6	8	6	8
Options — choosing backrow moves	4	7	2	5
PHYSICAL:				
Speed over 10-15 metres	8	9	9	8
Upper body strength	10	10	10	10
Aerobic fitness / endurance	9	10	8	8
Leg strength & line-out leaping	8	9	7	8
PSYCHOLOGICAL:				
Pre-game psych-up (activation)	5	9	3	2
Commitment	2	8	2	5
Team cohesion	5	9	5	7
Concentration	4	8	3	5
Confidence	9	9	9	10

Peak Performance Profile (II)

List and rate the performance skills / themes / qualities / characteristics of your **best** or **peak** rugby performance. Rate yourself on each of the skills / themes / qualities using the following scale:

	0	1	2	3	4	5	6	7	8	9	10

Current + Best: Poor Average Excellent

Improvement: Huge improvement needed No improvement possible

Stable: Unstable, needs control Very stable, maintain

Name: Bob Templeton *Playing position:* First five-eighth

	CURRENT	BEST	IMPROVEMENT	STABILITY
TECHNICAL:				
Goalkicking	2	9	3	5
Punting for field position/touch	8	9	9	8
Tackling at 1st phase	4	9	5	7
TACTICAL:				
Option-taking on attack	4	9	5	7
'Calling' backline defence	5	8	6	8
'Reading' holes in opposition defence	6	8	5	8
PHYSICAL:				
Speed on attack	8	9	7	9
Endurance fitness for 80 mins	5	9	6	7
Upper body strength (in the tackle)	2	6	3	7
Flexibility	8	9	10	9
PSYCHOLOGICAL:				
Motivation	8	10	9	10
Coping with pressure	3	9	2	5
Concentration & decision-making	4	10	5	7
Communication	6	10	5	7
Self-confidence	2	8	1	6

As you can see from the psych skills section of Jack's profile on page 40, at the start of this season he needed to commit himself fully to his rugby and his training, take control of his own pre-game psych-up, sharpen up his concentration, and be a more cohesive team player by improving his tactical skills and following the team's game plan. On the other hand, you can see from the psych skills section of Bob's profile on page 41 that he currently needs to gain some self-confidence, learn how to cope with pressure, get back his concentration, improve his decision-making, and pick up his on-field communication.

Jack was able to follow a PST programme that allowed him to improve his skill weaknesses. The first step he took was to sort his skill needs into different types of training, labelling them fitness/strength training, technical skills practice, and psych skills training. He decided that it was his psych skills that were most in need of improvement, and his next step was to categorise these needs into foundation, performance, and facilitative needs: these were (i) commitment (foundation skill); (ii) pre-game psych-up = peak activation (performance skill); (iii) concentration (performance skill); and (iv) team cohesion (facilitative skill). Based on this skill categorisation he concluded that he first needed to improve his foundation skill need for greater 'commitment' — for this he chose to use the PST methods of goal setting and self-talk.

Once Jack saw some gains in commitment he was in a position to work on enhancing his performance skills of pre-game psych-up and concentration. This time he chose to combine the methods of mental preparation, imagery and self-talk to work on both these performance skills together. He decided to use team goal setting, imagery and self-talk to help him stick with the team's game plan and be a more cohesive team player (the facilitative skill).

Bob needs some help to design his own PST programme based on his Peak Performance Profile on page 41. The first step is to separate Bob's skill needs — it would appear that he has some serious limitations in fitness and upper body strength (physical skills) that need to be addressed if his general play and especially his tackling is to improve. He also has some significant problems with his goal kicking (technical skills) that will need some specialist coaching, and finally he has some important areas of psych skills that need strengthening. Before making any definitive decisions it will be important for Bob to discuss his assessments with his coach and compare his assessments with the profile that his coach completed on him. Once Bob and his coach are in agreement, the next step is to categorise his psych skill needs — (i) self-confidence (foundation skill); (ii) coping with pressure (performance skill); (iii) concentration and decision-making (performance skill); and (iv) communication (facilitative skill).

Based on this classification of Bob's psych skill needs, we need to pick some likely PST methods to match with each psych skill. Following the logic of the PST programme we should sort out his foundation needs first — we would suggest to Bob that a blend of goal setting, imagery and self-talk could be a useful way to enhance his self-confidence. This decision would need to be discussed with Bob and his coach, then fine-tuned with his input as he starts to learn these three PST methods.

Once Bob is happy that his self-confidence is beginning to improve we would make some suggestions regarding PST methods for his need to cope with pressure — centring or relaxation, self-talk, and a CARS (critical action response strategies) plan are possibilities. At the same time as he is working on his coping skills he should also work on his need for improved concentration and decision-making — likely methods here are mental preparation, self-talk and maybe a modified version of a CARS Plan.

In chapters 3 to 15 you will see how Jack addressed his psych skills needs using various psych methods, and we will outline our suggestions for Bob. Finally, in chapter 16 we will show you a complete overview of the PST programmes for both Jack and Bob.

Planning your PST programme

Team PST programme. The team will have some general or common needs such as cohesion (teamwork), awareness of teammate needs, leadership, and communication skills. You may need to take these into account before you finalise the plans for your own PST programme.

Individual PST programme. Your personalised programme should take into account your need for foundation skills, performance skills, and facilitative skills — see the examples above for Jack and Bob.

Like physical skills and methods, psychological skills and methods need to be learned properly, adapted to fit your strengths and weaknesses, fine-tuned with initial use, and then practised, practised, practised.

Learning psychological skills

Education. Learning PST skills should initially focus on increasing your awareness of PST, increasing your understanding of PST principles, developing realistic expectations of PST, and understanding the need for PST for yourself. The Peak Performance Profile is vital in this self-education process. Indeed, you have already taken an important step in this process by reading this book. In the Recommended reading and resources section on page 227 you will find references for a number of other practical books and videos about PST.

Skill acquisition. Once you understand the PST programme fully you should focus on learning the specific PST methods you have selected to increase PST skill levels.

Practice. After you have identified the best PST methods you then need to practise them systematically.

Common psychological skill needs

Listed below are some of the PST skills that players commonly find they need to work on after completing a Peak Performance Profile. We have also included some suggested PST methods for developing these particular skills. Do not feel that you have to use all or any of the suggested methods for a particular PST skill: make your own choice based on your needs and preferences.

Motivation (a foundation PST skill). Motivation is both 'wanting to' and also 'having to' do something. You must identify rugby goals that you want to achieve — this is the long-lasting fuel for goal accomplishment — but also be realistic enough to realise that there will be times when you will need to motivate yourself to do something because you have to do it (such as training motivation). At such times you will need strong self-discipline to tough it out (see chapter 3).

PST methods:

★ Goal setting
★ Positive self-talk

Self-Confidence (a foundation PST skill). This involves the feelings and images you have about what you can and can't do. You need to develop and maintain a stable, realistic level of self-confidence (see chapter 4).

PST methods:

★ Goal setting
★ Positive self-talk
★ Mental preparation
★ Imagery

Controlling activation (a performance PST skill). Activation is your level of physical or mental activity and 'psych-up'. Controlling your level of activation enables you to manage your motivation and regulate aspects of your play such as heart rate, muscle tension and anxiety (see chapter 5).

PST methods:

★ Centring
★ Relaxation

* Mental preparation
* CARS plan (critical action response strategies)

Coping with pressure (a performance PST skill). This skill involves coping with the stress and anxiety that come with achieving challenging goals (see chapter 6).

PST methods:

* Centring
* Relaxation
* Mental preparation
* Self-talk, parking
* CARS plan (critical action response strategies)

Concentration control (a performance PST skill). This deals with the ability to 'tune in' what's important to performance and 'tune out' what's not. It includes the ability to maintain concentration as well as shift focus when needed (see chapter 7).

PST methods:

* Imagery
* Centring or relaxation
* Self-talk, parking
* CARS plan (critical action response strategies)

Communication and team cohesion (facilitative PST skills). These are the tools that allow you to interact and communicate effectively with other players, teammates, coaches, and managers (see chapters 8 and 9).

PST methods:

* Leadership self-talk and 'key words' for team communication
* Teamwork (task cohesion)
* Team spirit (social cohesion)

Practical considerations

Organisational considerations. There are a number of important organisational considerations to take into account when planning your PST programme: [6]

* Who should conduct the programme — sportpsych consultant, coach, or you?
* When should the programme be implemented — pre-season, early season?
* When to practise the methods — at home; before, after or during practice?
* How much time should be spent on mental training — is there a possible clash with physical practice time?
* How will you assess your psych skill needs? And how often? Who will do it?
* What PST skills to include, what methods to learn, and in what sequence?

There are no set answers to any or all of these questions. You have to be assertive and confident enough to make these decisions yourself. After learning the basics of the PST programme you should be in a position to make an informed decision on these matters — trust your own knowledge of yourself, your abilities, your strengths and weaknesses, your playing position; and now your knowledge of PST.

However, we suggest the following organisational recommendations. To learn PST properly you need to initially work with a sportpsych consultant. There are currently few coaches who have enough knowledge or experience with PST to teach it effectively. Nevertheless, it is vital that your coach gains a basic understanding of your programme so that he or she can reinforce what you are doing and lend advice and support (see chapter 16).

It is also important to approach your PST programme with the same commitment to planning and practice as you would put into your physical training. Ideally, PST should begin in the off-season and develop through the pre-season and early season with the goal of 'peaking' for the important games in the season. Experience has taught us that PST methods are best learned and practised during normal physical training or practice time, as the skills and methods must be integrated into the physical training in order to simulate the use of them during competition. Often you will need to do additional PST practice by yourself at home, just as extra physical practice is usually needed for fine-tuning of physical skills.

Training considerations. You need to understand the reasoning behind your PST programme — the what, why, when and how of your mental training. You must structure your team and individual situation for PST practice, stressing your own personal responsibility and commitment as a player; you must do the hard work and practise yourself. You must be flexible and individualise your programme and learning procedures to account for the team and your particular situation.

Evaluate the PST programme. Like any new skill development, your initial PST programme will probably not be perfectly matched to your individual needs. You should re-assess your Peak Performance Profile regularly, and use it to adjust your programme as necessary. There must also be a post-season evaluation of the programme for future recommendations, improvements and modifications.

Summary

Keep in mind that PST is not just for elite players, and that it is only one part of rugby performance. Be realistic: psychological skills will not replace a lack of physical skills or fitness. PST is not a quick fix — it takes time and effort.

The task before you is to identify the PST skills that you believe are needed to improve your performance (refer to Part II) and then choose the PST methods (in Part III) that you believe are the most appropriate. Don't try to do too much too soon, or you will struggle with the time and commitment necessary for practice.

Part II
PST Skills for Rugby

At the top everyone is multi-skilled. Props pass like half-backs, number eights kick; in those conditions the gaps between teams are really narrowed. That's where mental toughness comes in — the truly great players keep their heads when everyone else is losing theirs.

— ANDREW MEHRTENS (ALL BLACK 1995–)

3. Motivation and commitment

I think we have a mental toughness about us now which we never had when I first took over the side.

— Mac McCallion (Counties Provincial coach 1995–98) describing the Counties team that made the first division final in 1996– 97

Motivation

Success is getting what you want.
Happiness is wanting what you get.

Motivation is all-important for success in rugby. You need motivation for the season (dreams, vision, goals), for your fitness training, for your skill training/practice, and for your pre-game psych-up. Motivation is a foundation PST skill for developing mental toughness, so you need to have well and truly mastered it before you can expect to have consistent success at developing performance PST skills such as peak activation, peak concentration or coping with pressure.

Our job in this chapter is not to motivate you — the only person who can do that is you! Motivation must come from within — intrinsic motivation — to be effective and meaningful. Extrinsic motivation provided by someone else like your coach and captain or the opposition is unlikely to be always meaningful for you or have a lasting effect.

Too often, captains and coaches portray themselves as being able to motivate others. In reality, it isn't possible to motivate people unless they want to achieve the goals set for them. Captains and coaches can provide inspiration, but motivation must come from within. Motivation is both 'wanting to' and 'having to' do something. You must identify goals that you 'want to' achieve but also realise that there will be times when you'll need to motivate yourself to do something because you 'have to'. For this latter stage, you need strong self-discipline and mental toughness to 'tough it out'.

Mental toughness is all about self-reliance and personal responsibility, so you are responsible for your own motivation. Take some time to identify a dream (long-term goal) and a set of goals that excite you, have meaning to you, and will be satisfying and provide a sense of purpose for you.

> . . . the ideal of quality as the aim in life and on the field in training and during a
> game was something I valued and stressed . . .
>
> — GRAHAM MOURIE (ALL BLACK 1976–82)

What is motivation?

There are many different types of motivation:

★ Long-term motivation, such as commitment to training and practice.

★ Short-term motivation, such as motivation for an upcoming game.

★ Intrinsic motivation, such as playing for fun, enjoyment, and mastering the skills of your playing position.

★ Extrinsic motivation, such as rewards, trophies, money, recognition, and trips away with teams.

★ Pre-game motivation, such as the psych-up before your game.

Motivation energises, selects and directs performance, and is an important part of mental toughness and peak performance. Without adequate motivation you will not play well or train effectively.

Motivation is primarily made up of the direction and intensity of effort.

★ Direction — the tendency to approach or avoid a particular situation, such as competition. This represents the goals that you are trying to achieve, your reasons for playing.

★ Intensity — the activation of a person, on a scale from low intensity (asleep) to high intensity (all-out effort). This is the psych-up aspect of motivation (see chapter 5).

> Different games motivate people in different ways. I hate to lose, and that's another motivation. The fear of losing test matches is a powerful motivator.
>
> — CRAIG DOWD (ALL BLACK 1993–)

There are differing explanations of motivation in sport, often based more on guess-work than on successful experience or research. The first of the explanations below is common among players, while the second explanation is common among coaches — both are partially correct!

Person-centred model (intrinsic motivation). Player or personal factors determine motivation. People have underlying dispositions or traits that account for their level of motivation. The behaviours of players are viewed as signs of their underlying traits. This model suggests that you've either got motivation or you haven't, and that motivation isn't something that can be developed.

Situation-centred model (extrinsic motivation). Situational factors (coach, captain, opponents or spectators, for instance) determine motivation. Something in the situation causes a response in the person. This model suggests that the player has no drives or other motivational forces which affect behaviour; it's all up to the coach or captain to provide motivation.

A third, more useful explanation is the *interaction model* (person x situation). Motivation is a function of the person, the situation, and the interaction between these two factors — people actively change situations and situations change people. This explanation of motivation accounts for both the player's goals and the effect of the situation.

In the interaction model, players are motivated by both the situation and the goals and motives they bring with them. For example:

Player motives	Situational motivators
1. To beat my opponent/win	1. Crowd, spectators
2. To master the tasks/skills	2. Opponents
3. To get approval/praise	3. Coach
4. To get rewards (trophies/money)	4. Captain and teammates
5. Fun and friendship	5. Teammates

Many New Zealand studies have looked at motives for participation of rugby players in different grades.[1] Interestingly, whatever the level of player — from schoolboy up to Super 12 — the most important motives given for playing were 'to have fun', 'friendship' and 'achieving goals'. At representative level, 'winning' also becomes important, but these other motives suggest an emphasis on 'how to win' rather than winning as an end in itself.

To understand your motivation, you must know why you participate in rugby. What are your reasons for being involved? What is your definition of success in this great sport? Consider your motives, reasons, or goals, and the situation that you participate in. To help sort out your own definition of success, you need to understand the basic principles of a motivational factor called 'goal orientations'. Getting a handle on your goal orientations will enhance your levels of motivation and strengthen your commitment.

Goal orientations

People have different personal definitions of success, and these personal definitions are referred to as 'achievement goal orientations'.[2] Your goal orientations affect your perception of the situation and systematically affect your overall motivation in rugby.

Goal orientations are based on the principle that people are intentional, goal-directed individuals who operate in a rational manner.[3] Thus your motivation is the result of intentional and rational thought. The behaviour you choose has some meaning to you, and is influenced by your own subjective meaning of success — your individual perceptions of success and failure.

Individuals typically have multiple goals: your own combination of multiple goals forms your goal orientation for rugby. There are two major goal orientations that most players develop in sport (task and outcome), plus a third (social approval) that is less common, but can be important for some players.

Task orientation (or mastery). The focus is on succeeding at a task or mastering a skill; people with a task orientation are interested in the process — how competently you actually complete a particular task. These players are ability-oriented, but they focus on personal performance in relation to their previous level of ability or skill. Other ways to describe this goal orientation are mastery-focused, or intrinsically motivated. Such players assess performance on the task and the process of mastering the task. They also assess the effort needed to complete or master the task. Perceived ability is judged on task performance.

That's the thing about this team, we're always trying to get better.
— SEAN FITZPATRICK (ALL BLACK 1986–97) DESCRIBING THE 1997 ALL BLACK TEAM

Outcome orientation (or ego). The focus of success is social comparison. The player compares his ability with others or with a recognised standard. He is interested in the product — how performance is related to the final outcome or result (especially winning or losing), and how that relates to being better than someone else. The aim is to to claim high ability for yourself, so this goal orientation is very ego driven. Outcome-oriented players make three assessments in order to demonstrate high ability. The outcome of these assessments significantly affects their motivation:

★ Assess opponent's ability in relation to all other opponents; usually win/loss record.

★ Assess own ability in relation to opponent; social comparison. This assessment is usually based on the outcome of the game (win or lose).

★ Assess effort applied by yourself and your opponent; effort is emphasised and rewarded in sport. A minimal effort required to beat an opponent will enhance your perceived ability.

I'm sure that the negative motivation of fear of losing, which the All Blacks have often used, is a bad thing. Why don't we focus on the joy of winning instead?
— JOHN KIRWAN (ALL BLACK 1984–93)

Social approval orientation. The focus here is on demonstrating ability and effort to others and trying hard; these people want to gain approval and praise from others who matter to them, such as family, coaches, teammates, selectors or spectators. This goal orientation is especially relevant to players under twelve years[4] — but also applies to many senior players. Support from a respected figure can make a big difference to team performance in a key encounter.

Every player has acquired a little bit of each of these three major goal orientations. There may be other goal orientations as well, but these are the most common. It is your own unique combination of these goal orientations that determines your level and type of motivation.

For example, a player who competes at a senior club level may have a combination that is predominantly 'outcome', and to a lesser degree 'task'; while an individual who plays occasional social rugby with friends may have a combination that is predominantly 'social approval', with 'task' as a secondary goal, and some desire to demonstrate competitive ability ('outcome'). Goal orientations are dynamic; your combination of goal orientations may change from situation to situation and over time.[5] The competitive player mentioned above may change to a 'task' and 'social approval' orientation when they play social touch football with friends. Your combination of goal orientations and your emphasis among them represents your definition of success.

> At the end of the day you play rugby because you enjoy it, for what it gives you in satisfaction, physical and mental, and for what playing it well does for the country.
>
> — GRANT FOX DESCRIBING HIS GOAL ORIENTATION FOR RUGBY

It appears that Grant Fox mainly played for 'task' (enjoyment, satisfaction) as well as 'social approval' (doing something for your country) reasons. You need to identify your own goals for playing rugby if you want to maintain existing levels of motivation and create extra motivation.

Most elite players are highly task orientated and moderately outcome orientated.[6] So it would seem that the major goal orientation focus of elite rugby players is one that is high in mastery of skills or improvement, but also has a significant focus on winning or beating an opponent. Both goal orientations are useful for motivation in rugby and both contribute to mental toughness.

> There are a lot of things I know I can improve on. I know I can always do better. I expect improvement from myself. I never want to stop learning or stop improving.
>
> — CHRISTIAN CULLEN DEMONSTRATING
> HIS CLEAR TASK ORIENTATION

Goal orientations are also important in developing a number of other PST skills (such as self-confidence and peak activation), and are especially useful in learning the PST method of goal setting. Finally, an understanding of goal orientations is vital in achieving peak performance — to switch on the ideal performance state you need to primarily focus on a task orientation.

Jack (our number eight on page 12) has had a real problem with pre-game motivation for a number of seasons. Typically he had left his pre-game motivation and mental preparation to his captain and coach, assuming that it was their job to get him and the rest of the team motivated and psyched-up for each game. However, occasionally the captain and coach failed to do much to psych Jack up, so finally he decided to do it himself. Most of his coaches had emphasised winning in their pre-game motivation, but Jack felt better prepared when the captain or coach focused on the team's game plan and a 'how to win' approach to the pre-game psych-up. So he set himself goals before every game that were related to his jobs as a number eight and how they fit into the team's game plan. His goals were based on match stats such as tackle counts, forced turnovers, ball retention, effective backrow moves, and hit-up metres. He kept track of these match stats and goals by recording them in his Training Logbook (see chapter 20). He used a task orientation approach and it really paid off — he felt much more confident, motivated, and psyched-up before each game without being over-psyched or too nervous. He started playing much better and his improved play led to his selection in the provincial rep team.

Clearly, motivation is a key foundation PST skill for developing mental toughness. However, pursuing your goals will put you under considerable pressure to achieve success. This pressure to achieve can lead to anxiety and stress if you haven't carefully thought through your commitment to those goals. It is vital that you understand the role that *commitment* as well as motivation plays in peak performance.

Commitment

Winning the World Cup is a bit like shearing sheep, no other bastard is going to do it for you!

— ANDY EARL (ALL BLACK 1986–91)

One of the most important 'tough stuff' building blocks is commitment. This mental requirement is absolutely vital for achieving consistent peak performance and the Ideal Performance State.

The fully committed player is more determined, works harder, sets more challenging goals, and invests more time and energy in achieving peak performance than the less committed player. Complete commitment to peak performance is not possible without a positive level of self-esteem and an assertive approach to life and sport. However, complete commitment does not mean becoming over-identified with rugby as your only source of self-esteem. It means being committed to achieving peak performance in both sport and life.

> *Commit* To Win. Mental Hardness — work rate. Hunger. Urgency. Do your task at hand. Remember the 'state of mind' tasks. Scrum — Tackle — Drive — Concentrate. Win. Win. Win. Win. [Signed] *The Phantom*.
>
> — An anonymous note left on the whiteboard in the All Black team room before the third test against the British Lions in 1993[7]

Commitment as a psych skill

Sport commitment is a psychological skill representing the desire and resolve to continue sport participation and strive for peak performance.[8] We can look at it globally (as commitment to rugby in general) or specifically (as commitment to a particular team or a personal goal).

The concept of investment is a key one when trying to understand commitment. Your commitment to rugby will be a combination of your satisfaction with your investment in rugby, the attractiveness of the best alternatives to rugby, and your overall level of investment in rugby (for instance in time, effort or money).

In 1992 a comprehensive study revealed that commitment was a crucial psych skill for players in the All Black team of that year.[9] For example, when asked to offer

You have to have players with the desire, the passion, the absolute determination to succeed. If you haven't got that, you can't buy it — you can't make people do it. We're committed to continually improving our performance, on and off the field.

— Gordon Hunter (All Black selector 1996–99) previewing the 1997 All Black season

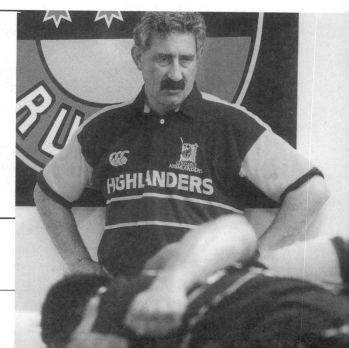

advice to younger players, one All Black said: 'I'd sit him down and say to make a commitment to himself about being honest about his sport.'

Some of the key commitment themes to emerge were: enjoyment; sacrifice; desire to be the best; set your goal; love of the game; thrill of playing; and friendship. The issue of sacrifice was a common theme for these All Blacks. 'You've obviously got to enjoy doing what you're doing, but there's got to be sacrifice, you know.' 'If you have a desire to be the best, then it takes a lot of sacrifice, and sacrifice comes into time. Time just on skills, fitness skills — sacrifice, you know, sacrifice . . .'

When asked 'How important has commitment been to your success as a player?' the following strong answers were recorded: ' . . . the overriding reason for [my] success has been the commitment . . . [it's] the number one reason anyone is in this team . . .' ' . . . it's probably the greatest lesson you could learn in life. . . . It's number one . . . it's the start of everything'.

Some players went so far as to place commitment at the top of the list for rugby needs: ' . . . overall 85–95 percent of my success is [due to] . . . commitment.' 'The start and finish of sport at an elite level is commitment.'

Sport enjoyment is a positive emotional response to the rugby experience — and greater enjoyment is likely to lead to greater commitment. Indeed, many sport psychologists consider enjoyment to be the cornerstone of motivation in sport. Knowledge of what makes the sport experience enjoyable and fun to the participant is the key to understanding and enhancing motivation.[10] So you need to ask yourself what is it that makes rugby fun — be very specific!

> The most important advice I can give is love the game. Enjoy and have fun playing it. Then put in the hard work and take it further.
> — CARLOS SPENCER (ALL BLACK 1996–)

A study of elite figure skaters found the following themes represented sources of enjoyment:[11]

★ Social and life opportunities: forming relationships with new friends and coaches; broadening experiences outside the routine of sport (such as travel).

★ Perceived competence: belief that you are skilled and competent derived from your achievement in sport.

★ Social recognition of competence: receiving recognition and praise from others for having sport skill competence; acknowledgement of your performances and achievements.

★ Physical exhilaration: sensations, perceptions, feelings of excitement and self-expression associated with the peak performance of sport skills.

Involvement alternatives represent the attractiveness of the most preferred alternatives to continued participation in rugby. While rugby may be a lot of fun you may decide that another sport or maybe some form of other recreation is as much fun, is a more attractive option for your spare time, or offers a better opportunity for you to achieve your goals. The more attractive the alternative, the lower the commitment to rugby.

Personal investments are resources that you put into rugby which cannot be recovered if you stop playing. These include expenditures of time, effort and money. Increasing investments creates greater commitment. The more you put into your rugby the more you want to get back out of it — you want a return on your investment!

Involvement opportunities are valued opportunities that are present only through continued participation in rugby. These may include such things as fun, the chance for sport mastery, the chance to be with friends, recognition by others of your skill and ability, or the chance to obtain extrinsic rewards (trophies, recognition, trips or money). As with personal investments in rugby, you may decide that the opportunities available are enough to keep you involved even when it may not be as much fun as it used to be — other opportunities (such as money, trips or recognition) may be enough reward for your investment of time, effort, and money.

Social constraints are social expectations which create feelings of obligation to remain in rugby, such as feeling you have to play to please your coach, teammates, friends, or parents. Sport commitment will likely be higher when social constraints are high. However, this is a negative reason for remaining involved since you have no control over your level of commitment — it is dictated by the expectations of others. Things that we feel we have no control over often become major sources of stress. In turn, stress usually detracts from fun and enjoyment, so your level of commitment will likely suffer in the long run if you rely on social expectations and obligations to others for your level of commitment.

Typically, individual players weight these five aspects of commitment differently. For example, you may be highly committed because of the intense enjoyment that you derive from performing the required skills of rugby, whereas another player might be equally committed because of his great investment of time and energy, despite low levels of enjoyment.

Jonah Lomu sought help from others to help him with the commitment needed to overcome his lack of fitness before the 1995 World Cup.[12] He found himself considering accepting one of the several offers he'd received from rugby league clubs. 'It seriously crossed my mind. What held me back were friends like Eric Rush who said the best way to deal with a situation like that was to prove them all wrong.' Lomu was enormously grateful to fellow All Black and rival winger Eric Rush for his support at that time. 'Eric's someone I knew I could trust. When you have to make a decision, it's great to have someone like him to turn to. He put my mind at ease, told me to believe in myself, told me to stick to my guns.'

> We desperately wanted him but because of our philosophy, we had to give the impression there could be no compromises. This was obviously hard to comprehend for a young man like Jonah who had found rugby so easy at school and who suddenly realised he was struggling to foot it with these guys. We knew we still had the time to prepare him, but we wanted him to confront the issue and understand that he had to do it if he was to make the World Cup. And he had to want to do it.
>
> — LAURIE MAINS TALKING ABOUT JONAH LOMU'S MOTIVATION AND COMMITMENT FOR THE 1995 WORLD CUP[13]

Jack's Peak Performance Profile on page 40 revealed that at the start of this season he needed to commit himself fully to his rugby and his training, before examining other aspects of his game.

His first action was to complete a Commitment Self-Assessment Worksheet (see pages 62–63). As you can see, this process of self-assessment helped Jack to realise that he really loved the game and that he was determined to enjoy his rugby and start playing to his potential. In an effort to improve his commitment (a PST skill) Jack chose to use the PST methods of goal setting and self-talk. In addition, he convinced his coach and teammates to develop a team vision, team goals based on that vision, and then specific goal achievement strategies devised to accomplish those goals (see team worksheets for these methods in chapter 8; pages 113–115). He felt that he could increase his personal commitment if he had a clearer picture of the team's goals and his role in achieving them.

Enhancing commitment

Identify commitment characteristics. Use Peak Performance Profiling (pages 38–39) and the Commitment Self-Assessment Worksheet (pages 60–61) to identify and rate the various aspects of your commitment to rugby — recognise these and consider how to use them to enhance your level of commitment.

Identify a team vision and team goals. Each team member must feel an investment in the team, its vision for the future, this season's team goals, and required teamwork and team spirit (see also chapter 8, Team cohesion).

A wonderful example of the usefulness of developing a team vision is evident in Team New Zealand's triumph in the 1995 America's Cup.[14] They used a team management system that employed a 'vision-driven model' to organise the sailing and on-shore teams during the 1995 America's Cup. As Tom Schnackenberg (Design Manager, Team New Zealand) pointed out, the use of a vision-driven model can achieve incredible results: 'We were dealing with normal, frail human beings; not super-beings by any means. And yet we achieved a super result.'[15] Use the Team

Vision Worksheet on page 113 as a starting point for your own team, and file copies of the team vision and team goals in your Training Logbook (see chapter 20).

Set challenging yet realistic goals. Use the goal setting procedures outlined in chapter 10 to identify difficult but realistic goals — set team goals first, then personal goals. Your personal goals should also focus on achieving the commitment characteristics identified as part of the Peak Performance Profiling process (record these in your Training Logbook too).

Use positive self-talk or affirmations. Use the self-talk and affirmation procedures outlined in chapter 11 to focus your thoughts on positive outcomes and persistent effort in pursuit of your goals. Even corny wee sayings or cliches can be useful if they strike a chord with you and your goal commitment. For example:

> *'The dictionary is the only place where success comes before work.'*

> *'There are three types of people in the world: those who make things happen; those who watch things happen; and those who ask "What the heck happened?" Successful people, people who reach their goals, **make** things happen.'*

Commitment Self-Assessment: Worksheet

Enjoyment

Enjoyment is a positive emotional response to the rugby experience, such as pleasure, liking, and fun. Greater enjoyment is likely to lead to greater commitment. Ask yourself what is it that makes rugby enjoyable and fun — be very specific!

....

....

....

....

....

....

Personal investments

Personal investments are resources that are put into goal achievement in rugby which cannot be recovered if you stop pursuing your goals. These include expenditures of time, effort, and money. Increasing investments creates greater commitment. What is your investment in rugby?

....

....

....

....

....

....

Involvement alternatives

Involvement alternatives represent the attractiveness of the most preferred alternatives to continued pursuit of your goals in rugby. The more attractive the alternatives, the lower the commitment to your rugby goals. What are the alternatives and how 'attractive' are they to you?

....

....

....

....

....

....

....

....

Involvement opportunities

Involvement opportunities are valued opportunities that are present only through continued pursuit of your rugby goals. These may include such things as fun, the chance for task mastery, the chance to be part of a successful team, or recognition by others of your skill and ability. What opportunities does pursuing your rugby goals provide for you?

....
....
....
....
....
....

Social constraints

Social constraints are social expectations by others which create feelings of obligation to remain in pursuit of your rugby goals, such as feeling you have to pursue a goal to please your coach, teammates, or friends. What expectations by others do you feel obliged or constrained to meet?

....
....
....
....
....
....
....

Overall assessment of your commitment

Typically, individual players weight these five aspects of commitment differently. For example, you may be highly committed because of the intense enjoyment that you derive from performing the required skills of rugby, whereas another player might be equally committed because of his great investment of time and energy, despite low levels of enjoyment. What is your overall level of commitment to your rugby goals?

....
....
....
....
....
....
....

Commitment Self-Assessment: Worksheet

Enjoyment

Enjoyment is a positive emotional response to the rugby experience, such as pleasure, liking, and fun. Greater enjoyment is likely to lead to greater commitment. Ask yourself what is it that makes rugby enjoyable and fun — be very specific!

I just love my footie! It's a really fun sport to play, I enjoy the team atmosphere and the challenge of being part of a team that operates like a well-oiled machine. It's also a real buzz to play in front of a vocal crowd of supporters in rep games. The challenge of matching up against elite players is also a lot of fun — trying to beat them one-on-one. Having a good game or doing something really well, like a big tackle or a good run is just a great thrill and a buzz!

Personal investments

Personal investments are resources that are put into goal achievement in rugby which cannot be recovered if you stop pursuing your goals. These include expenditures of time, effort, and money. Increasing investments creates greater commitment. What is your investment in rugby?

Rugby, especially rep rugby, takes up a lot of TIME. That's time away from work, away from my girlfriend, my family, and my mates. The training required to make it to the top also requires time, but it really requires a heap of bloody hard work — all the running and interval work for fitness, the weights sessions, the speed work, and of course the skill training, and team training sessions/practices. You have to be prepared to make big sacrifices if you want to succeed.

Involvement alternatives

Involvement alternatives represent the attractiveness of the most preferred alternatives to continued pursuit of your goals in rugby. The more attractive the alternatives, the lower the commitment to your rugby goals. What are the alternatives and how 'attractive' are they to you?

One thing I really miss is skiing in the winter at Queenstown. I'm not much of a skier, but I really enjoy the thrill of hurtling down the mountain, barely in control! Skiing is also a great social activity — good times and good people. Because rugby and rep rugby takes all winter and most of the spring I just don't get a chance to go skiing — but that can wait. I'd also like to have a crack at my old summer sport of cricket, but I just can't afford the time to play cricket when I should be doing my off-season and pre-season training for rugby. The other area of my life that I could devote my time and energy to, if I wasn't so involved in rugby, is my job — I really like my job, I'm pretty good at it and the opportunity to expand the business is quite considerable, but I can't afford the extra hours for work when I also need to do my footie training etc. My career development will just have to wait until my 'serious' rugby days are over.

Involvement opportunities

Involvement opportunities are valued opportunities that are present only through continued pursuit of your rugby goals. These may include such things as fun, the chance for task mastery, the chance to be part of a successful team, or recognition by others of your skill and ability. What opportunities does pursuing your rugby goals provide for you?

I probably wouldn't have my current job as a sales rep for the computer company if I didn't have a bit of a public profile through my footie. Being a rugby player opens a few doors. As I said before rugby is great fun to play and I got a real kick out of setting myself the goal of being a rep player and having achieved that goal — that's very satisfying! Also, I really enjoy the team atmosphere and all the mates I have made through footie. The other thing is travel — I enjoy being a tourist and through rugby I've seen most of New Zealand and been on tour to Aussie and the UK.

Social constraints

Social constraints are social expectations by others which create feelings of obligation to remain in pursuit of your rugby goals, such as feeling you have to pursue a goal to please your coach, teammates, or friends. What expectations by others do you feel obliged or constrained to meet?

I feel a bit of pressure from my club to play more club games and to help with coaching of junior teams. They have been really good to me — they helped me find my job and helped out with some spending money on my first tour with the rep team. I owe the club a big debt of gratitude. My parents have also been really supportive over the years and they get a kick out of coming to my rep games. But probably the biggest obligation that I feel is to my teammates and my coach for the rep team — he used to be my club coach and he's helped me heaps over the years, I owe him a lot. I do feel that I owe these people, but I figure the best way to pay them back is play really well and give them something to be proud of; besides I really enjoy playing for them as well.

Overall assessment of your commitment

Typically, individual players weight these five aspects of commitment differently. For example, you may be highly committed because of the intense enjoyment that you derive from performing the required skills of rugby, whereas another player might be equally committed because of his great investment of time and energy, despite low levels of enjoyment. What is your overall level of commitment to your rugby goals?

I am 110 percent committed to achieving my goals in rugby. It took a while to achieve my first goal of making the rep team, but having to work hard just made it even more satisfying! My next goal of cementing a regular place in the starting team (rather than off the bench) will also be a real challenge, but meeting that sort of challenge is what makes it so worthwhile and satisfying. Doing this Commitment Exercise has made me realise just how much I love playing rugby, especially at the rep level, and while there are some big sacrifices involved I reckon they are more than worth it. You're retired from the game for a long time, so you gotta make the most of it when the opportunity is in front of you!

4. Self-confidence

It just shows that when you have self-belief, you can't write people off.
— Peter Sloane (Canterbury Crusaders coach 1997–) explaining
the Crusaders' last minute win in the 1998 Super 12 final

Think of some of the great performances by players such as Christian Cullen and Zinzan Brooke of New Zealand, Tim Horan and David Campese from Australia, Joost van der Westhuizen from South Africa, or Jeremy Guscott from England — there are common characteristics of their play that would cause us to label them as confident players. All are or were willing to take risks in order to display their skills, and words like 'composure', 'timing', or 'effortless rhythm' can be used to describe their great performances.[1] They are never hesitant, rarely make unforced errors, and if they do, they are still willing to try a particular move again, even if it may not have worked the first time. They are confident players.

Basketball star Michael Jordan — the world's best-known sports person — puts his famous self-confidence down to the fact that he isn't scared of failure:

I've missed more than 9000 shots in my career. I've lost almost 300 games. Twenty-six times I've been trusted to take the game winning shot and missed. I've failed over, and over, and over again in my life — and that is why I succeed!
— Michael Jordan

So what exactly is self-confidence? Why is it so important? How can you learn to develop this skill for yourself, and how is it possible to instil confidence in other players?

In relation to rugby performance, we can define self-confidence as 'a player's belief in his ability to execute the various skills required for playing the game of rugby'. Essentially it is whether or not you expect to be successful when you attempt a particular skill.[2] If you expect to succeed, then you are confident. There is a difference between being confident in your ability to perform certain specific skills (such as tackling), which could be described as 'specific self-confidence', and a general belief in your ability to be successful overall in rugby. This could be described as 'general self-confidence'.

'If you think you can, or if you think you can't — you're probably right.'

Belief in your own ability is often a self-fulfilling prophecy — if you expect something to happen, then that expectation helps to make it happen.[3] For example, if you expect to be able to tackle an opposing player who is running straight at you, then you are more likely to successfully make the tackle than if you expect him to break through your tackle attempt. In other words, if your confidence in your ability to tackle is high, then you are more likely to be successful than if your confidence is low. The positive relationship between self-confidence and success is one of the most consistent findings in research relating to peak performance in sport.[4]

What are some of the other benefits of a high degree of self-confidence? To begin with, self-confident players are more likely to remain calm in pressure situations because they believe in their ability to do what is required. This is one of the reasons why team captains need to be self-confident players — they must remain calm when there is three minutes to go and their team is two points behind and stuck deep in their own 22 metres. They have to be able to cope with this kind of pressure and make the correct tactical decisions to get their team down to the other end of the field and score (see also chapter 6, Coping with pressure). In such situations, the ability to remain focused on the task is crucial, and confident players are able to do this. Their confidence allows them to focus on the task at hand, rather than worrying about the consequences of losing or playing poorly. Confident players will also be less likely to give up, and in fact will increase their efforts to overcome pressure because they believe that they can do it. So not only does confidence affect emotions (such as the ability to control anxiety), it can also have an effect on concentration, effort, and decision-making (team strategies). Players and teams that play with confidence are more likely to adopt positive tactics involving calculated risk-taking and taking control of their own performance rather than playing 'not to lose', which is often characterised by a more conservative and often tentative approach to the game.

Players who are not confident are afraid to make mistakes, don't take risks, and generally wait for things to happen rather than taking control over their own performance. If they find themselves in a position where they have several options available to them, they will typically pick the most conservative of these, and often perform this option tentatively anyway, which increases the likelihood that they will make a mistake. If this happens, their confidence can be further undermined, and a downward spiral begins to occur, with poor performance leading to less confidence, which in turn leads to further poor performance and so on. As a further consequence of this, the goals that the players set for themselves are likely to be less challenging than if their confidence was high, and they are less likely to realise their full potential as rugby players. Confident players, on the other hand, set far more challenging goals, and are more likely to exert a great deal of effort in attaining these goals. Their confidence helps them to realise their potential (see chapter 10, Goal setting).

However, being confident doesn't mean never having any negative thoughts or self-doubts. It's normal to be nervous or apprehensive about an upcoming game, whether it's five minutes, one week, or two months before the kick-off for that game! Confident players are still able to believe in their ability to perform well, despite any self-doubts they may have.[5]

Despite the advantages of having a high degree of self-confidence, this skill alone will not guarantee success. You need to have a realistic level of confidence that matches your ability levels. Players whose confidence exceeds their ability are likely not to succeed and will continue to fail until their confidence is eventually brought down to a more realistic lower level. The danger here is that while they are over-confident, not only does their own performance suffer, but that of their team also suffers as a consequence of their poor performance. And players who are under-confident, despite having the ability to perform well, are also likely to fail because their lack of confidence results in self-doubts, excessive nervousness, tentative performances, a lack of concentration, and conservative decision-making which restricts them from performing to their potential.

Developing self-confidence

How do players develop a high level of self-confidence? Is self-confidence something that can be further developed and improved upon? The best way to answer these questions is to look at the various sources of information that players use to assess their confidence levels, and the strategies that coaches use to boost a player's confidence. There are four major sources of information that will influence a player's level of self-confidence.[6] These are:

1. Whether or not they have performed successfully in the past (performance accomplishments).

2. Watching other players perform the skills (modelling or 'imitation').

3. Having other people tell them that they can perform a skill successfully (verbal persuasion).

4. How they interpret their physical and emotional feelings about an upcoming performance (activation levels).

These sources of information, and a few others, can be used by you and your coaches to develop and further improve your confidence. But how exactly can they be used? To begin with, there is no substitute for actually performing a skill successfully in order to build confidence, and the best way of accomplishing this is not during games (although that is the ultimate aim), but on the practice field. Here, you and your coach can work together to build up the confidence to perform the skills required for certain games, strategies, and individual moves, using a combination of PST methods and general practice techniques.

> Tackle bags and drills are OK for technique but the most important thing is to really want to tackle the guy. Most of it's mental, and if you go in confident then usually you do OK.
>
> — CARLOS SPENCER

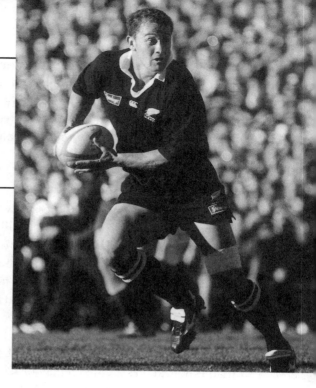

Performance accomplishment

The most powerful of the factors is whether or not you have been able to perform a skill in the past. For example, if Jack (our number eight) has been able to make the advantage line most of the time he takes the ball up from the base of the scrum during games, then he is likely to feel confident that he can do it again in subsequent games. If, on the other hand, he has been consistently tackled behind the advantage line, then his level of confidence for achieving the advantage line from an '8-up' call is not likely to be very high. Similarly, if Bob (our first five) has been consistently missing crucial penalty kicks during the last quarter of recent matches, then his confidence about goal kicking is likely to be rather low. On the other hand, if his kicking percentage has been up over 80 percent in the last few games, he is likely to approach future kicking opportunities with a lot more confidence. The message is clear — success breeds confidence, and vice versa.

Striving to achieve performance and process goals in games and during practice can be a very effective way to develop self-confidence (see chapter 10, Goal setting). One of the other ways to achieve success is to set up 'game simulation' drills in practice. The philosophy is simple: success increases confidence and leads to further success. Drills and techniques can be organised, taught, demonstrated, and practised to ensure that players experience success, and these experiences can be reinforced through encouragement from coaches and other players. You will undoubtedly be more likely to feel confident about performing a certain move or a certain skill during a game if you can successfully and consistently perform it in practice. This is also why practice conditions should often simulate the physical and mental requirements of actual competition, perhaps by setting up game-like scenarios during practice, so that the players get to experience performing the skills under the conditions that they are likely to experience during a game. There is nothing that is more likely to build confidence than experiencing in practice what you want to accomplish in a game.[7]

Modelling or imitation

By watching someone else successfully perform a particular skill during a game, or demonstrating how to perform that skill during a practice (modelling), you can learn how to perform the skill and gain confidence that you too can do it. Although this method of gaining confidence is nowhere near as powerful as knowing that you've successfully performed the skill in the past, it does work, especially if the player who demonstrated the skill is similar to you as the observer.

For example, if Jack is 1.80 metres tall, weighs 95 kg, and plays premier club rugby, he is more likely to believe that he can break the advantage line from the base of the scrum if he watches someone of a similar stature to him do it in a club game, than if he watches a video replay of Isitolo Maka (1.90 metres tall; 112 kg) doing it for the All Blacks against South Africa in a test match. The more similar the model is to you as the observer, the more powerful will be the influence it has on your confidence levels.

Verbal persuasion

If Jack's coach is someone that he trusts for his knowledge of the game, and he tells Jack that he is capable of breaking the advantage line from the base of the scrum, then Jack will gain some measure of confidence. In this case, Jack's coach has used verbal persuasion to try to instil some confidence in Jack about being able to perform this particular skill. Again, this kind of strategy would not be nearly as powerful as actually performing the skill successfully, but it will have an influence if Jack believes that his coach knows what he is talking about.

Controlling activation levels

The way that you interpret how you are feeling, emotionally and physically, about an upcoming performance will have an influence on your confidence levels. Most players would admit to feeling apprehensive or nervous before a game, and this is a normal reaction. In fact, for many players this is a desirable feeling to have because it means that they care about the game, want to do well, and are probably more focused on their own performance than if they were not feeling this way.

If you get butterflies in your stomach every time you think about an upcoming game, and interpret these feelings as pressure or fear, then your confidence about being able to successfully perform the skills required may be much less than if you interpreted those feelings as ones of excitement and being fired-up for the game (see chapter 5, Controlling activation).

How can you learn to control these feelings and perhaps even change them from feelings of fear to ones of excitement and eagerness to perform? One way would be to bring your physical feelings under conscious control by learning how to reduce your activation levels (if they are too high and result in feelings of fear and anxiety) through PST methods such as relaxation, imagery and stress management techniques (see chapters 13 and 14 for various relaxation and imagery techniques). Another method would be to change your perceptions of these feelings altogether, by training yourself to believe that the feelings are positive. This can be done through a number of PST methods including imagery and various self-talk techniques (see chapters 11 and 14 for a description of these methods). On the other hand, if you feel as if you are physically too relaxed going into a game, then you can increase your activation levels by a number of techniques such as imagery, self-talk, or simply by increasing your physical activity levels.

Goal setting

Focusing on achieving performance and process goals during a game will help you to stay focused on what it is that you have to do in order to perform well (task orientation; see chapter 3, Motivation), and by doing so you will be better able maintain your confidence (see chapter 10, Goal Setting). This is important because players can often doubt their ability and lose confidence if they focus on the outcome and winning as the only goal or think about how they would feel if they were to lose.

Imagery

The PST method of imagery is simply an extension of modelling (see chapter 14, Imagery). Instead of observing another person performing a particular skill, you can imagine yourself performing the skill. By imagining yourself successfully executing skills such as line-out throwing, goal kicking or tackling, or successfully shutting down opposition moves, you can approach an upcoming game with more confidence. But imagery should not only be restricted to situations or skills in a game setting. Players can imagine themselves successfully performing practice drills, or making it through an especially hard training run or fitness session.

Acting and thinking confidently

Even if you don't feel particularly confident, the more you act confident, the more likely you are to feel and perform with confidence. In addition, if you portray an image of confidence and seem calm and in control of the situation then your opponents may begin to lose some of their own confidence. By the same token, if you let it be known that you have lost your confidence, either by negative body language or self-talk, this can have the effect of boosting your opponent's confidence — they will believe that they've got the better of you. Acting confidently, even if you are not feeling confident, can also work to lift your own teammates' spirits if they have begun to lose confidence. It may not help you to win the game, but it will certainly go a long way towards preventing the team from giving up and conceding defeat.

Similarly, coaches should maintain an air of confidence because it will rub off on the players. Confidence, like enthusiasm, is contagious. Coaches should remain calm and focused, and when they have the chance to communicate with the players at half-time, they should maintain that air of confidence. This can be accomplished by briefly emphasising the positive aspects of their team's performance, making them aware of some of the things that they may need to improve upon, and encouraging them to do some specific things in the upcoming half. A coach who yells at his players at half-time, and appears to be panicking, will go a long way towards successfully destroying the team's confidence.

'Tell someone they're brave and you help them become so.'

Players should also try to maintain a positive attitude, whether in practice or during a game. Negative thoughts can quickly undermine confidence, so players should actively encourage each other and themselves through the use of positive self-talk and affirmations (see chapter 11, Self-talk). If a mistake is made, it's no use getting down on yourself for making it; if you do, you should quickly replace the negative thought with a positive one (see chapter 15, CARS Plan). For example, if Bob misses touch from behind his 22 metre line, or knocks the ball on during an attacking backline move close to the goal line, rather than saying, 'You idiot, you couldn't catch a cold at this rate,' he should immediately refocus and say something positive like 'Hang in there, things will get better. Focus on the next job.'

Self-talk should either be motivational ('You can do it') or instructional (as Grant Fox used to say to himself when kicking goals, 'Head down, follow through'). It is self-defeating to always be judgmental, and can even result in boosting the confidence of opposition players if they hear a player getting down on him or herself. The bottom line is that thoughts translate to action, and so players who are more positive in their thoughts and self-talk are more likely to be confident and positive in their play (see chapter 11).

Preparation

Being as well prepared as possible for a game, or even a practice, will give you confidence that you have done everything that you can to maximise your chances of being successful.[8] Going into a game with a well-prepared and well-practised game plan, with well-rehearsed moves and techniques (e.g., scrummaging, back-row moves, backline defensive screens, tap penalty moves), and with well-learned and practised individual skills, can only increase your confidence about an upcoming performance. An integral part of this preparation is the preliminary fitness training that you have done during the off-season. Players who know that they are as fit, fast, strong and powerful as they could possibly be when the season starts will be undoubtedly be confident in their ability to play at maximum intensity without fatigue, to handle the physical aspects of the game, and to focus on their own performance in the game.

A well-rehearsed pre-game routine of mental preparation is also important (see chapter 12, Mental preparation). If you know the exact routine that you will follow in the build-up to a match, then you will be confident that you are as prepared as possible. For example, if Jack and Bob know that they should arrive at the ground at least one hour before the kick-off, and then follow a pre-set routine of mental and physical activities leading up to the kick-off, then they will start the game knowing that they have not left anything to chance in their preparation, and will be more confident about performing well. All players like to prepare for a game in their own way, and there should be enough flexibility in a pre-game routine to allow time for individual as well as team and sub-unit warm-up activities. These things should be discussed and agreed upon by the players and coaching staff early in the season (or ideally before the season begins).

Self-confidence is crucial for peak performance in rugby. You need to develop a realistic level of confidence in your ability to perform the variety of skills needed during a game. This can be achieved in a number of ways, most of which involve use of the four main sources of information that determine your level of confidence. PST methods such as goal setting, imagery, self-talk, relaxation, and mental preparation can all be used to develop, maintain, and /or improve your confidence levels. These PST methods, when used in conjunction with good practice and training habits, and hard work on fitness and physical skills, can have a significant impact on your levels of confidence.

To adapt from the French writer Alexandre Dumas:

> *When you doubt yourself, it's like joining your enemy's army and bearing arms against yourself. You make failure certain by being the first person to be convinced of it.*

Strive to have a strong level of self-confidence without being over-confident or arrogant. This will help you perform to your potential and also help you cope with any slumps in performance. Believe in yourself!

5. Controlling activation

> Yeah, I was pretty nervous on the bus! I couldn't stop shaking! When I got to the dressing room I just sat there. I had no idea what an All Black did to warm up, so I just watched the boys and copied them; before long I learned to just do my own thing.
> — CHRISTIAN CULLEN DESCRIBING HIS FIRST TEST MATCH

Hand in hand with the need for self-confidence goes the need to learn how to control your levels of mental and physical activation — how active you are. For many players, this means controlling their nerves and learning how to reduce their levels of physical activation (such as heart rate, breathing, butterflies in the stomach) and emotional activation (anxiety, stress, fear) in order to maintain a realistic level of confidence. Remember, if you perceive that your nervousness is a sign of fear, then this can undermine your confidence and lead to poor performance on the field (see also chapter 6, Coping with pressure).

For most players, being nervous is a normal and expected part of the build-up to a rugby match.[1] However, the additional psych-up routines that coaches and other players sometimes use can make a player's nervousness even worse, so that by the time the game begins, they are over-psyched, or too fired-up. This often means that they don't perform well because they are too busy trying to calm themselves down! However, for some players the problem is not that they get too nervous or over-activated for a game, but just the opposite — they can't seem to get themselves psyched up enough. They feel that they just can't get into it!

What can players and coaches do to ensure that their level of activation (psych-up) is just right for them, and that they don't take 20 minutes to settle into a game? How can you psych-up or calm down enough so that your level of activation is optimal for you? What exactly *is* activation, what causes it, how can it affect your performance — and how can you control it?

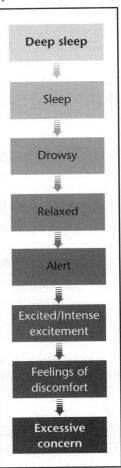

What is activation?

Activation is the level of physiological and psychological activity that a player experiences in a particular situation. It is represented in the scale to the left.

Activation is *not* the same as anxiety. Anxiety represents a high activation level that produces feelings of discomfort and concern, and is a response to a specific situation. Stress, which is the basis of this excessive concern, results from the player thinking that they cannot perform a particular task successfully when it is important for the team to do so at the time — it is a perceived imbalance between situational demands and the person's abilities, under conditions where failure to meet the demand has important consequences.

Bob's team is down by 2 points with time up on the clock in the club final, and the referee has awarded them a penalty right in front of the posts, but 45 metres out. Bob's captain has indicated that they will attempt a shot at goal, knowing that this will be the last play of the game, and has asked Bob to take it. Given that Bob has already missed three shots at goal in the game from close range, and has only ever slotted three goals in his life from this far out, he doesn't believe he can do it, but has to make the attempt because there is nobody else who can kick goals, and the referee has indicated that a shot is about to be taken. As he places the ball on the tee Bob is aware that his activation levels are high — his heart is racing, his stomach is churning, and his palms have suddenly become very sweaty. He is over-activated, anxious, and definitely under stress. He starts to worry about how the other players will respond if he misses, and wonders if anybody else can hear his thumping heart. He thinks to himself, 'I can't do this — it won't have the distance and we're gonna lose!' He steps back to his mark and tries to clear his head and calm his body; but it doesn't work. He moves in, and at the point of contact with the ball, lifts his head and miscues the kick, sending it short and wide, and sinking his team's chances of taking the championship.

Bob's situation illustrates how a perceived imbalance between task demands and player ability can affect concentration, self-confidence and activation, which in turn affects performance. Compare this with the Ideal Performance State described in chapter 1. The Ideal Performance State results from a perception of a balance between the situational demands and the player's abilities. This perceived balance or imbalance is also related to the 'perceived ability' discussed in chapter 3.

Activation and motivation

Many common coaching sayings used with regard to motivation indicate the use and/or control of activation and anxiety: 'psych-up', 'fire-up', 'get psyched',

'psyched-out', 'put them under pressure', 'attack of the nerves', 'choke'. Have you ever seen a player 'choke' in an important game because of the pressure? Have you ever 'choked' yourself?

The relationship between activation (psych-up) and performance

There are two types of activation. Emotional psych-up (mental) represents excitation, apprehension, and nervousness, whereas physiological psych-up (physical) represents bodily responses such as increased heart rate, increased breathing, muscle tension, sweating, and 'butterflies'.[2]

There are a number of theories about the relationship between activation and performance. The first of these, drive theory, states that there is a direct relationship between performance and activation, in that the more highly psyched-up or activated the player is, the better they will perform.[3] This approach to motivation suggests that more is better — that if a certain level of psych-up is followed by a good performance, then a greater degree of psych-up will increase performance even more!

Traditionally many coaches and captains have adopted the drive theory approach in preparing for a game, and have used such strategies as emotional pre-game speeches, pre-game yells, and team chants to psych-up the players. Unfortunately, this theory doesn't explain why players often perform poorly when they are super psyched-up. In such cases, it is clear that more is definitely not better.

Nerves can give you the edge, the tension makes you more focused and the pressure makes you perform. When two players are physically equal, it's the one who prepares the best that wins the battle.

— Jeff Wilson (All Black 1993–)

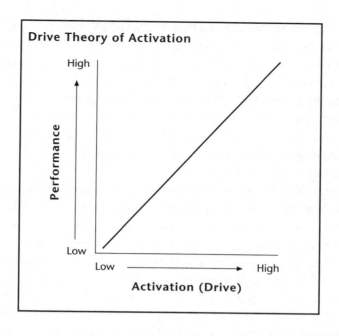

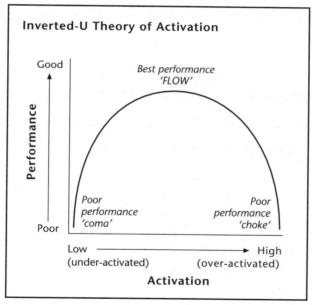

In an attempt to explain the relationship better, the inverted-U theory (named after the shape of the curve on the graph) was developed. This theory states that performance will increase in proportion to increases in activation up to a certain optimal or peak point, beyond which performance will begin to decrease (see diagram above).[4]

This theory seems more accurate than drive theory, because it accounts for the fact that a player can produce a less than satisfactory performance because of over- or under-activation, but could produce their best performance under conditions of optimal or peak activation.[5] However, it has been criticised for being over-simplistic, and for failing to account for the fact that many players experience dramatic decreases in their performance once they become over-activated. These are called performance catastrophes — peak activation levels can be regained only after the player has reduced his (or her) activation levels to a very low level and has built up to peak levels once more (see diagram below).[6]

Under-activation can lead to boredom and poor performance, whereas over-activation can lead to 'choking' or anxiety. There is a fine line between getting psyched-up to peak activation levels and being uptight (over-activated). The relationship between activation and performance can perhaps be more easily understood in terms of an activation 'thermometer'. If you imagine your activation level in terms of temperature, you can imagine that you will have an optimal temperature at which you perform best, just as your body has an optimal healthy temperature. If you are under-activated, or cold, you will perform poorly; if you reach your optimal temperature or activation level then you will perform to your best; and if you are over-activated (or choke) you will perform very poorly.

Key points:
★ Peak performance results from peak activation levels.
★ Peak levels of activation are task-specific (e.g., line-out throwing).

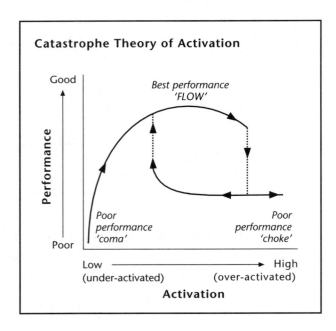

76 PST Skills for Rugby

★ Each of us has a different peak level of activation that will produce peak performance. You need to recognise when you are at peak activation, over-activated or under-activated.

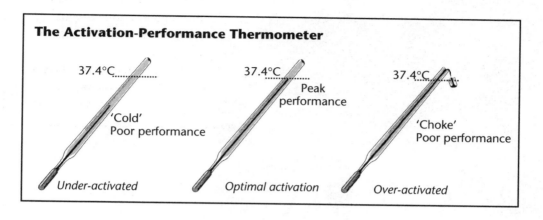

The Activation-Performance Thermometer

37.4°C ....
'Cold'
Poor performance
Under-activated

37.4°C ....
Peak performance
Optimal activation

37.4°C ....
'Choke'
Poor performance
Over-activated

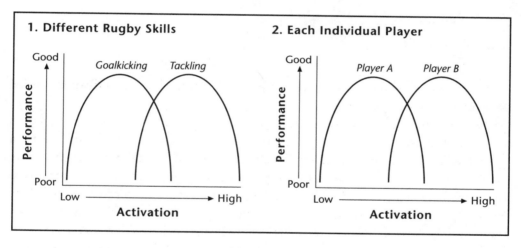

1. Different Rugby Skills

Performance — Good / Poor

Goalkicking *Tackling*

Activation — Low → High

2. Each Individual Player

Performance — Good / Poor

Player A *Player B*

Activation — Low → High

Different skills or tasks within the game of rugby require different peak levels of emotional and physical activation.[7] For example, the tasks of goal kicking and tackling require very different physical skills. Goal kicking demands a very high level of precise control over physical movement, force, strength, and timing. Tackling requires a high level of strength, and the players often have to use large amounts of force and effort to successfully execute a tackle. Both skills require high levels of concentration and motivation, but the type of motivation will be different. For example, if you were Andrew Merhtens standing over a 45-metre penalty kick, with the score at 15 all and time up on the clock, you would not want to be as psyched-up as Olo Brown would be when preparing to pack down in an attacking 5 metre scrum in the last seconds of the same test match with the scores still tied! Both

I changed into my playing gear as soon as we got into the changing room . . . just kept quiet, hoping no-one would notice me dry retching discreetly in the corner . . .
— JOHN KIRWAN (ALL BLACK 1984–93)
DESCRIBING THE BUILD-UP TO
HIS FIRST TEST MATCH

players would be equally determined to succeed, but the level of activation needed for each skill is vastly different.

In addition, all players have their own slightly different peak levels of activation for each of the skills required for their position in the game.[8] This individuality of peak levels of activation is clearly evident in the difference between the calm, controlled level of activation exhibited by All Black Michael Jones, the 'Iceman', and the hyped-up, almost out-of-control level of activation exhibited by Wallaby Michael Brial. Both of these players are successful, test-level loose forwards, but their 'peak levels of activation' would appear to be very different. Every player needs to identify their own personal level of activation and establish a pre-game routine to match that peak level.

Signs of over-activation

To control activation and over-activation and consistently achieve your peak level of activation, you have to learn to recognise the signs of peak activation and over-activation for yourself. Some of the immediately obvious physical signs of over-activation are: butterflies in the stomach, racing heart rate, increased breathing or hyper-ventilation, uncontrolled and increased muscle tension, feeling tired, dry mouth, clammy hands, frequent desire to urinate, trembling or twitching muscles, flushed face, voice distortion, yawning and nausea or vomiting.[9]

Some of the obvious mental signs include: being abnormally irritable and/or confused, forgetting details, inability to concentrate and make decisions, self-doubts, fear, worry, and changes in communication levels.

Obviously if you demonstrated all these signs at once you would be a complete wreck! Typically, most players have an individual pattern or combination of physical and mental signs that indicate when they are over-activated — it is vital that you learn to identify your own personal over-activation signals.

What happens when players become over-activated?

Players differ in how much their performance is affected by over-activation. You need to be aware of the effects of over-activation on your own mental and physical performance.

Mental effects of over-activation. Negative thoughts such as self-doubt, loss of self-confidence, worry and fear usually accompany over-activation, and often lead to anxiety, which is very detrimental to performance.[10] Over-activation is also commonly associated with a shift in concentration; your focus of attention becomes too narrow and important cues or pieces of information (such as an unmarked player outside you shouting for the ball) can be missed (tunnel vision). As activation increases, the amount of information that you can 'scan' becomes less. Different tasks require different concentration demands (compare throwing to the middle of a line-out versus 'reading' the opposition's defence pattern), and you must voluntarily control your activation levels to match the concentration demands of your current task. Over-activation can interfere with your control of your concentration levels (see chapter 7, Concentration).

Over-activation can also cause a concentration shift from task-related concerns to other factors such as the score, the crowd, or the expectations of others. Further increases in activation can then shift your concentration to internal factors such as worry and self-doubt, which in turn, leads to stress and anxiety and further decreases in performance.[11]

Physical effects (muscle tension). Over-activation commonly results in decreased co-ordination and 'timing', and tight jerky movements as a result of uncontrolled increases in muscle tension. If you can recognise when you are in this state you will then know when you need to relax both the mind and body, and bring unwanted muscle tension under conscious control in order to achieve success.

What causes over-activation?

Over-activation leads to problems with concentration and muscle tension. These problems can inhibit performance, and destroy the enjoyment and satisfaction that comes with achieving peak performance and the Ideal Performance State. But . . . why? Why would you perceive a situation as stressful? What factors cause stress and high activation?

In competitive sport other people (coaches, other players, spectators, selectors) make comparisons between your abilities and those of other players, or with your previous performances. This 'threat' of social comparison can cause stress before, during, and after the game.

Stress results from a perceived imbalance between situational demands and your ability to meet those demands. If you feel unable to successfully meet the demands of the game, but want to be successful because of the perceived 'threat' to self-esteem and self-confidence that comes with failure, stress occurs. This is linked to the 'perceptions of ability' that you make in the process of deciding if you have achieved your goal (see chapter 3, Goal orientations).

There are a number of sources that affect your perception of your ability to meet the demands of the situation.[12]

Person/player factors. These include high levels of anxiety, low self-esteem, low team performance expectancies, low personal performance expectancies, fear of failure, and lack of fun.

Situational factors. Factors such as the game's importance, the presence of significant others (coaches, selectors, family), and the actual outcome of the game can cause uncertainty in your mind about your perceived ability.

> Shield [Ranfurly Shield] matches are not unlike tests, and often success is a question of how well you react under pressure.
>
> — ANDY DALTON (ALL BLACK 1977–87)

Significant other factors. These include parental and family pressure, unrealistic expectations from coaches, teammates, administrators or selectors, worry about negative social evaluation by others, and the importance that other people place on winning.

The critical feature of these sources of stress is that it is *your perception* or interpretation that determines whether you will be vulnerable to stress and 'choking'.

Two factors most often cause players to become stressed. The first is the importance that is placed on the outcome of a game — the more important the outcome, the more activated you become. The second major factor is the uncertainty you feel about the outcome of the game, your ability, and your relationship with other people involved in the game — the higher the uncertainty, the higher the activation.

Practical implications

Know yourself as an individual. Recognise your individual level of optimal activation and individualise your motivation techniques. Remember, not everyone needs to psych-up for a game. In fact, many players would benefit more from learning to relax before a game (see chapter 12, Mental preparation, and chapter 13, Relaxation).

> I don't like being too tensed up before a match. When you're tensed up you can make a mistake early on. I'm a great believer now in going into a match as relaxed as possible.
>
> — JOHN ASHWORTH (ALL BLACK PROP 1978–86)

Reduce the importance of the outcome of the game. Accept that wanting to win is the aim of most players when they take the field for a game of rugby, but place your emphasis on the process of performing to achieve that aim (task orientation; see chapter 3, Motivation). In doing so, emphasise effort and doing your best, and set technique or performance goals (see chapter 10, Goal setting). Place trust in the fact that if you achieve these goals, then you will have done all that you could towards winning the game.

Reduce uncertainty. Do as much as you can to create a supportive atmosphere within the team. Make sure that your individual and team goals are clear and specific. Ensure that your coach knows what 'pre-game coaching' you would like so that you get consistent coach support leading up to a game. If everybody is clear about their goals, their role in the team, and the way that they like to interact with other players and the coaches leading up to a game, then a great deal of uncertainty can be eliminated and stress can be reduced.

Emphasise and develop positive mental attitudes. You should focus on what you *can* do in a game, rather than what you can't. This will help you to set more realistic and appropriate goals. Identify what can be learned from a loss or poor game; analyse mistakes, learn the lesson, then forget them.

Develop your 'coping skills' for dealing with pressure. The following chapter outlines a number of methods for 'coping' with pressure and developing the ability to control your activation levels (see also chapter 15, CARS plan).

6. Coping with pressure

A self-inflicted stressful situation . . .
— Graham Mourie's definition of sport

Playing the game with commitment and pride means putting pressure on yourself to succeed and achieve your goals — pressure which can lead to over-activation, anxiety and stress. All players, regardless of ability, must learn to cope with stress and pressure in order to regain or maintain their 'composure'. Even All Blacks feel stress and pressure — it is part of the challenge of playing competitive rugby.

In general, coping with pressure means managing stress, anxiety, and activation for peak performance.[1] So how do you psych-up without psyching-out?

You can use PST methods to try to prevent stress or over-activation, but you will also need to use some PST methods to try to cure or manage pressure and over-activation when it occurs before, during, and after the game. These coping methods and techniques take time and effort to learn correctly. They must be practised, and need to be 'tailored' to your individual needs. They are essential to consistently reach your peak level of activation (see chapter 5, Controlling activation).

Pressure and stress are a common part of competitive rugby. Their effects can be positive (such as reaching and maintaining peak activation before and during the game), or negative (such as over-activation, anxiety, burnout). Pressure and stress can be both long-term and short-term. Long-term stress is ongoing and persistent; for example, the pressure that comes with a nagging injury or the pressure to retain your place in the starting team. Short-term stress is temporary; for example, making a mistake or error during the game.

Long-term stress requires you to utilise coping resources such as PST methods, nutritional habits, lifestyle management, time management, and social support,[2] and to develop other PST skills like self-confidence, self-esteem, motivation, and commitment. It is important to have a balanced lifestyle and be able to 'switch off' when away from rugby.

One of the most important mental skills is to be able to just switch off. It's actually really hard to train your brain to get away from the training mindset when training's over for the day, but that's certainly what I had to learn to do.

— Zinzan Brooke

> I'm still taking it game by game. With so many talented players around, there's so much pressure on your position and you can't take anything for granted.
>
> — Taine Randell (All Black 1996–)

Short-term stress can negatively affect your concentration, motivation, effort, energy expenditure, and peak activation.[3] Short-term stressors can create emotional turmoil and/or distract your concentration during the game.[4] In extreme cases, the inability to cope with repetitive short-term stress may lead to demotivation, unpleasant emotions, poor overall performance, and eventually to psychological burnout and giving up competitive rugby completely.[5] Short-term stress is inherently negative for your immediate skill performance unless you have mastered appropriate coping strategies (see chapter 15, CARS Plan).

Successful coping requires you to be able to regain composure, to establish the proper mental set, and to maintain your peak levels of activation and concentration. Managing short-term stress primarily depends upon your self-control in a stressful situation.

Examples of short-term stressors in rugby include committing a physical or mental error, experiencing pain, observing an opponent cheat, reacting to the sudden success of an opponent, contending with a poor call by the ref, an unfavourable game score, adverse weather or ground conditions, and receiving unpleasant comments from opponents, teammates, coaches, or others.[6] For instance, players sometimes have to deal with unpleasant verbal abuse during the game. Your opponents may be using it as an outlet for their anger and frustration, or simply to intimidate and distract you. The coach represents another potential source of distraction if they serve up verbal criticism before the game, unwanted advice from the sideline during the game, and negative comments at half-time. Clearly, it is to your benefit to ignore such verbal comments or abuse.

It is important to keep in mind that pressure, stress, and anxiety are not automatically 'bad' (see chapter 5). Some anxiety can be useful: many players report that the 'nervous butterflies' are a sign that they are going to be psyched-up for the game — in fact they get worried if they don't feel nervous before the game! Indeed, research in rugby has pointed out the positive effect that a controlled level of anxiety can have on motivation and commitment for peak performance.[7] To 'control' anxiety you need to learn how to cope with the stress that causes it in the first place.

The process of coping

Coping refers to the process of using PST skills and methods to manage stressful demands that you perceive as pressure (that is, as exceeding your skills and ability).[8] Different types of stress require different coping strategies. Most coping strategies can be categorised as task-focused or emotion-focused,[9] and these two types of coping strategies can be further subdivided into approach and avoidance coping.[10] You need to understand these categories to identify coping methods that fit your personal needs.

Task-focused coping ('problem-focused' coping) is the use of problem-solving, tactical decision-making, physical activity and extra effort to control the cause of the stress and achieve a specific task or skill objective. It can include methods like tactical changes, re-setting goals, channelling your frustration into extra determination for your next skill (such as scrum, line-out, tackle, ruck or maul), seeking social support, becoming verbally assertive, or possibly deliberately avoiding the pressure situation.

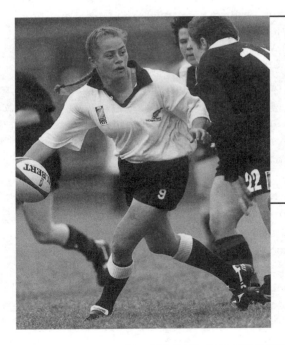

The only people to put pressure on us will be ourselves, because we know we're good and we'll be out proving to ourselves, first and foremost, that we are the best.
— MONIQUE HIROVANAA (BLACK FERNS 1997–) TALKING ABOUT THE TEAM'S PREPARATION FOR THE 1998 WOMEN'S WORLD CUP

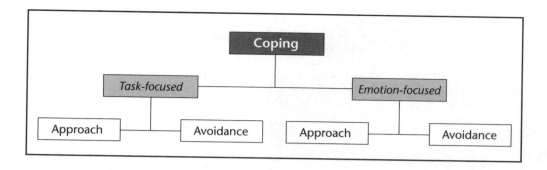

In other words, get on with the game and try to fix the problem, but don't dwell on the sources of stress and pressure. For example, a mistake or error during the game (a potential form of short-term stress) may require additional effort, determination and concentration to maintain a good performance. On the other hand, you may cope with unpleasant comments from your coach, captain, or teammates by attempting to distance yourself physically from that person. In other situations, you may cope with an opponent's verbal abuse by becoming increasingly assertive, vocally and/or physically. PST methods such as self-talk, imagery and mental preparation can be particularly useful for task-focused coping by helping to increase effort, determination and improve concentration. Task-focused coping is primarily directed at solving, changing or fixing the cause of the stress and pressure.

Emotion-focused coping, on the other hand, consists of using thoughts to feel better about performing the task or skill and to cope with the negative and unpleasant emotions that result from the stress/pressure. For instance, if you feel upset after committing a physical error during the game, PST methods such as positive self-talk ('Keep at it', 'Concentrate on your job', 'Stay calm, nail it next time'), thought-stopping, blocking distractions, rational thinking, seeking social support, imagining successful skill execution, and relaxation or centring may be used to reduce interfering thoughts and muscle tension.[11] In general, emotion-focused strategies are designed to help you develop a 'mental readiness' for any eventuality during the game. In this sense, 'readiness' reflects a general confidence about your preparation for the game, and includes mental readiness, physical readiness, and performance expectations based on previous games. Perceived readiness is a key issue in preventing stress and coping with anxiety.[12]

Emotion-focused coping is not used to solve the stressful situation, but rather to deal with the emotional consequences of feeling pressure and stress.

Coping strategies can also be categorised into approach and avoidance categories.[13] An approach strategy consists of confronting the source of stress and attempting to reduce it deliberately — this can be achieved by using either a task-focus or an emotion-focus (or both). At times, however, avoiding pressure situations and their

I get nervous, certainly, but you make your own pressure, and I try to concentrate on the things that I've got control over, and the things I can do to help the players.

— Tony Gilbert, left (Otago Highlanders and 1998 NPC Champion Otago team coach)

consequences is preferable to an approach strategy.[14] Each technique has its advantages and disadvantages.

Approach coping is preferable when the pressure situation is controllable, the source of stress is known to you, or there is a need to remain 'on task' after a period of inactivity following the stressor (such as after half-time or an injury break).[15] For example if Jason verbally abuses his opponent Jim to intimidate or distract him, Jim can ignore it and use the abuse as an incentive for further action. Given Jim's control over the pressure situation and the likelihood of continuing interactions between the two players during the game, an approach coping strategy might be preferred — Jim using a task-focus to confront Jason. Avoiding or ignoring Jason may simply encourage him to continue abusing Jim.

Approach coping is effective when direct action is required to deal with the cause of the pressure. In this sense, it focuses on situation-relevant information (such as reading a defensive pattern), while ignoring any distracting and irrelevant information (such as dummy-runners, verbal comments or abuse from the crowd).[16]

Avoidance coping is appropriate when the most effective coping response is to ignore or dissociate from the pressure situation. It is most useful when emotional resources are limited (low self-confidence), the source of stress is not clear, the pressure situation is uncontrollable, or when time is of the essence as the game 'moves on'.[17] For instance, you cannot afford to become distracted if the referee makes a wrong call while play is ongoing (perhaps an offside interception or an illegal turnover at a ruck). In such cases approaching the stressor will rarely improve the situation or the outcome — the ref won't change their call and the game has continued! Avoidance can be achieved by using a task-focus (such as applying extra effort to the next job at hand) or an emotion-focus (such as deliberately shifting your thoughts and concentration to other skills or to upcoming tactical options). The most effective method of coping with stressors that are outside your control is to ignore them or quickly forget them and mentally 'move on'. The game has carried on to the next phase and so must your thinking and concentration if you want to play well and enjoy yourself rather than become annoyed and frustrated.

Certain pressure situations require you to be more objective. An avoidance coping strategy called 'psychological distancing' consists of maintaining a detached and distant view of a difficult person while he or she is in the process of being difficult.[18] Mentally dismissing someone as a 'whinger' or 'negative' allows you to view that person's behaviour more objectively and less stressfully. For instance, rather than being intimidated or upset by negative comments from an opponent, you may be able to quickly explain or rationalise these actions to yourself (this is an emotion-focused method of avoiding the source of stress). The objective of this strategy is to see others as truly separate from yourself.

Avoidance coping also has its disadvantages. Denying responsibility for the causes of a pressure situation (an avoidance coping strategy) may lead you to dismiss valuable information such as a coach or captain's instructions, or your opponents' tactical weaknesses. And if you don't take proper responsibility for your own actions you may fail to improve or learn from previous mistakes.

Using approach and avoidance coping techniques is not an either/or choice. You might use a combination of both to cope with a particular source of pressure, whether by switching rapidly between the two, or avoiding certain aspects of a pressure situation while approaching others.[19]

For example, if you miss a simple midfield tackle from scrum ball, you will likely feel frustrated and angry at yourself for letting yourself and your teammates down. You may attempt to cope with such a major mistake by using centring and self-talk to avoid the stress and pressure that comes with the temptation to mentally criticise yourself. If the game has carried on to the next phase this coping strategy is likely to be the most effective, since trying to solve your tackling problem by using approach coping would not be appropriate — you need to move on to your next job! But at the next scrum or other break in play you could attempt to cope by approaching the cause of your mistake, quickly using imagery to replay the situation in your head and figure out what you did wrong in your defensive lines and your tackling technique.

In competitive rugby, avoidance coping may be more productive when performing ongoing tasks such as decision-making at second and third phase play. Worrying or dwelling on unpleasant emotions will interfere with your concentration and your decision-making, resulting in poorer performance. Instead, to be a successful player you must use PST methods to keep your activation levels under control under adverse circumstances.

Prevention or cure?

Although you should focus on minimising or preventing 'stressful' factors or situations in rugby, you will also need to learn coping techniques to counter or cure uncontrollable factors. Prevention is better than cure, but there will always be a need for the 'cure' techniques.

Prevention

There are two major perspectives to 'prevention' coping — person factors (what you bring with you in terms of coping skills and abilities), and situational factors (what coping methods the situation allows you to use).

Person factors. Goal setting is a common PST method for preventing stress and pressure. By setting performance and process goals you can control the standards used to judge your success — having a sense of control allows you to resist possible sources of pressure. Try to match yourself with realistic task demands and goals for each game (see chapter 10, Goal setting). If you can increase your self-confidence you will also reduce stress and anxiety (see chapter 4, Self-confidence). Mental preparation strategies are effective methods for increasing confidence and reaching peak activation without becoming stressed (see chapter 12, Mental preparation). All of these examples are approach and task-focused methods of preventing pressure and stress.

Situational factors. This is primarily the role of the coach and captain. You can reduce pressure and stress by encouraging your coach and captain to reinforce performance and technique goals. Match stats such as tackle counts, ball won at first phase, ball won at second phase and turnovers can be used to set performance goals for the team and for individual players in each game. Encourage your coach and captain to emphasise doing your best, and encourage your coach to reward effort and goal attainment through use of match stats, not just the outcome of the game. Winning or losing are important, but you need to emphasise effort and goal attainment — these are aspects of the performance that are in your control. These situational factors are primarily examples of avoidance and task-focused coping.

> I don't know what people's expectations are, but to me you feel pressure when you can't control what you're dealing with. What we have to attempt to do is control as many of the variables as we can.
> — ROBBIE DEANS (CANTERBURY NPC TEAM COACH 1997–)

Cure

The same two perspectives — person factors and situational factors — apply to 'cure' coping.

Person factors. To control the mental and muscle tension that often results from pressure you need to learn the PST method of relaxation (see chapter 13, Relaxation techniques). You can use thought-stopping to reduce negative thoughts by rationally eliminating stressful factors or cues, and then focusing on positive thoughts and performance goals (see chapter 11, Self-talk). These techniques are both approach coping methods, but are a mixture of task-focused (muscle relaxation) and emotion-focused (thought-stopping and self-talk) coping strategies. It can help to focus on the basic goal of 'enjoyment' — too often we forget this while we are working hard to enhance our performance and seek success.

> I always go out with the idea of wanting to enjoy myself. It is, after all, a game. You just take enjoyment from the fact you're out there doing what you want to do, trying to beat the best teams in the world, especially if you are standing in the middle of Ellis Park playing the Springboks. The stadium is such a cauldron. Everyone is looking down on you and there's not that many Kiwi supporters. But you stand there and you look around and think, 'It doesn't get any better than this.'
> — FRANK BUNCE (ALL BLACK 1992–97)

Situational factors. Once again this is primarily the role of the coach and captain, who both need to be good role models. They should act confident (emotion-focused, avoidance coping strategy) and focus on performance goals in discussing the game (task-focused, approach coping strategy). It is helpful if your coach can recognise your signs of stress and over-activation, but unfortunately research shows that most coaches are poor at this.[20] The coach must 'individualise' their motivation techniques — not everyone needs an emotional pep talk. The coach may also need to initiate and reinforce relaxation and thought-stopping techniques for certain players (emotion-focused, approach coping methods). Finally, it is vital that the coach and captain focus on performance goals (task-focused, approach coping strategy) to establish a sense of control.

> I thought the discipline of the All Blacks was outstanding under provocation and I just wanted to get the message across that we need to keep our composure and not get sucked into the off-the-ball stuff that was starting to happen.
> — JOHN HART (ALL BLACK COACH 1996–99), EXPLAINING WHY HE SENT INSTRUCTIONS TO THE TEAM AFTER A TENSE SITUATION DURING A TEST AGAINST SOUTH AFRICA

Specific coping methods

Most players use a number of coping methods to deal with different sources of stress. You need to learn your coping methods so well that they can be executed automatically.

Mental preparation strategies. These techniques are useful for both prevention and cure of over-activation and pressure. Depending on the type of mental prep used, this PST method can be both an approach and an avoidance technique, and both task- and emotion-focused. The goal of mental prep is to help you reach your peak level of activation — to psych-up without being psyched-out. (See chapter 12, Mental preparation.)

Self-talk. Identify the appropriate concentration 'signs' or cues to focus on, and learn to maintain that focus[21] (see chapter 7, Concentration and decision-making). The use of silent 'self-statements' can be useful for maintaining concentration ('watch the ball'), for increasing self-confidence ('I can do it', 'I can do no more than give 100 percent'), and for controlling activation levels ('centre', 'stay calm', 'you are in control'). (See chapter 11, Self-talk.)

Parking (thought-stopping). Practise stopping negative thought patterns by using silent instructions or 'triggers' such as 'stop!' , 'park it!' , or 'bin it!' (see chapter 11, Self-talk). Some players slap their leg, or slap the ball to 'park' the negative thoughts somewhere else so that they can refocus their concentration on the task at hand. 'Parking' is just like parking a car: when you don't need or want a negative thought you can 'park' it somewhere and come back for it after the game!

Relaxation. Use mental and physical relaxation procedures such as mind-to-muscle (centring) and muscle-to-mind relaxation to decrease your heart rate, breathing rate, and muscle tension. Relaxation also demands a change of mental focus away from anxiety-producing thoughts; therefore it helps to cope with mental stress and pressure. (See chapter 13, Relaxation techniques.)

Imagery. Also known as mental practice, this technique can increase confidence and move your focus to task cues or thoughts. Imagery allows you to cope with stress mentally before competition, so that you can develop ways to prevent or manage pressure situations during the game (see chapter 14, Imagery).

CARS plan (CARS = critical action response strategy). This is an individualised combination of a number of the PST methods mentioned above (see the sample CARS plans in chapter 15). One player's CARS plan might involve a combination of imagery, self-talk and relaxation; another's may include a mixture of self-talk and mental prep. CARS plans are designed to help you cope with the stress and pressure associated with critical actions in a game. Critical actions are situations such as defence and tackling, goal kicking, your own mistakes, refereeing decisions, adverse weather conditions, physical or verbal intimidation by opponents, and coming on as a substitute. A CARS plan is vital for a continuous, interactive sport like rugby where typically you must cope with stress and pressure 'on the go'.

Bob (our first five) desperately needs to learn how to cope with the pressure that he is experiencing (see his Peak Performance Profile on page 41).

He's been working on his foundation skill need of self-confidence (see chapter 4), so now it's time to look at PST methods for his need to 'cope with pressure' — in this case, relaxation or centring, self-talk, parking, and a CARS plan. Bob's completed worksheets for self-talk and his CARS plan for coping with pressure are shown on pages 147 and 196 respectively. Bob may wish to use imagery here as well, but the type of images would need to be a bit different from those he used to improve his self-confidence. At the same time as he is working on his coping skills Bob can also begin to work on his need for improved concentration and decision-making: see chapter 7.

No Worries

Ain't no use worrying about things beyond your control,
because if they're beyond your control ain't no use worrying, . . .
. . . ain't no use worrying about things within your control,
because if you have them under control, ain't no use worrying . . .

— AUTHOR UNKNOWN

7 . Concentration and decision-making

You have to concentrate on what you are doing. The moment you start looking at the opposition the focus goes and you drop the ball.

— ROBBIE DEANS

Dave is half-back for his club's under-19 team. He's been selected for his strong passing and aggressive running, but lately his coach has noticed that his option-taking from scrums and from rucks and mauls has been poor. He has been told that he is too tunnel visioned, in that he runs when he should pass the ball, passes when he should run, and doesn't seem to see the gaps on the blindside. Dave is aware of the problem and worries that he might be dropped because of it, yet he can't seem to see the options that open up to him during a game. He still either passes to his first five, or runs himself from the base of a scrum or a ruck/maul when this is the wrong option (*too narrow focus — inability to scan the play*).

Sara is the coach of the provincial women's team. During the selection trials for the team, Sara finds it difficult to watch particular players because she gets distracted by the actions of other players or the team with the ball. She tries to focus solely on the player that she is interested in at the time, but seems to always end up following the progress of the ball-carrier (*external distraction*).

Paul is a hooker for his senior club team. He often finds that he gets distracted by spectators yelling out on the sideline, or by the opposition's half-back yapping to his own forwards when he is about to throw the ball into the line-out. As a consequence, his throwing has been rather inaccurate this season. His team has slipped to mid-table, and according to the local sports reporter in the newspaper, their poor performances are mainly due to their inability to gain quality line-out ball. Try as he might, Paul just doesn't seem to be able to block out these distractions when he throws into the line-out. Opposition teams have begun to sense this and are deliberately trying to put him off. It seems to be working (*external distraction*).

Bob (our first five) gets distracted by worrying about what his teammates will think if he misses important kicks at goal. He is very aware of his heart rate, butterflies in his stomach, sweaty palms, and tense muscles as he prepares for a kick, and his kicking percentage has been down on previous years (*internal distraction*).

On the other hand, Jack (our number eight) has recently developed good concentration and decision-making skills. In ruck situations during a game, Jack always seems to know when to 'pick-and-go', when to 'blow over' the ball, and when to 'pick-and-feed' to another player on the burst. His ability to 'read the play' has been a major factor in his selection for the rep team this season (*good concentration and focus of attention*).

In all these situations the individual's concentration has a powerful influence on their performance, either positively or negatively. It is clear that the ability to concentrate is an important feature of successful performance in rugby. Coaches, players and spectators are often heard telling other players to 'concentrate', 'pay attention', or 'focus' at various times during a game — usually when the player has just made some kind of unforced error. Although these comments are probably made in an attempt to be helpful, it can be difficult if you don't know *how* to concentrate, pay attention, or focus on the right cues (pieces of information) on the field. So what do these terms actually mean, and how can you improve your ability to concentrate and make smart decisions?

Attention can be described as 'selective thinking'. We have a limited capacity for handling and processing (thinking about) information, and so we need to selectively focus our attention onto the information that we decide is appropriate, choosing among the many visual cues and voices that can be seen and heard by a player at any one time. For instance, a lock running towards a ruck must not only look for where he might hit the ruck, but he should also ignore the calls of the crowd and the opposition players, and selectively pay attention to the voices of his own support players, especially the half-back, who is probably yelling out instructions to either drive into the ruck, get out of the way, wait for a pass, or to 'pick-and-go'. He probably shouldn't pay attention to the alignment of the opposition backs, the position of the referee, or whether or not the player lying on the ground 5 metres away from the ruck on the blindside is hurt, although he could if he wanted to. The point is that the player must choose what information to pay attention to and what to ignore or disregard.

Concentration is the ability to sustain the appropriate attentional focus for the required period of time. The lock in the previous paragraph should focus on the appropriate cues for his role in that ruck situation until it is over and a new situation requiring a different attentional focus occurs. During that time he must block out any distractions, or refocus immediately if those distractions draw his attention away from what he has to do. Concentration is a skill, and must be developed and practised just like other PST skills such as confidence or motivation.

Attentional style

There are two key dimensions of attention:[1]

Breadth of focus (width). This represents the amount of information that you pay attention to at any one time, and can be categorised as either broad or narrow. A broad focus means that you pay attention to a number of different cues at any one time, whereas a narrow focus means that you pay attention to only one or perhaps two cues at a time.

Direction of focus (direction). This represents the location of the information that you pay attention to: whether it is external to you, or remains as an internal focus of attention. An example of an external focus is simply watching an opponent coming towards you with the ball; an internal focus would becoming aware of the fact that you are worried about your ability to tackle the player bearing down on you.

Research in sport suggests that there are four major attentional styles, of which one will be the preferred style that forms part of your personality. For example, you might tend to focus on one or two cues at a time rather than seeing everything that is going on around you. However, a well-rounded player needs to be adaptable. Different situations — such as a line-out (first phase) or a ruck (second phase) — mean you often have to change your attentional style to match the demands of that situation. A prop's preferred attentional style may be to focus on one cue at a time (narrow focus), such as lifting his lock in a line-out, but in open field play he must be able to broaden his focus to pay attention to a number of different cues like 'reading' the lines of attack or defence while anticipating where the next ruck or maul will be.

Broad-external. This style is used to rapidly assess a situation with a large number of relevant cues. You might be a player who is good at 'reading' the game (especially opposition strengths and weaknesses) and strong in your ability to use a broad-external focus. This style is also used to develop and use 'anticipation' in situations such as counterattacking from broken play, or reading play for an interception. Former All Black number eight Zinzan Brooke was known for his uncanny ability to read a game. During a 1997 Tri-Series match against Australia he fielded a high kick on his own 10 metre line (using a narrow focus of attention), and then had the vision to immediately make a wide pass to Christian Cullen on the counterattack, who proceeded to run through the Australian defences and score underneath the posts. Brooke's ability to switch to a broad-external focus enabled him to 'see' Christian Cullen over 20 metres away, and rapidly to assess that there was an opportunity to counterattack from an essentially defensive situation. This ability to rapidly switch

Model of attentional style

EXTERNAL

Broad-external	**Narrow-external**
To rapidly assess a situation	Required at the moment a response is given
For 'reading' the game, especially in first phase attack and defence	Focus, non-distracted, on one or two pieces of external info
To develop and use 'anticipation'	
e.g., choosing a backline attacking move	*e.g., kick a ball, pass to a teammate, react to 1 opponent*
Broad-internal	**Narrow-internal**
Used to analyse and plan	Required to 'tune-in' and be sensitive to your body
To make game plans, tactics	To centre and calm yourself
To anticipate the future, and recall past info	To rehearse mentally (imagery) skill or move
e.g., coaching; tactics, strategy	*e.g., activation regulation; centring, imagery*

BROAD ... NARROW

INTERNAL

from a narrow-external focus to a broad-external one was clearly something that separated Brooke from other less skilled players in his position.

Narrow-external. This style is required at the moment a response is given. Players who have a strong ability in this attentional style are able to focus on one or two external cues such as passing, kicking or catching a ball, or reacting to one opponent (such as when controlling the ball in the back of a scrum while going for a pushover try, or making a head-on tackle on a tight forward on the burst).

Broad-internal. This style is used to analyse and plan. It is often used by coaches and captains to develop game plans and tactics, to anticipate the future, and to recall past information. For example, coaches must use a broad-internal focus of attention at some time during the first half of a game in order to provide the players with feedback on their performance at half-time, and to decide upon the best tactics to use in the second half.

Narrow-internal. This style is required to 'tune-in' and be sensitive to your body. It can be used to calm yourself down, or to mentally rehearse (imagery) a skill or move. This style is useful for controlling activation (see chapter 5). By using a narrow-internal focus you can recognise when you are too psyched-up for a match and then use PST methods such as imagery, relaxation or self-talk to re-establish your peak activation levels for the game.

Stable versus situational components of attentional style. Although you will have a 'preferred attentional style' that forms a stable part of your personality, you must also be able to adjust your attentional style to match the particular demands of the situations in which you find yourself.[2] Indeed, the ability to switch attentional styles is something that you must be able to do in order to perform well, otherwise you will not be able to perform to your potential. If you can match your attentional style with the demands of the particular situation in the game, you are more likely to deal with it successfully, and less likely to be criticised for 'taking wrong options', being 'tunnel-visioned', or becoming 'distracted'.

Normally you will be better at using your preferred attentional style, but the demands of rugby are such that you need to use them all at one time or another, and you should train yourself to become better at using all of them. You should also learn to quickly switch between attentional styles as the situation demands. However, a player who has a strength in one particular style will often find themself playing in a position that best suits that style. For example, rugby research has shown that half-backs and first five-eighths are significantly better than other players at using a broad-external focus.[3] An important component of playing well in these positions is the ability quickly to assess a large number of situational cues (to 'read the game') and to make swift decisions about what to do, so players who have a strong broad-external focus are more likely to play well in these positions.

Attention-activation interaction. Peak attention or concentration is very much related to peak activation. Increased activation can lead to a 'narrowing' of your attentional focus (this is an involuntary response). This in turn can lead to a decreased ability to pay attention to peripheral cues (such as being able to see a teammate out of the corner of your eye), and you find that you cannot scan as much of the field as you could before.[4] Probably you will also be less able to switch between attentional styles because your increased activation has begun to control your attentional ability. If you become over-psyched or extremely anxious, your attention becomes focused internally as well as narrowly, and you become solely concerned with how you are feeling inside.[5] Obviously this is detrimental to your performance, so in order to regain your attention you must control your activation level.

Effect of fatigue. Many mistakes occur during the last quarter of a match when players are tired or fatigued. Fatigue has the effect of making it more difficult for players to focus on critical situational cues because everything simply takes more effort.[6] This is one of the reasons why fitter players are able to perform more effectively in the latter stages of matches — they can remain focused on the task at hand, while their less fit teammates and opponents are perhaps more concerned with internal cues (such as how 'bad' they are feeling) and find themselves so distracted that they miss important external cues that might influence the outcome of a tightly contested match.

Distractions. The ability to deal with potential distractions is an important factor in maintaining your concentration skills. Distractions can be of two types, internal and external.

Internal distractions occur when you are thinking about something that is unrelated to the task. A women's team fullback could be thinking about the pass that she dropped in the previous play, a number eight could be worrying about whether or not she can control the ball at the next attempt at a pushover scrum, a prop could be angry at the ref for penalising her at the last scrum when she was doing nothing illegal, and a centre could be thinking about how sore her thumb is after the last tackle she made. Focusing on internal cues like these could potentially distract them from what they should be doing at the time.

External distractions occur when you are unable to stop yourself paying attention to cues in the situation that may have nothing to do with the move or the skill that you are executing at the time.[7] For example, a midfield back may allow herself to be distracted by the defenders instead of focusing on the ball as it is passed to her. On the other hand, a player who is appearing in his first ever first class match in front of 50,000 people might suddenly notice the roar of the crowd during a particularly exciting passage of play and be distracted from the task at hand.

Common attentional errors

Having a preferred or dominant attentional style has its disadvantages. You can come to rely too much on your preferred style, and if this is inappropriate for the situation at the time, mistakes can occur. If you are unable to voluntarily shift from one style to another as the situation requires ('limited attentional flexibility'), errors will also occur.

There are common errors associated with each of the major attentional styles.

Broad-external. These players are sometimes too busy reacting to the situation unfolding in front of them to think about what they should be doing at that moment. They often repeat the same mistakes, and can be fooled by their opponent because they react too quickly and 'buy the dummy' or 'take the fake'. Their behaviour is externally rather than internally controlled. These players often become distracted by unimportant information such as crowd noise or verbal intimidation from an opponent.

Narrow-external. Players who are dominated by this attentional style often fail to adjust to changing situations. They get a plan, strategy or response in mind and stick to it no matter what. Such a player often focuses totally on the ball and fails to notice changes in positioning by teammates and opponents. This can be a big problem if the player is in a key decision-making position such as half-back, first five-eighth or loose forward, or finds themself in a situation that demands that they make a decision based on a large number of situational cues ('read' the game).

Broad-internal. These players often over-analyse and out-think themselves, rather than focusing on the game. For example, players who dwell on a mistake that has just been made will find that they end up making more mistakes during the game because their attention has been diverted away from the task at hand.

Narrow-internal. These players are often seen as 'chokers'. They sometimes become so focused on their own feelings that they can't function. For example, the second five who is concentrating so hard on trying to control his activation and anxiety levels that he forgets to catch the ball could be said to be inappropriately focused on narrow internal cues rather than having a focus of attention that matches the situational demands at the time.

Overloading. Attentional errors can sometimes occur from what is termed external or internal overloading. External overloading occurs when the player becomes confused by trying to concentrate on too many external cues at once.[8] As a consequence they get distracted by things that have nothing to do with the task that they should be doing, and their performance drops off. Internal overloading occurs when a player becomes preoccupied with too much self-talk or 'internal coaching', missing important external cues during the game, and taking the wrong options in critical situations.

Limited flexibility. Successful players can voluntarily shift their attentional style to match the situational demands at the time. Over-activation, pressure and stress can often result in concentration being totally focused internally, so that you become inflexible and unable to switch your attention-concentration to match the situation.[9]

Developing concentration skills

Before you can improve your ability to concentrate, you must first determine what exactly you should be concentrating on, and make an assessment of your own attentional strengths and weaknesses. You should also assess your ability to switch your attentional focus at the right times during a game or during practice, so that the attentional style you use matches the demands of the task that you are about to perform.

Assessing concentration skills

The first step in any assessment of your attentional abilities is to assess the attentional demands of rugby in general, and then more specifically the demands of your playing position. In doing this assessment you should ask yourself a number of questions, such as:

★ What are some of the basic skills that every player needs in order to play well?

★ What are the specific skills involved in playing my position?

★ When do these skills usually occur during a game?

★ What should I be focusing on when they do occur?

★ When do I need to switch my focus of attention during a game?

You may wish to use the Peak Performance Concentration Profile sheet on page 105 to help you categorise the skills and demands you have identified in terms of the four basic attentional styles. This will help you to understand the type of attentional style that you should adopt when performing these skills (see Bob's Concentration Profile on page 106).

The next step in the process is to analyse your own strengths and weaknesses in performing each of the skills that you identified as being important to playing the game, and especially your position. You should ask yourself:[10]

★ How good am I at focusing on the critical aspects of each of these skills?

★ When does my concentration tend to break down?

★ Does this breakdown occur at certain times during a game, or when performing certain skills?

I think tackling is a timing thing really if you are going to make big hits. Anticipation is a big part of it. You can see what is developing with players on the field. If someone is running up field you can see one player that he is going to draw, but he has a support player. You know he is going to draw his man and pass it inside so you just head for the inside player and if you are a few metres away at the time, the guy with the ball isn't going to see you coming and the guy who is receiving it has got his eye on the ball and he's not going to see you coming. He catches it, turns and wham!

— FRANK BUNCE DESCRIBING THE DECISION-
MAKING SKILLS USED IN BACKLINE TACKLING

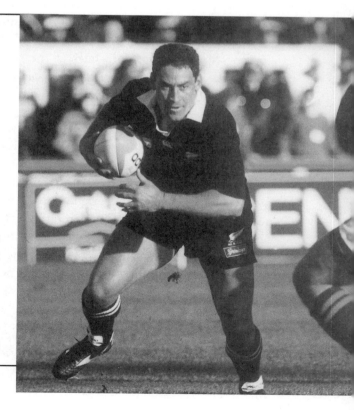

Again, you may wish to use the Peak Performance Concentration Profile on page 105 to help you rate your ability. Developing your own Concentration Profile will help you to:

★ become more aware of the attentional demands of the game;

★ become more aware of your own attentional strengths and weaknesses

★ decide which skills you need to work on to match the attentional demands with your own attentional abilities.

Another approach would be to ask players or coaches who you respect and trust about what to focus on when performing each of the skills involved in playing the game. Ask them about the strategies and techniques that they use to remain focused in the face of possible distractions. You might also wish to observe top level players during practices or games and assess what they focus on when playing, and how they seem to know what to do in certain situations. It may be that these top players are simply able to concentrate on the right cues and therefore can react quickly to situations that develop during a game. This ability, coupled with their own high ability to execute the skills of their position, is often part of what separates them from those players who are unable to make that step up to the next level. Their concentration skills are a key part of their mental toughness.

Most top level players agree that the pace of the game increases considerably as you move up the grades, and therefore the ability to make the right decisions quickly is critical.[11] A large part of your ability to do this will be determined by your ability to concentrate on the right cues at the right times, and to ignore those that are irrelevant. For example, anticipation is a big part of the skill of tackling, so it needs to be part of your attention-concentration skills.

Techniques for developing concentration

The ability to concentrate is very much affected by fatigue and activation levels. Consequently, your fitness levels are an important factor in your ability to concentrate. If you are as fit, fast, strong and as powerful as you could possibly be, you will be less likely to experience lapses in concentration due to fatigue, especially towards the end of a match when fatigue is often a factor. If you can control your activation levels and remain at peak activation you will be less likely to suffer from concentration lapses caused by a narrowing of your attentional focus as a result of over-activation (see chapter 5, Controlling activation).

Some more specific techniques to develop concentration could include:

Attentional cues.

These are specific cues (or combinations of cues) that you can use as a signal to focus on specific things, or to intensify or relax your concentration whenever you need to do so.[12] They can take various forms, but in general terms can be categorised as listening, visual or physical cues.

> Every individual knows what makes them perform best and whether it is superstition or just trust, no one likes to break their routine. For me, the routine I follow is very simple and easy to do, there are no long concentration periods, no patterns I go through. I just do what needs to be done and what I feel like doing.
>
> — JEFF WILSON

Listening cues can be verbal cues such as particular calls by players (perhaps to signal a backrow play or a backline move), or specific individual self-talk strategies such as affirmation statements, cue words or phrases, positive self-talk, thought-stopping, or countering (see chapter 11, Self-talk). They can also take the form of verbal team signals or codes. For example, a specific, pre-agreed word (such as 'ICE') could be used by anyone in the team at any time to signal an increase in Intensity, Concentration, and Effort (see also chapter 15, CARS plan). As well as these verbal cues, other listening cues could be used. For example, the blast of the referee's whistle during the game could and should be used as a cue to switch your concentration on or off as the situation demands. If you find yourself dwelling unnecessarily on a previous mistake you can use the ref's whistle as a signal to shift your focus back onto the task at hand after quickly assessing what has just happened and deciding on your actions for the next play.

Visual cues involve focusing intently on something within the situation as a signal to concentrate on a specific task or skill that is about to be performed. In rugby a goal kicker might focus intently on the posts or the spot where he will place the ball as he is walking up to prepare for the kick.

Physical cues involve doing specific physical actions to focus yourself on the task at hand. A hooker could twirl the ball in his hands as part of his preparation to throw the ball into a line-out. A prop might clean the dirt from his boots, even if it is a dry day, before he packs down in a scrum, and a half-back might wipe her hands or spit on them before the ball is thrown into a line-out as a signal to focus on the throw. These physical cues can form part of players' pre-performance routine, another effective method for developing concentration (see chapter 12, Mental preparation).

Routines. [13]
Preparation is a key ingredient in successful performance. The use of consistent physical and mental preparation routines before and during a game will help you to block out irrelevant cues (internal and external distractions), and increase your chances of performing consistently well (see chapter 12 for mental preparation routines). Routines must be carefully planned and practised before you use them in competition games.

Simulated practice
By simulating the conditions under which you will be playing you can become used to the potential distractions that you may be exposed to during the game. There are various ways that players and coaches can simulate these conditions:

★ You can practice at the same time during the day as the game will be.

★ If possible, practice on the field at which you will play.

★ Have opposed practices, with other players taking on the role of opposition players.

★ Wear your playing jerseys during practice.

★ The coach could set up situations to simulate unfavourable conditions that might occur during the game, such as playing with a player in the sin bin, asking the players to imagine that they are 4 points down with two minutes to play, or asking someone to adopt the role of a referee who makes unfavourable decisions at crucial times during opposed practice drills.

If you practise under simulated conditions you will be less likely to be distracted by these situations if they arise during the game. You will be able to remain focused on your job, and will be better able to react quickly to anything that your opponents may try (provided it is something that has been simulated in practice). The more prepared and confident you are about your ability to deal with situations that arise, the less likely you will be to become anxious and experience the attentional narrowing that accompanies this (see also chapter 15, CARS plan).

Imagery training (mental rehearsal)
Create clear and vivid images of yourself successfully performing the various skills of your position, and learn to control these images as much as possible. By imaging (or 'visualising') yourself performing well, coping with distractions and quickly switching your focus to the appropriate cues for different tasks, you will

automatically be practising your concentration skills. Imagery practice can be done at almost any time during the days leading up to a game or practice, immediately before and during practices, before games, and even during games at certain times (such as during breaks in play, before the ball is thrown into a line-out, or immediately before kicking goals). It is also useful after a game as a means of reviewing your performance and deciding whether your focus was appropriate (see also chapter 14, Imagery).

> One of the practical ways that Michael Jones has developed his physical and mental demands of lines to be run is illustrated by his 'rehearsal time' [imagery]. On a rugby field, often at night, Jones will lean into a goalpost and visualise field situations and the resultant lines he is required to run. He then physically runs these lines, noting to himself any 'changes' in the opposing team's tactics or play. Thus, he rapidly adjusts his line, speed and placement. He may run 30 or 40 metres and then go to ground, or simulate being tackled.
> — A DESCRIPTION OF 'IMAGERY' TRAINING METHODS USED BY MICHAEL JONES (ALL BLACK 1987–98)

Focus-loop[14]

Many situations on the rugby field during a game will require you to use all four of the attentional styles in a particular sequence or 'loop'. For example, as soon as the referee whistles for a scrum, the half-back who will be putting the ball in must quickly assess the situation using a broad-external focus, taking into account the field position, the alignment of the opposition defences, the calls from his first five, and whether or not there is the opportunity for a blindside move. He must then decide upon a strategy for that scrum that fits into the team's game plan (broad-internal focus), perhaps taking into account the score, the amount of time left, and the success or otherwise of previous attempts at particular scrum moves. Then he must prepare himself for the execution of the move decided on, perhaps by visualising the move or using a centring technique to control his activation levels (narrow-internal focus). All his attention must then be focused on executing the move and ignoring any potential distractions (narrow-external focus). As soon as the ball has been passed (or the move executed), he must quickly broaden his focus and assess whether the move has been successful (broad-external focus), and thus the process begins again. You should get into the habit of using this focus-loop process, which may only take a few seconds to complete each time.

Goal setting

Focusing on achieving performance and process goals during a game will help you to stay focused on what it is that you have to do in order to perform well, and help you to remain focused on the present moment (see chapter 10, Goal setting). It is easy to get distracted if you focus on winning as the only goal, dwell on a mistake that you have just made, or think about how you will feel at the end of the game. It is important to be aware of the 'big picture' regarding your team's game plan, but during the execution of particular moves you should be focused on what you have to do at that time! Having performance- and process-based goals will help you to achieve this.

Overlearning

By learning each of the individual and team skills to the point where they become automatic responses, you will be more likely to be able to perform them in the face of whatever situations arise during a game. Once the skills have become 'second nature', you should not have to think about their execution, and your attention can then be directed towards deciding when to use them — you can 'just do it!'

Peak Performance Concentration Profile

List and rate the attention/concentration characteristics of your **best** or **peak** rugby performance. Rate yourself on each of the concentration qualities using the following scale:

```
              0   1   2   3   4   5   6   7   8   9   10
Current + Best:  Poor              Average           Excellent
```

Name: . . . .   Playing position: . . . .

	CURRENT	BEST
BROAD-EXTERNAL:		
. . . .	| . . . . |	| . . . . |
. . . .	| . . . . |	| . . . . |
. . . .	| . . . . |	| . . . . |
. . . .	| . . . . |	| . . . . |
BROAD-INTERNAL:		
. . . .	| . . . . |	| . . . . |
. . . .	| . . . . |	| . . . . |
. . . .	| . . . . |	| . . . . |
. . . .	| . . . . |	| . . . . |
NARROW-EXTERNAL:		
. . . .	| . . . . |	| . . . . |
. . . .	| . . . . |	| . . . . |
. . . .	| . . . . |	| . . . . |
. . . .	| . . . . |	| . . . . |
NARROW-INTERNAL:		
. . . .	| . . . . |	| . . . . |
. . . .	| . . . . |	| . . . . |
. . . .	| . . . . |	| . . . . |
. . . .	| . . . . |	| . . . . |

Peak Performance Concentration Profile

List and rate the attention/concentration characteristics of your **best** or **peak** rugby performance. Rate yourself on each of the concentration qualities using the following scale:

0	1	2	3	4	5	6	7	8	9	10

Current + Best: Poor   Average   Excellent

Name: Bob Templeton   *Playing position:* First five-eighth

	CURRENT	BEST
BROAD-EXTERNAL:		
Goal kicking: Evaluating conditions (e.g., wind)	6	10
Kicking for field position	8	9
'Reading' holes in opposition defence	5	10
Option-taking: Opposition & field position	4	9
BROAD-INTERNAL:		
Goal kicking: Recalling other kicks in similar conditions	8	9
Option-taking within the 'game plan'	6	10
Recalling 'weaknesses' in opposition defence	7	9
NARROW-EXTERNAL:		
Goal kicking: Watching the ball in the run-up	4	10
Punting for touch: Watch ball onto boot	6	10
'Calling' backline defence to one teammate	4	9
NARROW-INTERNAL:		
Goal kicking: Imagery rehearsal of kick	4	10
Self-talk for coping with pressure	3	8
Imagery & centring for activation control	4	9

8. Team cohesion

Rugby is a team game which requires the fifteen players on the field and the rest of the squad to work together toward common goals. Individuals, no matter how talented, who don't accept that the team must always take precedence, who aren't prepared to function within the framework of standards and disciplines, eventually become an enemy within, undermining the colllective effort.

— JOHN HART OUTLINING THE KEY ASPECTS OF TEAMWORK AND TEAM COHESION IN RUGBY

Team versus individual

A common rugby cliché is that 'a champion team will always beat a team of champions'.[1] A considerable amount of coaching wisdom is reflected in this claim — rugby is a genuine team sport where each player is totally reliant on their fourteen teammates (plus the reserves bench and coach). A champion 'team' should indeed beat a team of champions — the integrated, coordinated effort required to be successful in rugby can only be achieved by a high degree of teamwork. On the other hand, the 'team of champions' is more of a loose group of talented players than a real team.

As a coach or captain, how do you identify the key differences between these two types of team? As a leader, how can you develop a champion team? To answer these questions, we need to understand some of the principles of 'group productivity' from the area of corporate team-building; we'll then integrate these principles with findings from research on team performance in sport.

What is a group?

A group is defined as a collection of individuals who have connections with one another that make them interdependent to some significant degree.[2] The key requirements of a group are interaction, mutual awareness, interdependence, and continuity over time. Groups are dynamic not static; they exhibit life and vitality, interaction and activity.[3]

A collection of individuals is not necessarily a group.[4] Group members must all be aware of each other and be able to interact and communicate with each other.[5] A collection of people who swim for fitness during their lunch hour is not a group — they are not necessarily aware of each other and nor do they interact in a structured manner. On the other hand a collection of competitive swimmers who meet for early morning swim training is a group — they have a shared purpose (training for competition); they are aware of each other (they belong to the same swim team or club); and they interact with each other (they pace each other and share coaches and training programmes).

> As I grew to understand the structure of the game I was more and more absorbed by its reliance on teamwork with player working for player, a mutual reliance which placed team before individual.
>
> — BRIAN LOCHORE

What is a team?

A team is a special type of group. It is a group of players who have a well developed collective identity and who work together to achieve a specific goal or set of goals: the goal makes the team members interdependent.[6] A team must have a shared sense of purpose, structured patterns of interaction, interdependence amongst teammates, team spirit, and a collective identity. Each team member must view membership as being rewarding and satisfying, and consider that such rewards and satisfaction would not be attainable without membership of the team.[7]

A common assumption about team performance is that 'the best players make the best team' — but if this were true a team of champions would *be* a champion team by default. Simply summing the abilities of individual team members does not accurately describe the team performance. We must consider the team process as well as individual ability:[8] team motivation, team cohesion, and captaincy are processes that have a significant impact on team performance.

General observation of any rugby competition reveals that few teams consistently perform to their potential. A team that appears 'on paper' to have the best players does not necessarily perform well. Individual skill performance should *not* be the only factor for team member selection — rugby requires high interaction and communication skills that are not present in individual performance. Team dynamics research focuses on explaining why teams do not always effectively harness the individual abilities of their players.[9]

Team performance

A useful framework for explaining team performance in sport is expressed in the following equation.[10]

Actual performance = Potential performance — Losses due to faulty process

Actual performance (or productivity) is what the team actually does. Potential performance is the team's best possible performance given its resources which are relevant to the task and the demands of that task. Process is everything the team does while transforming its resources into a performance. In rugby, process is basically each player's individual skill development combined with teamwork skills developed by the coach, including team tactics and strategies.

Faulty process is the ineffective use of available resources, and can result from two types of 'loss': coordination losses and motivation losses. Coordination losses include poor timing, teamwork or strategy, while motivation losses occur when all or some members of the team lack effort and desire.

While this model is useful as a general description of team performance, it is the role of team leaders and coaches to decrease faulty process by developing and practising organisational strategies, or teamwork, that reduce coordination losses and maintain high motivation levels. As you are probably aware, this is nowhere near as easy to achieve as it sounds! So why do teams not always perform up to their potential?

There is an aspect of team dynamics commonly referred to as *social loafing*. Social loafing means that the average individual performance decreases with increases in team size. Although the number of coordination losses may also increase as the number of people in the team increase, social loafing is usually not the result of coordination losses. The key psychological reason seems to be motivation losses.[11]

Social loafing occurs when the 'identifiability' of individual performances is lost in a team performance.[12] Performances decrease because each player has less apparent responsibility for the overall performance ('not my job'; 'not my fault').[13] If players believe that their own performance within the team can be identified (perhaps by individual statistics, tackle counts or video analysis), and that they will be held accountable for their contribution, then social loafing typically does not occur.[14] Therefore players need to have their individual performances monitored and they need to be made accountable for their personal contribution to the team performance.

As a coach or a captain you need to increase each team member's sense of responsibility for the team performance by increasing team interaction, commitment to the team goals, and task cohesion.[15] Developing a sense of team pride and a collective identity will ensure that each member feels personally involved in team effort and success.[16] Finally, you need to use systematic goal setting for the team as a whole and for individual members.[17]

Clearly other factors can also increase individual effort in the team. Social incentives such as peer pressure and social support from teammates can have a powerful effect. Coaches can develop a record of 'match stats' as a means of identifying, measuring and rewarding each player's performance contribution to the team.

General implications for teams

Individual skill performance should not be the only factor determining team selection. Rugby requires many skills that are not present in individual performance,

We can't just have two or three guys doing all the shit work. We've all got to take our share. It's no good having guys hanging off waiting for a run.

— Todd Blackadder (All Black 1996– , captain Canterbury Super 12 and NPC teams)

such as interaction and communication. Also, loss of motivation can be avoided by identifying and rewarding behaviour that contributes to a good team performance, both at an individual and a teamwork level. Contrary to the coaching cliché, it may be useful to put the 'I' back into the 'team' so that individual contributions are identified and desired teamwork patterns are recognised, encouraged and rewarded.

Team motivation

Teamwork and team process on their own do not lead to peak performance in rugby. You also need to consider team motivation if a team is to consistently perform to its potential. The basis of team motivation are the team's goals and each member's desire for team success.

The main factor in developing team motivation is the identification of one single, unifying team vision — performance (not outcome) goals that all team members agree upon and commit themselves to achieving.[18] Your teammates have to agree freely that membership of the team is important to them as individuals and to their self-esteem.

Emphasise a 'pride-in-team' approach:[19]

★ Use the worksheets on pages 114–15 to set your team goals and objectives to achieve that team vision.

★ Ensure that the individual contribution of each of your teammates is valued and recognised by you as the coach or captain and other teammates.[20] Keep the reserves and substitutes involved as well.

★ Place strong emphasis on good leadership from yourself as the coach or captain.[21]

★ Actively work to encourage and develop team cohesion; both social cohesion (team spirit) and task cohesion (teamwork).

★ Encourage unified commitment to the team effort — teammates have to be prepared to invest time and energy to achieving the overall team goal.[22]

★ Expect and reward the pursuit of high standards of excellence.

★ Use effective communication to keep all of your teammates informed and feeling 'part of the team' (see chapter 9).[23]

While you and each of your teammates need to feel a strong identification with the team, you also need to feel accountable and responsible for playing your key part in the team's success. This sense of responsibility is related to the important issue of team cohesion.

Team cohesion

Team cohesion is the dynamic process that makes your team stick together and remain united in the pursuit of its goal.[24] Cohesive teams are able to ignore distractions and avoid disruptions while staying firmly focused on their team goals.[25]

There are two general dimensions associated with team cohesion. Social cohesion (interpersonal attraction) reflects the degree to which the members of your team like each other and enjoy each other's company.[26] Social cohesion = team spirit: you and your teammates need to respect each other, trust each other, and be willing to make sacrifices for each other and the team, perhaps by giving up personal time for fitness training, skill training or extra unit practice such as line-out practice.

Task cohesion reflects the degree to which your teammates work together to achieve specific and identifiable goals or tasks.[27] Task cohesion = teamwork: synchronising the technical and tactical skills of fifteen individuals requires a well developed level of psych skills from each of those players, and the leaders in particular.

Team cohesion research involving New Zealand rugby teams showed that for a professional rugby team (Super 12 team) task cohesion was very important for team success, but that social cohesion was not necessary for success on the field.[28] However, social cohesion was clearly a vital ingredient in creating a positive team environment for training, team practices, and the travel that is a part of top level rugby. The clear implication is that every team should put considerable time and effort into developing both task (teamwork) and social cohesion (team spirit).

> The sense of belonging, of comradeship through a common team aim with its ability to meld many diverse personalities into a cohesive group is a rare thing; one which I imagine many people never experience.
>
> — GRAHAM MOURIE

After working on his foundation and performance skill needs, Jack was ready to tackle his facilitative skill need of team cohesion (see Jack's Peak Performance Profile on page 40).

He decided to use the PST methods of goal setting, imagery and self-talk to help him stick with the team's game plan and be a more cohesive 'team player'. Jack chose a variation on goal setting that focused on team goal setting and convinced his coach and teammates to develop a team vision, team goals based on that vision, and then specific goal achievement strategies devised to accomplish those goals. In addition, Jack talked his teammates into having some fun with a 'what if . . .' session called the 'Mission Impossible' exercise. (See these worksheets on pages 116–17.) Jack's plan was that the act of sorting out the team's goals so specifically would help him as a player to identify his role and become committed to proving his contribution to the team's game plan. Finally, he used imagery to mentally rehearse the team's game plan and his role in it, and he practised self-talk to help keep his concentration on the correct options within the team's game plan.

The acronym of 'Pride in the Team' serves as a useful review of a number of the key points in this chapter.

PRIDE	*in the*	TEAM	
P Personal		**T** Together	
R Responsibility		**E** Everyone	
I In		**A** Achieves	
D Delivering		**M** More	
E Excellence			

We broke the players up into 'workshop' groups, mixing seasoned campaigners with newcomers, front rowers with three-quarters. They were sent away to assess themselves, their fitness programmes, and the All Blacks generally, and to report back. . . . We invited comment on the performance of the selectors and team management as well. . . . From the top down, we literally tore ourselves apart and started putting the pieces back together. Some of the new players must have wondered what on earth they had got themselves involved in!

— LAURIE MAINS (LEFT) OUTLINING THE TEAM ASSESSMENT PART OF THE FIRST
TRAINING CAMP BEFORE THE 1995 WORLD CUP

Team goal setting session

Outline

Team vision — the *why* of this team; why are we together?) (page 113)

Team goals — *what* is this team aiming to achieve? (page 114)

Goal achievement strategies — *how* are we going to achieve our goals? (page 115)

'Mission Impossible' exercise — *'what if . . .'* planning; coping with problems or weaknesses (pages 116–17)

Team vision

★ The *why* of this team.

★ Why are we together?

★ What team values do we want to emphasise?

. . . .

. . . .

. . . .

. . . .

. . . .

. . . .

. . . .

. . . .

. . . .

. . . .

. . . .

. . . .

Team goals

★ *What* is this team aiming to achieve for the season?

★ Make the goals: long-term and short-term, specific and measurable, positive, tied to a deadline.

1.

....

....

....

....

2.

....

....

....

....

3.

....

....

....

....

4.

....

....

....

....

Goal achievement strategies

★ *How* are we going to achieve our goals?

★ Be very specific: precisely what do we need to do in order
   to achieve each of our goals?

Goal 1.

....

....

....

....

Goal 2.

....

....

....

....

Goal 3.

....

....

....

....

Goal 4.

....

....

....

....

'Mission Impossible' exercise

Imagine you are part of the management team for our main opponents — your mission ('should you decide to accept it') is to send a saboteur or spy into our rugby team for the season in order to sabotage and destroy our season.

★   What would your instructions be?

★   What would you get the spy to sabotage?

★   What would you get the spy to do in order to destroy this team and stop us achieving our goals?

This instruction sheet will self-destruct in 5 seconds.

1. ....

   ....

2. ....

   ....

3. ....

   ....

4. ....

   ....

5. ....

   ....

6. ....

   ....

7. ....

   ....

'Mission Impossible': Counterattack Options Plan

★ What plans can be put into place to *prevent* these problems or issues happening or *cope* with them if they do arise?

1. ....
....

2. ....
....

3. ....
....

4. ....
....

5. ....
....

6. ....
....

7. ....
....

9. Captaincy and communication

The first thing you have to remember as captain is while rugby is very much a team concept you are dealing with individuals, who are all different in attitudes, temperament and experience. Thus you have to find out each person's strengths and weaknesses . . . And you have to find out which players best respond to the carrot and which to the stick.

— ANDY DALTON (ALL BLACK CAPTAIN 1983–87)

Captaincy

Unlike sports such as basketball, softball or American football, rugby is a sport in which the team's performance is almost entirely under the control of the players once the whistle to start the game has sounded — there are no timeouts for the coach to contribute to decision-making. The role of the captain is crucial — not only must captains demonstrate competence in their own playing role, they must also inspire confidence in other players, remain calm under pressure, call the appropriate moves at the right time, change tactics when required, and communicate effectively with referees and teammates. The captain is a decision-maker and a communicator as well as a player,[1] and the responsibilities do not end once the final whistle has been blown. The role of captain in a rugby team is potentially the most powerful and most challenging of all for a player.

In the history of New Zealand rugby, no position has been more prestigious than that of All Black captain. Arguably the most successful and the most respected of these have included Wilson Whineray, Brian Lochore, Graham Mourie, and more recently Wayne Shelford and Sean Fitzpatrick. What was it about these players that made them so successful and so respected as captains? Were there certain characteristics that each had in common? Why were they chosen ahead of the other players in the team at the time? What did they do or say as a captain that caused them to be labelled as a good or even great captain? If you were asked to be the captain of your team (maybe you already have been), how would you respond to the challenge? What extra skills might you have to learn in order to do the job well? What exactly does being a captain mean?

No matter what you think may be the best way to approach the role of captain, the bottom line is that you will be required to be a leader: captaincy is simply one form of leadership. According to All Black coach John Hart, leaders can be very different, but they need the basic credentials of integrity, being good at their job (that is, playing their position within the team), and excellent communication skills.[2] Hart believes that the captain's role is an extension of the coach, and is a key appointment within the team. Some of the most successful rugby teams in history have included strong partnerships between the captain and coach of those teams. Think of Graham Mourie and Jack Gleeson on the 1978 Grand Slam All Black tour to Britain, or Sean Fitzpatrick and John Hart in the 1996–97 period when the All Blacks won 22 tests, lost one, and drew one.

What sort of player makes a good captain? What qualities and skills must they possess, and what sort of behaviours do they need to demonstrate? Many rugby coaches, administrators, players and spectators have offered their views on this issue, and a great deal of research into leadership in sport has been conducted. The following is a sample of the opinions and findings of these groups of people.

★ There are no identifiable personality traits that characterise an effective captain.[3] Good captains are as different in their personalities as they are in their playing position. For example, David Kirk and Buck Shelford were seemingly very different in personality, yet both were successful All Black captains. In choosing a captain, coaches and/or the other players in the team (if they have input into the selection) should decide upon the person that they believe is best suited for the job, given the particular situation in which the team finds itself. The mix of players in the team (their personalities, experience and ability), the style of play that the team wishes to adopt, and the player's compatibility with the coach's philosophy must all be considered.

★ Speak only when necessary. What the captain says should be short and to the point.[4] The captain's on-field communication should be more positive than negative (see pages 124–28 on communication skills). It is a myth that all players are motivated by being shouted and sworn at. While this may work on occasion for some players, most players would prefer a positive approach.

> I keep orders simple. I sow one seed in their minds and it grows. Defence is important so I tell the backs 'Make a tackle.'
>
> — ZINZAN BROOKE

★ A sense of humour is important.[5] You should be able to laugh at yourself and with others, rather than at other players. Remember that sarcasm is not always a desirable form of humour: it can serve to alienate other players and undermine your ability to lead them.

★ Deal with each player as an individual.[6] You must get to know what individual players prefer to do to mentally prepare themselves for a game, and learn how to

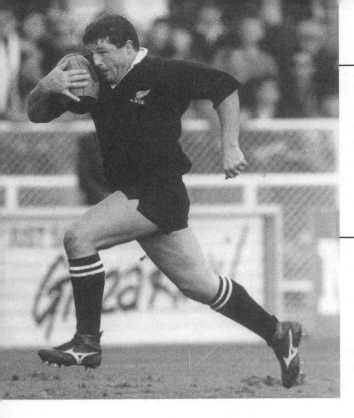

best deal with each player. Some players will respond better to a gentle reminder about your expectations of them, others will need a more forceful expression of what you require of them during practices or games, and others still will be best left completely alone. By observing and talking to each player both on and off the field, you will be able to gain an insight as to which strategy you should use.

★ Be good at what you do! You should not only demonstrate competence in your own playing position, but make a point of gaining knowledge (not necessarily ability) and an appreciation of the skills involved in playing other positions, and of the techniques and strategies involved in the performance of the various sub-units of the team (such as scrummaging, line-out play, counterattacking strategies, backline defensive patterns).

★ Have an appreciation of the dynamics of the team, and how the players interact with each other both on and off the field.[7] This will be useful for identifying how you might deal with individual players as well as the team as a whole (see chapter 8, Team cohesion).

★ Act with the utmost integrity in all your dealings with players, coaches, administrators, fans and the media.

★ Be a role model.[8] Don't expect other players to follow you or to listen to you if the example that you set is less than what you expect of them. For example, don't expect your players to accept refereeing decisions without question if you are not

He was able to read moods as well as moves.

— TAINE RANDELL ON SEAN FITZPATRICK'S STYLE OF CAPTAINCY

prepared to do so yourself. Similarly, captains who are prepared to cheat or to commit acts of violence on the field are sending the message to teammates and spectators alike that this kind of behaviour is acceptable. Look, speak and behave in the manner that you would expect of your players.

★ Demonstrate self-confidence.[9] Not only will this help you in your own performance, but it will instil confidence in the players around you. Even if you don't feel confident about the way that you or the team are performing, you should give the impression that you are. This will be evident in your body language and your interaction with teammates and the referee. Look and act confident, and sooner or later you will be confident (see chapter 4, Self-confidence).

★ Learn to control your emotions (see chapter 6, Coping with pressure). If you lose control and become angry at an opponent, teammate, or the referee, you will undoubtedly lose your ability to make rational decisions about strategy. Your own play will also suffer: a loss of emotional control will not only affect your coordination and timing, but also your ability to read the play because you are likely to become more narrowly focused (see chapter 7, Concentration). A visible

> The captain's job is to ensure that each [player] . . . is in the frame of mind to contribute all that they have to the team effort.
>
> — GRAHAM MOURIE

loss of emotional control will also set a poor example to your own teammates, and will signal weakness to your opponents. This will undoubtedly give their confidence a boost, and undermine that of your team. (See chapter 5, Controlling activation, and chapter 15, CARS plan, for more on dealing with anger and other emotions.)

★ Demonstrate planning and commitment.[10] Careful planning will ensure that the team functions more effectively, that your responses to the various situations that arise in a game will be immediate and appropriate, and that your teammates will be more confident in your leadership ability. It is important that you spend some time planning for each game, and this is best done in conjunction with the coach and/or some of the other senior players in the team (see chapter 12, Mental preparation). This planning should take the form of clarifying the game plan and preparing responses to the various situations and scenarios that may arise during the game (what to do in certain situations, how tactics might change depending on different weather or ground conditions, when to substitute players, and so on). (See also chapter 15, CARS plan). On your own you should think about and prepare your team talk before the game, decide how to deal with certain players before and during the game, and mentally rehearse the way you will respond to the situations that are likely to occur on the field. The better prepared you are, the more you will be able to change tactics if required, because you will have maintained a state of mind that can cope with such events (see chapter 6, Coping with pressure).

> To change a team's tactics midway through a game is far harder than most journalists would have the watching public believe. The best that I could ever do was to always maintain a state of mind in which I was prepared to be flexible. To be open to suggestion and to the fact that there are always more solutions than problems.
>
> — GRAHAM MOURIE

★ Show concern for team members as people, not just players. You will achieve greater loyalty and respect from your players if you make the effort to know something about their lives outside of rugby.

★ Don't be afraid to seek advice from other people, especially if you believe that they have more experience or expertise in an aspect of captaincy or performance than you have, and even more especially if you trust their judgement. Seek the advice of other players on aspects of strategy or technique. Captains who are confident and secure in their role should look to empower others with leadership responsibilities, rather than trying to take on all of the responsibilities themselves. As an example of this type of leadership structure, the modern All Black philosophy is that certain players are given leadership roles in their particular areas of expertise. For example, in the 1996–97 All Black team Olo Brown lead the scrummaging drills, Ian Jones took responsibility for line-outs, Michael Jones called loose forward defensive patterns from scrum and line-out, and Frank Bunce called the backline defence.[11] According to coach John Hart, this philosophy of shared responsibility developed confidence within the team in terms of decision-making both on the field and at training.

> The need, then, is to be honest with them [the players], but sensitive too. The telling point is that you have invited their confidence. If I had success as a captain of New Zealand this would have been the most identifiable reason why — and it had absolutely nothing to do with leading players on the field.
>
> — BRIAN LOCHORE

★ You must have excellent communication skills.[12] This is one of the cornerstones of good captaincy, and is a feature of successful rugby teams. Gone are the days when the only voice expected to be heard was the captain's. Most modern rugby teams encourage a great deal of on-field communication between players, and it is regarded as a crucial aspect of overall team performance. (See pages 124–28 on communication skills.)

The best players do not always make the best captains. Indeed, New Zealand rugby has a number of examples of excellent provincial captains who have successfully led their provincial teams despite having numerous All Blacks in their teams. This is a tribute to the coaches of these sides, who have recognised the qualities in these players.

How can you develop the skills needed for captaincy? Many captains learn these skills simply through experience, but if you are able to do so you should observe other captains in your club or in other teams, and ask them how they cope with the responsibilities of the role. Discussing this with your coach and other former players and/or captains is also a good idea. You may want to model yourself on a captain that you admire and respect, but eventually you should develop the leadership style that works best for you. Be patient, and accept that you will make mistakes, but persevere — and try not to make the same mistake twice.

Communication skills

On attack, the most important thing is communication. The backline needs to think as one.

— Jeff Wilson

Good communication skills are very important ingredients of peak performance in rugby teams. There are several important strategies that players, captains and coaches can use to enhance the quality of their communication and deal with communication problems.[13]

One of the biggest problems that players have with communication is that we often expect other people to be mind readers, to understand our thoughts and feelings without our ever expressing them.[14] 'Why doesn't he understand my feelings, my perspective?' 'Why doesn't she know when I need some feedback or encouragement?' If you express your feelings and perceived needs, there is at least the possibility of someone understanding and responding; if they are made aware of your feelings they have the chance to act.

The ability to express feelings, to communicate clearly, and to criticise constructively is not easily acquired. The communication skills of consistency, staying expressive, refined listening, clear speaking, and giving and receiving criticism need to be developed and refined over time.

Be consistent. Inconsistency in communicating with others destroys credibility.[15] Be consistent over time and be consistent in your communications with different team members: avoid having 'favourites' or 'scapegoats'. Avoid double messages: they often result in confusion. For example, avoid the confusion that can arise when you try to soften the blow of dropping or criticising a teammate by making complimentary comments only to follow them by the required criticism. While your goal of considering the player's feelings is admirable, the double message ('you're a good player, but . . .') is often confusing to the player concerned and it may also limit your credibility in his eyes.

Staying expressive. For a team to perform to its potential and for players not to interfere with each other's psychological preparation in important games, you need to have open discussion with one another well before the game.[16] Each member of the team (players, coaches and support staff) should know the pre-game needs and preparation idiosyncrasies of the others. Pre-game worries about what teammates are doing, or conflict between members of the same sub-unit (such as forwards or backs) just before the start of the game can easily lower your team's performance. Do not let your teammates' varied ways of preparing affect your own preparation and performance. What is best for them before kick-off is not necessarily what is best for you. Each player doing what is best for them will create the best team performance.

Staying expressive within the game is also very important in rugby. That means talking to each other and encouraging each other on the field while playing the game. Calling out plays, giving each other verbal and physical support, and being genuinely positive on the field ('good play', 'we're in control', a clap of the hands, or a pat on the back), can help a team to achieve its goals. A team meeting should be held to clarify what is meant by staying expressive, to set some expectations, to encourage each other, to indicate when it will happen, to rehearse it in practice, and to do it in games.

Giving criticism constructively. There is immense value in explaining the intent of your criticism before giving it.[17] Good examples are, 'I'm telling you this in the hope of improving our teamwork'; 'I need to get something off my chest that has been bothering me'; 'My intent is to help and not to hurt, regardless of how it might come out'. Explaining your intent first is probably the single most important thing you can do when giving criticism.

Deciding to state your intent before you state your criticism will force you to think about your own purpose, and should help you phrase the criticism appropriately. If you can think about how the criticised person is likely to react, it may help you to phrase the criticism more constructively. Phrasing a criticism constructively includes expressing your intent and delivering your message in a clear, open and concerned way, without attempting to put the other person down or build yourself up. You gain most from delivering criticism if you express it as constructively as possible, and if the criticism is face-to-face rather than behind your teammate's back.

Stab each other in the stomach, not in the back.

Receiving criticism constructively. A person receiving criticism gains most if they can receive it as constructively as possible.[18] But often we take criticism badly — we interpret it as a personal attack, a put-down, rejection, or lack of appreciation for all of our good qualities. When you are being criticised, the anger or irritation that surfaces may result from a misperception or misunderstanding of the other person's intent. It is true that someone is pointing out what they perceive as an imperfection, and that, in this instance, they did not see you as perfect or as skilled as you would like to be (or have them think you are). But why are they telling you this?

When criticism comes from a person who cares about you and your performance, the intent of that criticism is usually constructive or helpful, regardless of how it might be delivered. The criticism is usually aimed at resolving a perceived problem, correcting a performance error, or improving a relationship. The hope is to make things better. Listen to criticism in this light. Learn from it instead of putting up protective barriers, and you will have a much better opportunity to gain from it, personally, interpersonally, and performance-wise.

In case criticism and advice still occasionally comes through in a less constructive fashion, especially before the game or at half-time, you should have your own plan to translate it into positive action (a CARS plan; see chapter 15). For example, 'stop, breathe out, relax' (centring; see chapter 13). Translate the message into what you have to do to set up properly for that skill. Take on that responsibility yourself. Run the correct image through your head several times. 'Feel' it going well. Then set it aside. The action should unfold as you imagined because you have focused on what to do and secured that message in your head through your repeated imagery (see chapter 14, Imagery).

The more proficient you become at self-direction and self-criticism, the less you need to rely on the criticism of others. But at times, direct, honest and objective criticism from another person can give you a perspective for improvement that you may not see in yourself.

Build credibility. Become as knowledgeable as you can about all aspects of rugby. Be reliable, fair, honest, and consistent in your dealings with others, and express warmth, friendliness, and empathy towards them. Be spontaneous and open so that you demonstrate your 'trust' in others, which is vital for credibility. Trust is a two-way street — you need others to trust you in order to establish credibility.

When talking to others, you should *own* your messages by using 'I' statements as often as possible. Avoid using vague terms like 'we', 'they', or 'most people' when stating what you believe.

Send messages high in information.[19] Use specific information about 'how to do it'. Focus on one message at a time to avoid information overload. Be knowledgeable or keep quiet. Separate fact from opinion; facts give a basis for opinion, so explain them first. For example, instead of just stating your opinion about a teammate's play, take the time to first outline the facts about the strengths and weaknesses of their play. This approach helps to avoid any misunderstandings or resentment.

Clear speaking. When you speak to teammates, be sure that you express yourself clearly. When your captain, coach or manager gives you instructions, how clear is the message? It is best for a coach to say exactly what he or she wants ('be more explosive onto the ball', 'take the pass earlier', 'focus on staying in synch with the rest of the backline'). If you are not getting this exact feedback ask your coach to be more explicit so that what you think the coach is saying and what the coach thinks they are saying are one and the same when translated into action. Express your own messages and suggestions as clearly as possible — players too are often unclear in their verbal messages.

Develop nonverbal communication skills. At least 70 percent of all communication is nonverbal.[20] Become aware of your body language, body motion, physical characteristics, touching behaviours, voice characteristics, body position (the space between you and others), and clothing. Ensure that your verbal and nonverbal messages agree.

For example, offering praise and encouragement will not be particularly effective if you avoid eye contact, shake your head or give the player the 'cold shoulder' at the same time as your comments.

Refined listening. This is probably the most important and yet least developed communication skill. Listening involves your ears, your eyes, and your heart.[21] What is this person really saying, and what are they really feeling? It is not always written on the surface. If you are not sure how someone is feeling about a decision or a performance, you may have to ask, 'How are you really feeling about this in your gut?' Becoming a keen observer also allows you to listen better.

To listen well, you should forget about how you see the situation and focus fully on how the other person sees it. Don't interrupt; don't judge; let the other person express their feelings while you focus on listening and understanding. Eliminate the 'yeah buts'. Just listen and feel that person's perspective. Soak it in before responding.

Key words and phrases (see also chapter 11, Self-talk). These are essential for clear, controlled and unambiguous communication immediately before and during the game.[22] This is especially important between teammates and between the coach and players during a game (for instance, instructions relayed via the physio, or during injury timeouts and at half-time).

> They're really switching on when they have to and they're using the key words well and communicating well . . .
>
> — Wayne Smith talking about the 1992 New Zealand sevens team's preparation

Improving your communication skills is a lifelong process. Like other skills it requires a plan, practice, reflections, and refinement. You will do yourself and your teammates a favour by beginning that process now.

Media skills

Developing effective communication skills is also useful for dealing with the media.[23] If you are successful enough to reach an elite level of rugby it is likely that you will be sought after by the media. Obviously, media exposure is necessary for raising the profile of rugby as a sport, for recruiting new players, for attracting sponsors, and for marketing the sport. However, it is vital that you know how to express your thoughts clearly so that you are not misquoted or misinterpreted. Media exposure can become a major source of pressure and stress if you do not have effective communication skills.

> Players should be taught how to handle themselves with the media and how the media works. People in other walks of life who are exposed to the media, like politicians and business people, get professionally advised so why shouldn't rugby players? I'm sure the All Black captain has more dealings with the media than most chief executives and many politicians.
>
> — John Kirwan

Part III

PST Methods for Rugby

If other nations follow our methods in physical development
then it is by moving into the area of sport psychology
that our edge can be maintained and increased.

— LEE SMITH (NZRFU DIRECTOR OF COACHING, 1987–95)

10. Goal setting

Performing well at any level is possible providing the individual has his goals clear in his mind and is prepared to do the work necessary to reach them.
— GRAHAM MOURIE

Goal setting is a very effective PST method for developing motivation, commitment and confidence. Select your goals by identifying the qualities from your Peak Performance Profile that you believe to be the most important or give you the most room for improvement. If you have your goals clear in your mind, then peak performance becomes achievable on a regular basis.

What is a goal?
Briefly, a goal is an aim, objective, target or dream. More exactly, a goal is a specific standard of performance, usually to be attained within a specified time limit.[1]

Why set goals in rugby?
Achieving goals helps create and maintain motivation by reflecting improvement. In addition, your goals are linked to your levels of self-confidence, activation, and stress — appropriate goal setting will assist you in maintaining optimal levels of each of these psych skills.[2] For example, when a player is solely focused on outcome goals (such as winning), unrealistic and unattainable expectations often result. This leads to lower self-confidence, increased mental anxiety, decreased effort and consequently poor performance. Goal setting also helps you to make key decisions about how you should manage the time you have available for training.

Goal setting and time management

Time is nature's way of making sure everything doesn't happen at once.

The process of goal setting will help you to identify your strengths and weaknesses, which is the ideal starting point for designing a training plan. Goals help you determine what is important in your training by providing direction and forcing you to prioritise your needs. Goal setting is like a 'road map'; the long-term goal is the destination, while the short-term goals are 'pit stops' along the way, and the goal

I really put it on myself this tour to show a lot of personal discipline, to set myself goals each week, and I've tried to achieve those. That's what has helped me most.

— SCOTT McLEOD, RIGHT (ALL BLACK 1996–)
TALKING ABOUT HIS ROLE ON THE
1997 ALL BLACKS' TOUR OF THE UK

achievement strategies (that is, training methods) are the choice of route you take to your destination.

What types of goals should you set?

Set performance and process goals rather than outcome goals (task orientation; see chapter 3, Motivation). These performance and process goals should be based on the peak performance needs identified in your Peak Performance Profile. In competitive sport there is enormous pressure from many sources, especially the media, to set outcome goals such as winning, or beating an opponent. Indeed, coaches often emphasise and teach outcome goals. However, outcome goals are not in your control, and consequently can become a major source of pressure and anxiety.[3] Performance and process goals should be your main focus for motivation and self-confidence.

Performance goals

Performance goals are all about mastering specific tasks or skills. The nuts-and-bolts of playing well and being successful depends upon doing basic tasks and skills correctly (passing, kicking, tackling, scrums, line-outs, second-phase ball retention). If you perform these tasks well then you are likely to achieve the 'outcome' that you are seeking. Performance goals encourage you to focus on 'how to win' rather than winning itself. The beauty of these goals is that you have control, because they are based on measuring your mastery of specified tasks or standards of performance (such as increasing your tackle count by 5 percent over the next two games). The criterion for success is being better than you were last time at the specified task (such as number of first time tackles, or goal kicking percentage) or better than a standard that you set for yourself on a task. Rather than comparing yourself to your opponents to determine your success, performance goals allow you to compare yourself to your own previous performance.

Performance goals are a very honest and demanding way to measure success. Even when you win easily against poor opposition you will have your performance goals as a more demanding evaluation of your 'real' success on the day. On the other hand, when you lose to a good team you still have a measure of success that provides you with information about performance improvements and about the effectiveness of your training. Outcome goals are just too crude and imprecise as a useful measure of 'success'.

> Goal-setting definitely works. I've found that if you write down your goals and what you've done, see what you've achieved, you feel your goals are more attainable.
>
> — ZINZAN BROOKE

Process goals

These goals are a variation on performance goals — the focus of achievement is on the actual 'process' of playing well, as opposed to the resulting 'performance'. You need to break down complex skills into the key components or actions that combine to produce successful execution of the complex skill. This provides you with a primary focus for attention and effort — a focus that you have more 'control' over.[4] For example, a process goal for a goal kicker might be to maintain balance on the non-kicking foot and have a full follow-through on every kick at goal. This 'process' goal helps the player to concentrate on good kicking technique. A performance goal for the same player might be to succeed with 90 percent of all kicks at goal within the range of 40 metres.

Process goals should form part of your technical and tactical skill development. Eventually these skills will become second nature to you.

Both performance and process goals utilise a task goal orientation, but there is a distinct difference in emphasis. Both types of goals are useful for motivation, self-confidence, and concentration and many players utilise both types of goals at the same time.

Set long-term and short-term goals

Goals should be out of reach, but not out of sight.

> We took this season just step-by-step, establishing short-term goals as we went along.
>
> — TODD BLACKADDER TALKING ABOUT THE 1997 CANTERBURY NPC CHAMPIONS

A long-term goal is a 'dream' goal. It is the ultimate objective and provides direction for your season and for your training. Short-term goals allow you to regularly see how much you have improved and can increase your intensity of effort in training and games. Achieving short-term goals also lets you reward yourself for effort and hard work in training and games.

Set specific, measurable goals

Specific, numerical goals are easy to measure and thus make it simple to determine whether or not you've achieved your goals. These goals need to be very specific to the skill that you are trying to improve. Write down a detailed description of each goal so that you can see whether you've attained it or not.

Poor goal: I want to be faster.

Good goal: I will reduce my average time for 40-metre sprints by 1 second by the end of a 4-week training phase.

Poor goal: I want to be more accurate in my passing.

Good goal: I will be able to hit a 30-cm square target, on the run, 9 times out of 10 after receiving a pass from another player.

Set positive rather than negative goals

Instead of focusing on 'I won't fail', focus on 'I will succeed'. For example, rather than saying to yourself, 'I will not blow my cool every time a refereeing decision goes against me,' say, 'Whenever a refereeing decision goes against me I will remember to remain composed and stay focused on my game.' Or instead of saying, 'I will not miss any more than 10 percent of my line-out throws,' say 'I will strive to hit my jumpers with 90 percent of my line-out throws.'

Areas in which to set goals

★ *Physical goals* — health and fitness goals (such as improving endurance, power, strength, flexibility, weight, diet, sleep patterns).

★ *Technical goals* — related to performance of the particular skills of your playing position (such as keeping shoulders relaxed when sprinting; passing accurately with both left and right hands; following through when goal kicking).

★ *Tactical goals* — related to an understanding and appreciation of appropriate tactics, attacking and defensive strategies, and game plans (for instance improving ability to 'read' opposition backline defensive pattern and quickly identify the best point of attack; improve ability to read the right 'lines' to run in support).

★ *Psychological goals* — psych skills and methods (such as planning to practice mental preparation techniques; practising imagery of performance in pressure situations; coping with poor refereeing).

Goal setting staircase

The goal setting staircase involves the steady progression through short-term goals to reach your ultimate long-term goal. You should make up a staircase for each long-term goal.

Prioritise goals. Choose the key areas in your Peak Performance Profile that need improvement. First set long-term goals for each area, then set short-term sub-goals for each long-term goal. Each key area has its own staircase of sub-goals.

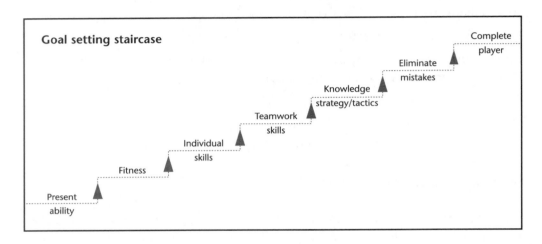

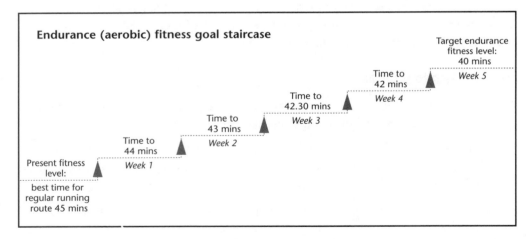

Use your SMARTS

Talk to your coach. Before you talk to your coach about the results of your Peak Performance Profile (see pages 38–39) make sure that you have asked yourself some key questions regarding your rugby performance. These should include:

★ Where am I now?

★ Where do I want to be in one week, next month, six months, two years?

★ What are my strengths and weaknesses?

Select key areas: prioritise needs. Using your coach's advice decide on long-term and short-term goals for each area. Then based on these 'priorities' use the SMART(S) system to actually 'set' your goals.

S = Specific
M = Measurable
A = Adjustable
R = Realistic
T = Time-referenced
S = Strategy to achieve goal(s)

Specific: Set specific goals. These need to be difficult to reach, but still realistic. They should be performance and process goals, stated positively, and should involve a detailed description of the goal so that it can be measured.

Measurable: Set numerical goals. Readily measured, numerical terms make it simple to determine whether or not you've achieved your goals.

Adjustable: Goals and goal schedules may need to be adjusted or changed. Sickness or injury may interfere with progress towards your goal. The goals initially selected may be too hard or too easy. You must be prepared to modify and change goals, strategies, and target dates as required. Like any activity that you attempt for the first time it will take time to develop effective, accurate and realistic goal setting. Monitor your progress regularly, and check your target dates as well. Record these in your Training Logbook (see chapter 20). They may need to be adjusted according to how well you are progressing towards your goals. The effectiveness of your training methods and strategies should also be periodically reviewed. Remember, setting goals in itself does not improve performance — the hard work and training detailed in the strategy is what allows for goal achievement and subsequently improves performance.

Realistic: Set difficult but realistically achievable goals. Know your own limitations, but aim to stretch your capabilities. Goals should be out of reach but not out of sight! Make sure that they are achievable if you put the work in. If you set goals that are unrealistic and too hard to achieve then you are virtually guaranteeing failure, rather than increasing your chances of success.

Poor goal: I want to make 100 percent of my goal kicks from within 40 metres.

Good goal: Because I'm only currently making 50 percent of my kicks from within 40 metres, my goal is to average making 75 percent of my kicks from within 40 metres over the next five games.

Time-referenced: Set target dates for achieving goals. Again, these should be difficult but realistic. If you don't set a target date, you can always use the excuse that you're still working towards achieving the goal if somebody asks you how you're progressing. But if you have a target date set, then the closer to that date you find yourself, the more effort you are likely to put into making sure you achieve the goal.

Strategy: Outline a strategy of training methods to achieve the goal (be specific). For example, a goal strategy for improving punting accuracy (kicking for touch) might be: 'I will practice an extra 50 kicks punting for touch after training on Mon/Wed/Fri, and ask for an extra hour of one-on-one coaching each week.'

Complete the Goal Achievement Worksheet on pages 138–39. Striving to express yourself in writing on the worksheet will help you think through your goals in depth. Make sure that the goals you set are specific and numerical, with specific target dates for attainment, and with a specific strategy of training methods to achieve each goal (record these in your Training Logbook — see chapter 20).

Ensure your commitment to your goals

You must have the desire, motivation and commitment to pursue your goal strategies. Writing a contract with yourself can be helpful (see worksheet on page 139). Social support from significant people in your life is also vital (teammates, parents, partner, friends, boss). Ensure that you inform these significant people about your goals and training plan. They can't support you if they don't know what you are trying to achieve and why it matters to you!

To ensure your commitment to your goals and your training plan you should do the following.

Write down your goals. Write out both long-term and short-term goals (see the example opposite). Write down at least one goal achievement strategy for each short-term goal. Use the Goal Achievement Worksheet on pages 138–39 to record this information (photocopy extra worksheets as you need them). Write down target dates as well; deadlines provide added incentives and help to plan the time frame of goal achievement. Finally, the goal evaluation procedures should also be recorded for use with a Training Log. (See chapter 20 for sample daysheets for your Training Logbook).[5]

> On the morning of my test debut I spent an hour and a half writing out what I wanted to achieve in the game and how I wanted to feel afterwards.
>
> — PAUL HARRAGON, AUSTRALIAN RUGBY LEAGUE PLAYER

Remind yourself of your goals. Keep a Training Logbook (see chapter 20). Other options include making a wall poster as a visual reminder of your goals, target dates, and overall training plan, or writing your goals on index cards and sticking them somewhere visible; such as on your mirror or on the fridge door.

Skill/Area needing improvement	Specific goal	Goal achievement strategies	Target date evaluation
Goal kicking accuracy	I will consistently be able to make 8 out of 10 shots from all angles within 40 m.	1. Before practice I will spend 30 minutes practising my kicking, taking at least 30 shots at goal (Tuesday and Thursday). 2. I will take extra instruction once a week (Sundays) from a goal kicking expert (45–60 minutes).	8 May, fourth weekend of the season. Then reset goal to 10 out of 10 by 12 June.

Ask yourself periodically: 'What did I do today to become a better player?'

Monitoring is your job, not your coach's. Self-monitoring and self-evaluation lead to self-motivation. Be organised, be responsible, be committed and be assertive. 'If it's to be, it's up to me!'

Common goal setting problems

★ Goals that are not specific or measurable.

★ Goals that are not realistic.

★ Setting too many goals at one time.

★ No goal achievement strategy.

★ Poor goal monitoring or evaluation.

★ Lack of commitment.

Once you have identified your Peak Performance needs and written them out as performance or process goals you will be on your way to improving motivation, commitment, and self-confidence. Goal setting is the first step in prioritising your needs and becoming fully committed to success.

Goal Achievement Worksheet

My 'dream': . . . .

Statement of my goal: . . . .

. . . .

. . . .

. . . .

Target date: . . . .

What is the *payoff* from achieving my goal? . . . .

. . . .

. . . .

. . . .

What are the consequences of *not* achieving my goal? . . . .

. . . .

. . . .

. . . .

What is my *strategy* to achieve my goal? . . . .

. . . .

. . . .

Possible *obstacles* in the way of my goal achievement: . . . .

. . . .

. . . .

. . . . *continued:*

Strategies for *overcoming* the obstacles: ....

....

....

....

....

What *excuses* do I usually make? ....

....

....

....

....

Is it worth the time, effort, and commitment to reach my goal?:

Yes/No

Why? ....

....

....

....

....

Goal Setting Contract

I . . . . hereby do solemnly swear that I am committed to achieving the goal that I have set out above. I will achieve this goal by following the goal achievement strategy that I have developed and outlined above.

I am fully committed to this goal and my achievement strategy.

Signed: . . . .   Date: . . . .

Witness: . . . .   Date: . . . .

11. Self-talk

> I have in my mind a picture of the ball going through the posts. The deep breathing, the shaking of the hands, are to rid the body of tension so that all is crystal-clear and unperturbed in the mind — the picture is in focus. I command myself, 'Head down. Follow through'
>
> — GRANT FOX RELATING HIS PRE-KICK PREPARATION

Self-talk may be described as conscious thinking, as an inner conversation, or as intentional thinking.[1]

Self-talk/thoughts ⟶ Feelings ⟶ Behaviour

Your level and type of self-talk is clearly linked to your motivation and self-confidence. Confident players 'think' they can, and they do! They imagine themselves being successful and focus on positive things, on successfully mastering a task rather than worrying about performing poorly. Self-talk is also a useful method for developing the performance PST skill of concentration, and players like Grant Fox attribute part of their success to using this technique.

Players with low self-confidence think they can't and invariably they don't. The effect of positive versus negative self-talk will be obvious to you if you complete the exercise 'Self-test: positive versus negative self-talk' at the top of the next page.

Too often players and coaches use the word 'worry' incorrectly, as in, 'All I have to worry about is playing to our game plan.' The correct word to use would be 'think' or 'focus'. Using words like 'worry' indicates to the player that there is indeed something to worry about!

Intentional thinking is the basis of 'controlled' self-talk. You can learn to replace negative, self-defeating thoughts with positive ones, thoughts that build confidence and expectations of success. Positive thoughts and expectations can become self-fulfilling prophecies; if you think positive you will likely play in a positive manner.[2]

Self-talk does not mean having a long conversation with yourself during the game. Self-talk words and phrases need to be brief and precise, short and sharp. Self-talk is like having your own cassette player in your head; you make your own 'tapes' and then play them when you need them! It is designed to enable you to create and maintain your Ideal Performance State; good self-talk helps you switch on your 'automatic pilot'.

Uses of self-talk

Skill learning. Self-instructional talk or 'cue words' are very useful in learning and practising physical skills. For example: 'Head down, follow through' for goal kicking; 'Hit the dartboard' for line-out throwing. Keep the talk brief but precise; work towards 'automatic' execution of the skills. Automatic use of self-talk is needed for you to play in your Ideal Performance State.

Attention control. Use a specific set of self-talk cues to 'hold' the appropriate focus on the task at hand. For example: 'Here and now !' ; 'Watch the ball into your hands'; 'Run good lines'; 'Watch the drift defence'.

Creating 'mood'. Use words or phrases with a clear, specific emotional message. For example: 'go' or 'explode' for sprinting the first 10 metres from a scrum; 'smooth' or 'easy' or 'oily' or 'rhythm' for goal kick leg-swing.

Controlling effort: Use phrases to maintain energy and persistence — for the direction of effort and sustaining that effort. For example: 'Go for it'; 'Push it'; 'Pick it up'; 'Guts it out'; 'Hold onto it'.

Coping with distractions: Self-talk phrases can be very helpful when you need to hold your concentration in the face of an external distraction (such as your opponents) or an internal distraction (such as negative thoughts about failure or mistakes). See the section on page 143 on 'parking', or 'thought-stopping'.

Mental preparation: Use cue words or phrases to assist with mental preparation pre-game, during the game, or refocussing after the game (see chapter 12, Mental preparation).

I've always used my mind-talk when I'm training or playing. It might be as simple as saying to myself, 'Come on, come on', or grunting. And I've got no time for negative thoughts.

— ZINZAN BROOKE

Affirmations for building self-confidence. 'Affirmations' are self-statements that reflect positive attitudes or thoughts about yourself. You are only able to do what you think you can do. To be an achiever, you have to be a believer! Affirmations help you believe in yourself and develop self-confidence. For example: 'I'm fit and ready for a hard 80 minutes!' ; 'I play well under pressure'.

Identifying self-talk

The first step in gaining control of self-talk is to become aware of what you say to yourself. Surprisingly, most players are not aware of their thoughts and their impact on performance. It is especially important to identify and then eliminate negative and self-defeating thoughts such as 'I always struggle against this opponent', or 'I never play well in the rain'.

How do you identify self-talk?

Retrospection. Recall past situations of good and bad performances, and try to re-create the thoughts and feelings. Use the Self-talk Log on page 145 (see also Peak Performance Profile, pages 38–39).

Imagery. 'Relive' past performances through imagery; record the recalled thoughts, phrases and self-talk from good and bad performances.

Self-talk log. Keep a daily diary or self-talk log of thoughts used during games and practice over a period of weeks. For example, ask yourself: When do I have negative thoughts? What seems to cause negative thoughts? When and why do I have self-doubts? Record the frequency and content of both positive and negative thoughts. (See the Self-talk Log on page 145).

Techniques for controlling self-talk

Once your awareness of negative thoughts and feelings is heightened, you need to learn techniques to deal with the negative thoughts and to focus on positive thoughts.

Key word or phrase list. Develop a list of key words and phrases that have specific purposes (such as self-instruction, creating mood, holding attention, affirmation or confidence statements). See the Self-talk List worksheet on page 146, and Bob's Self-talk List on page 147.

'Parking' (thought-stopping).[3] Practise stopping negative thought patterns by using silent instructions or 'triggers'. For example, 'stop!' , 'park it!' , or 'bin it'. Some players use imagery to mentally write the negative thought on a piece of paper then throw it in the rubbish bin ('bin it') or set fire to it! Other players mentally write the thought on a blackboard then wipe it clean. Some players slap their leg, or slap the ball to mentally 'park' the negative thoughts somewhere else so that they can refocus their concentration on the task at hand. 'Parking' is just like parking a car — when you don't need your car you park it in a carpark; and when you don't need or want a negative thought you can 'park' it somewhere and come back for it after the game! You may want to get your coach to initiate parking and thought-stopping during training. For example, the coach could ask, 'Where is your head — past, present, or future?' , or state, 'Here and now!' Parking can also be very useful as part of a CARS plan (see chapter 15).

Changing negative thoughts to positive thoughts. Make a list of typical negative and self-defeating thoughts (use your completed Self-talk Log). Then design a substitute positive thought for each negative thought, and couple this process with relaxation and centring. For example:

★ I don't want to fail; I don't want the responsibility of this penalty kick. — 'Relax . . . all you can do is give your best effort; accept the responsibility; enjoy the challenge!'

★ I can't believe it's raining, I never play well in the rain . — 'Relax . . . no one likes playing in the rain, but it's the same for them as it is for me. I can handle it better!'

★ This referee is useless, he's picking on us! — 'Relax . . . the refereeing is not in my control; focus on my job and playing well, then the standard of refereeing won't matter.'

Reframing irrational thinking. There are a number of common irrational thought patterns: perfection is essential; worth = achievement ('unless we win I'm not a good person'); fallacy of the 'fair deal' (the ref isn't being fair to us at ruck or maul) ; polarised thinking (either/or thoughts — absolute terms); catastrophising ('what if . . .'); personalisation (*'my* fault!'); blaming ('it was the ref/weather/conditions'); and one-trial generalisations ('I missed that line-out throw so now I'm going to miss for the whole game!'). Practise recognising these thoughts as irrational and reframing them into rational, positive thoughts (see also chapter 15, CARS plan).

Personal affirmation statements. Construct a 'success list' of your strengths, skills, and qualities. Create positive action-oriented self-statements; for example: 'I have trained hard, I deserve to succeed'; 'I play well under pressure'; 'I am an excellent scrummager'; 'I always make my first-time tackles'. It can be useful to print these on index cards and carry them in your gear bag or stick them to your mirror as consistent visual reminders of your affirmations.

Coping and mastery self-talk tapes. Create an audio tape with affirmation statements, cue words, and refocussing or coping statements. Repeated listening to positive self-talk tapes helps programme your mind for positive thoughts during training and performance.

Your self-talk is linked to your concentration, self-confidence, and stress. Self-talk is not an in-depth conversation with yourself or a long list of self-instructions. Effective self-talk is short and precise — the minimal amount of thought required to correctly complete a skill or affirm confidence in yourself. Self-talk = inner conversation, self-statements, intentional thinking.

Confident players think they can, and they do!

Self-talk Log

Positive self-talk	Negative self-talk

Self-talk List

Statements I will use	When?	Purpose?
Focus words/phrases *e.g.* *'Pass in front at chest height'* *'Hit the dartboard'* *(line-out throw)*		
Mood words/phrases *e.g.* *'Calm and relaxed'* *'Strong & aggressive'* *'Feelin' fine'*		
Positive self-statement *e.g.* *'I have trained well, I deserve to play well'* *'I'm ready'*		

Self-talk List

Statements I will use	When?	Purpose?
Focus words/phrases		
'Pass in front — chest height'	Before a miss-2 pass; especially to my right.	To help me avoid having negative thoughts — I sometimes doubt my ability on these 'miss' passes.
'I.C.E.' (Intensity, Concentration, Effort)	Concentrate and focus my attention when I'm setting up at first phase ball.	To help with my mental prep during the phases of the game.
'Smooth follow through'	Technique reminder for goal kicking.	I have to resist the tendency to 'self-coach' myself during my goal kicking — I need simple self-talk to help me to 'trust' my technique.
Mood words/phrases		
'Calm and relaxed' <u>or</u> 'Smooth and easy'	At the start of my goal kicking routine.	To set the pace and mood for each and every goal kick.
'Boots on, switch on'	15 mins before kick-off.	To help kickstart my 'kick-off countdown' prep plan.
'Chop down the tree' (tackle)	Facing a big second-five on a 1-out defence.	To help me focus on good tackling technique against the 'big boys'.
Positive self-statement		
'I've worked bloody hard, I deserve to play well'	During my pre-game mental prep.	To remind myself of one of my sources of self-confidence — all my training!
'I'm ripped and ready'	During the 'kick-off countdown' part of mental prep.	To 'gee myself up' for physical contact (I'm just a wee guy!).
'Stay in the PRESENT!' <u>or</u> 'Start your CARS'	After a mistake or a loss of concentration.	To cope with pressure and keep my concentration.
'P.R.I.D.E.' (Personal Responsibility in Delivering Excellence)	'Kick-off countdown' part of mental prep; & when I need to use my CARS plan.	To fizz on 'my' contribution to the TEAM; play with pride and guts.

12. Mental preparation

> Motivation comes from within the individual. If it is not in the player to motivate himself, if he has not prepared himself mentally for what is to come, an 'inspirational' team-talk is not going to make the difference. Preparation is the vital ingredient.
>
> — GRANT FOX

Mental preparation is a method vital to the development of the foundation PST skills of motivation and self-confidence, as well as the performance PST skills of peak physical activation, peak mental activation, and peak concentration. Quality mental preparation is a key element of sporting success.

Mental preparation strategies are used to organise a consistent and systematic psych-up period before the game. Mental preparation will help you psych-up without becoming psyched-out or over-activated. The purpose of mental prep is to help you consistently reach your Ideal Performance State of optimal activation and mental readiness.

Pre-game mental preparation means psyching-up, without psyching-out. This needs to be individually designed to suit your needs and your peak level of activation. There is no one perfect mental prep plan, it depends on your needs and preferences and the particular situation you are competing in.

> I will get myself mentally attuned in the morning. But it won't be too intense because I want to remain relaxed. [However] I will get slightly nervous. It helps to be a bit on edge.
>
> — LINDSAY MCLACHLAN (FORMER INTERNATIONAL REFEREE) DESCRIBING HIS PRE-MATCH ROUTINE

Performance plans

There are three types of performance plans designed to help you achieve optimal mental preparation. These are the pre-game plan, game focus plan, and coping plans (distraction control).[1] Planning sheets for developing these are on pages 152–56. Make your own photocopies for writing out your ideas and plans.

To develop your performance plans you need to ask yourself the following questions:

★ What kind of preparation do I like — how much, when, and why?

> In the changing room, you can feel the atmosphere and you tense up a bit, but I purposely keep a focus on the game, my job is clear, I'm very clear-minded. I don't go shouting around. I don't like sitting too close to the door. I usually sit near a corner. I'm free to focus there . . .
>
> — MICHAEL JONES

★ What do I like and dislike about events leading up to game day, 24 hours before the game, and during the game itself?

★ Do I already have a routine for game day — how, when, and where do I warm up?

★ Do we have a clearly defined game plan of tactics going into each game?

★ What, if anything, makes me anxious and uptight before a game?

★ How disciplined am I about my mental preparation and my concentration focus for each game?

You may be very happy with your current mental preparation plans. If it ain't broke, don't try to fix it! But we encourage you to use the worksheets at the end of this chapter to write down your current plans — that way if you have any problems with your mental prep in the future you will have a record of what has worked for you in the past. You can compare your mental prep with your written plans to check for any subtle changes that may have crept into your pre-game routines. Often players get a little 'lazy' in following their pre-game and game plans and the small changes they have inadvertently made can have major effects on their mental preparation and performance.

Once you have developed mental plans that you are happy with, be prepared to adjust them and modify them as your sporting career continues. Like many things mental plans can become a bit boring unless you are always looking for ways to keep them fresh and meaningful. Be wary of the danger of hanging on to a good mental plan that has worked well for you but that has lost some of its meaning — if you just go through the motions during your mental preparation you will likely play the same way!

Be prepared to tinker with your mental plans for quite some time. It will take time for you to get them right. Write out your best guess, then try it out, make changes, try it again, and modify it some more until you are happy that you have developed a set of mental plans that will allow you to get into your Ideal Performance State regularly.

Finally, be wary of letting your mental plans become a superstition. If you get too attached to a detailed plan you are guaranteeing yourself stress in the future — some day your plan will be upset by some hassle (you lose your Walkman, the batteries go dead, your teammates decide they want to practise extra line-outs during the warm up . . .), and become a source of stress rather than a way to create a calm, focused period of mental preparation. While it is important to have a structured mental plan, be careful to not overdo it and create a superstition. This is where coping plans are vital!

Pre-game plan. Plan, organise, and structure your thoughts, actions, and behaviour leading up to the game — develop a 'mental warm-up' to go with your physical warm-up. Often this is referred to as 'segmenting' since you organise your mental warm-up in distinct 'segments' that give your mental prep a sound structure, like a checklist to go through before kick-off. For example, Zinzan Brooke used the following self-talk phrase as part of his pre-game plan: 'Boots on, switch on.'[2] See the pre-game planning sheet on page 152. Jack's pre-game plan from the start of this season is shown on page 153. This is actually Jack's third version of the pre-game plan — he found that he needed to modify it after the first two games of the season.

You should also have a 'short' Pre-Game plan (approximately 2–3 minutes) for use in situations where you don't have as much time as you would prefer for your mental preparation, such as going on as a substitute or an injury replacement (see also the CARS plan on page 193). This should be linked with your coping plan. 'Short' plans are also useful after half-time or after an extended injury break. In these time-pressured situations, you must have a plan to help you psych-up without being psyched-out or over-activated.

You could tell some players were trying to force themselves, saying 'I'm ready', and 'I'm going to do this'; and that's a waste of time, because it's too late trying to force things five minutes before the game.

— ALEX WYLLIE (ALL BLACK COACH 1987–91) DESCRIBING PROBLEMS BEFORE A TEST MATCH

Game focus plan. Plan and organise how you want to think, feel and focus during the game ('the how for now'[3]). If you like having a lot of structure, do some 'segmenting' to help organise your thoughts during the game. For example, you may segment your game into the first five minutes of each half and the last five minutes of each half, as well as having a structure for your thoughts at every scrum and line-out. See the Game focus planning sheet on page 154.

Coping plan (distraction control). Plan and organise methods, strategies, and thoughts that will help you deal with hassles and distractions before, during, and after the game. For example, you may choose to include self-talk, parking, imagery, relaxation or centring as part of a coping plan. This coping plan may also be integrated into a CARS plan as described in chapter 15. Thought-stopping procedures like 'parking' can be very useful as part of your coping plan. See the Coping plan sheet on pages 155–156.

There is no one perfect set of mental prep plans — your plans should be individually designed depending on your needs and the particular team you are playing in. In order to be fully mentally prepared, you need to develop a complete set of mental prep plans: a pre-game plan, a game focus plan and a coping plan. As Alex Wyllie notes, you can't leave your mental preparation to the last minute; you have to be organised!

Mental preparation: pre-game plan

Write out your pre-game plan in the sequence that you want it to occur on game day. List your physical 'warm-up' in note form and develop a 'mental warm-up' to go with it. List stretches, drills, activities, self-talk, self-suggestions, imagery, centring, etc., in the sequence that you intend to do them.

'General' warm-up: Physical and mental (approx. 45–60 mins before kick-off)		'Kick-off' preparation: Physical and mental (approx. 10–15 mins before kick-off)	
Physical	Mental	Physical	Mental

Mental preparation: pre-game plan

Write out your pre-game plan in the sequence that you want it to occur on game day. List your physical 'warm-up' in note form and develop a 'mental warm-up' to go with it. List stretches, drills, activities, self-talk, self-suggestions, imagery, centring, etc., in the sequence that you intend to do them.

'General' warm-up: Physical and mental (approx. 45–60 mins before kick-off)		'Kick-off' preparation: Physical and mental (approx. 10–15 mins before kick-off)	
Physical	**Mental**	**Physical**	**Mental**
FRIDAY NIGHT: Video or movies.	Keep my mind off the game: 'Don't play the game on Friday night.'	30 mins: Grids with team – Upper body stretches Kick-off countdown	Psyching-up: focus on 'my' goals & 'my' standards.
SATURDAY MORNING: Read the paper. Go for a walk. Pre-game meal. Check gear, mouthguard.	Think over my 'goals for today'; focus on 'standards'. – Take it in, but keep psych-up under control. – Build psych-up toward kick-off.	15 mins: 2nd pee stop – re-check gear & mouthguard – put boots on: 'Boots on, switch on.'	Think: MUST DOMINATE my opponent, be physical, but be smart – stay focused on accurate technique; do MY jobs 100 percent effort every time.
AT THE GROUND: 60 mins: Team talk – coach / captain.	Think a/b opposition – their weaknesses & strengths. – our game plan against them: backrow moves; 'runners'; etc	12 mins: Jogging on spot & stretches – stay warm & loose	Use imagery & self-talk to replay key 'jobs' to be done: backrow moves, line-outs, 2nd phase. – Use imagery to psych-up if needed; OR use centring to calm down if needed.
50 mins: Change gear – strapping – rub down (1st pee stop)	'Scrum thinking' – backrow moves – running lines from scrum in attack	5 mins: Last pee stop	– Avoid talking to others until on the field: 'Stay inside my bubble.'
40 mins: Stretching – hamstrings – neck & shoulders at same time. – calves	'Line-out thinking' – jump selection – support of '5' jumper. – line-out defence	4 mins: 'Stay warm & loose' – stretches/jog.	Enjoy the adrenaline! Briefly review general game plan.
– groin	Support play & 'lines' – accurate lines – speed & urgency – backline 'targets'	2 mins: Take warm-up gear off.	After the toss; focus solely on my first job at kick-off.
35 mins: Jogging on spot for 3–5 mins			'Keep the fizz' 'Be focused & disciplined'

Game focus plan

Write out your segmented plan of tactics, strategies, thoughts, cues, self-talk, imagery, centring, activities, etc. as you intend to use them during the game.

First five minutes:

Last five minutes of the half:

First five minutes of the second half:

Last five minutes of the game:

Critical skills or critical moments, such as before set plays, actions (e.g., line-out throw, scrum, backline move . . .):

Coping plan

Write out the coping plans that you intend to use if you are faced with distractions before and during the game. Identify possible things that could 'go wrong', then develop possible solutions to help you deal with the problem/distraction — to help you cope and refocus. List stretches, drills, activities, self-talk, thought-stopping, self-suggestions, imagery, relaxation, centring, etc., in the sequence that you intend to do them to help you cope.

Below are some possible sources of problems/distractions — use these as a basis for developing your coping plan.

Not psyched-up enough:

Being over-psyched (over-activated):

Pre-game distraction:

Change in start time (earlier or later):

Non-ideal ground or weather conditions:

continued:

Early mistake or error by you in the game:

Early mistake or error by a teammate in the game:

Loss of ideal focus in the game:

Repeated mistakes or errors during the game:

Poor performance in the first half:

Poor overall performance (i.e., need to cope and re-focus for next game):

13. Relaxation techniques

I always get nervous before any game. It's just a matter of trying to relax.
— MARK MAYERHOFLER (ALL BLACK 1998–)

To many people, rugby has traditionally been associated with fifteen fired-up players going out onto the field and giving their all. Indeed, a long-standing myth is that players have to be as psyched-up as possible in order to play well, but this has led to many players being over-psyched and playing poorly as a result (see chapter 5, Controlling activation). Consequently, an often-heard observation among coaches, commentators and players is that a team took twenty minutes or more to settle down and start playing according to the game plan, and to their ability.

As we've seen in chapter 5, every player, every game, and every situation within a game, requires a different level of activation in order to perform optimally, so your ability to control your level of activation is an important skill to master. For most players, the problem lies not so much in being able to psych themselves up for a particular game or a situation within a game, but in preventing themselves from being psyched out by being too activated.[1] They are unable to cope with the pressure of the situation, and can experience not only a decrease in performance but real physical illness (some players have been known to vomit before games) and mental distress.[2] It is their inability to effectively control their activation levels that is the problem. Their limited control seems to be entirely in one direction — they can easily raise their activation level, but have a problem lowering it when required.

Given that controlling activation is a key skill in maintaining peak performance through peak activation, and that most players need to lower their activation levels rather than raise them, the ability to physically and mentally relax is an important weapon in a player's arsenal. If you are aware of what it feels like to be totally relaxed, then you are more likely to recognise when you are over-activated. And if you know *how* to relax, there will be less chance of you becoming even more activated when a teammate or your coach tells you to 'relax' — which often has the opposite effect to that intended; the player thinks 'there must be something to panic about', or 'I must be too uptight', and because they don't know how to deal with the situation, the problem simply becomes worse. Players who know how to relax, on the other hand, can perform a relaxation procedure and lower their activation to a more appropriate level for the task that they are about to perform. As a result, they play better!

Knowing when and how to relax will allow you to become physically and mentally free from uncontrolled activation, tension, anxiety and negative thoughts before, during and after games and practices. A player who is relaxed might describe the feeling as one of ease, looseness, and readiness to perform. This involves both physical relaxation and mental relaxation. The overriding notion is one of being able to calm the body and clear the mind.

> The body brought to an edge of expectation. At the best, completely relaxed and coiled, ready for the first few moments of action . . . A light warm-up, a few muscle stretches, and sit completely relaxed, letting the mind dominate. The mind. The driving force.
>
> — GRAHAM MOURIE

Purposes of relaxation training

The most obvious purpose of relaxation is to calm the body by decreasing muscle tension, as well as decreasing your heart rate and breathing rate. In addition, relaxation can help to shift your concentration from anxiety-provoking thoughts to a more relaxed and focused mindset (that is, to the Ideal Performance State) by helping you to reach your peak level of physical and mental activation, before and during the game.

Being able to relax can also help you sleep the night before a major game, a concern for many rugby players. It is also used as a mechanism for helping to develop other PST skills and methods (such as peak concentration, and imagery).

Relaxation techniques

Some of the most common relaxation techniques are described here. Not all of the techniques will be appropriate in every situation, so you should become proficient at using a number of them. For example, a technique that takes several minutes to perform will be of no use to you during a game when you only have a few seconds between the end of one passage of play and the start of the next, but might be very useful as part of your pre-match preparation. On the other hand, a technique such as centring can, with practice, be performed in a few seconds, and therefore may be useful as a means of reducing activation levels during a game.

Centring

Centring is a relaxation and concentration exercise in which you focus on your breathing in a particular way; that is, on breathing from your 'centre of gravity', which for most of us is just behind the navel/stomach. It combines the use of abdominal breathing and key words, and is described as a mind-to-muscle relaxation technique.

How can centring help you? In martial arts such as judo and karate, centring is

> I haven't got any real superstitions. I've just got a routine I usually go through. It's mainly about polishing my boots on the day of the game, packing my gear, doing my warm-ups properly. . .
> — MARK MAYERHOFLER ON STAYING RELAXED

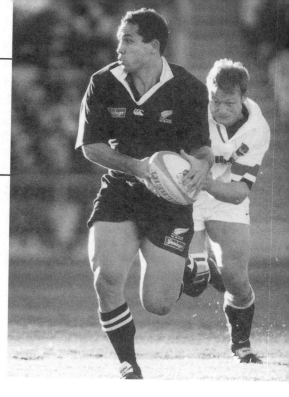

used as a method to reduce unwanted tension and to increase concentration powers for body control. Likewise, you can use centring to stay loose under pressure and to focus attention on your centre of control. Whoever controls the centre of gravity controls where the body moves. If it's your opponent, he controls you! Learning to centre helps keep you in control.

Physical effects of centring: These include decreased heart rate, decreased breathing rate, increased oxygen to the muscles, decreased negative tension, better control of hips, and better balance.[3] Movements that are initiated and controlled from your centre of gravity will generate better timing and better coordination.[4] This can help your rugby in a number of ways, ranging from the simple act of running more efficiently to being better able to tackle, pass, jump, and push! A scrum made up of eight players who can effectively control and initiate power and force from their centres of gravity will potentially exert more pressure on their opponents.

Psychological effects of centring: Players who are able to centre effectively may feel stronger, more confident and more in control of their actions on the field.[5] Their attention will be focused on their centre of gravity and therefore on body control, which will direct their attention away from negative thoughts or other distractions.

Everyone can centre to at least some degree right now. However, centring under game pressure requires practice. It may be appropriate for you to relax yourself before kicking a penalty for goal, or before throwing into a line-out, but if you don't know how to do that, and if you haven't practised doing it beforehand, it can lead to a poor performance. The following two phase learning process will help you learn and practise centring.

Phase 1: *Breathing skills and centring of attention.*
Focus on a point just about behind your navel. Concentrate upon this point and then feel your entire body in relation to it. Remind yourself that your strength, power, balance and control all come from this point.

★ The easiest way to learn this technique is to lie down on your back with your legs uncrossed.

★ Place one hand on your stomach just below your navel and rest the other hand on top of it.

★ Breathe in through your nose so that your stomach and your hand rise as you inhale. Breathe out through your mouth so that your stomach and hand fall as the air goes out. Keep breathing in and out in this manner with your attention totally focused on your breathing and nothing else.

★ Try to make the inhalation and exhalation last the same amount of time. The transition between the two should be very natural and unforced.

★ Every time you breathe out repeat the word 'one' silently to yourself. If your mind drifts just refocus on your breathing and your concentration word (eventually replace the word 'one' with a word that is meaningful to you). It can also help to visualise each muscle group loosening up, like light bulbs being turned off one by one.

★ At first spend about 10 minutes on this exercise each day. Gradually decrease the time to 3–5 minutes and change your position from lying down to sitting, and then standing. Eventually practise the exercise in a position that is relevant to your rugby playing position (for example, waiting for the ball to be thrown into a line-out, preparing to throw the ball into a line-out, waiting to receive a pass from your half-back from a scrum, or waiting to field an up-and-under).

Build in a mental cue for centring. As you breathe in, say a cue word to yourself (such as 'centre'), to remind yourself to centre, and as you exhale say another cue (such as 'relax'), to remind yourself to stay loose. At the end of one breathing cycle many players like to cue their attention towards their opponent or the next task while staying centred; a word like 'concentrate', 'focus', or 'action' works well. Use the Training Log for Centring sheet on page 166 to record your centring practice.

The entire sequence might be:

$$\text{Breathe in (nose)} \longrightarrow \text{Breathe out (mouth)}$$

$$\text{'Centre'} \longrightarrow \text{'Relax'} \longrightarrow \text{'Focus/Action'}$$

Phase 2: Centring during practice or training.

Practice centring between drills or between periods of practice. Later, make it a habit to centre before each set piece (such as scrum, line-out, kick-off, 22 metre drop-out).

Use cue words to reinforce the centring drill. As your skill improves, try centring in low pressure games, gradually working up to more important games. The more automatic your centring skills become, the more they can be used in important games. The better centred player will have more strength, speed and balance; and better timing, concentration and confidence. Centring helps you switch on your 'automatic pilot' and the Ideal Performance State.

Example

Whenever you are feeling too uptight or you are distracted from your present task, use the centring procedure.

★ Stand comfortably with your feet shoulder distance apart and your knees slightly flexed.

★ Consciously relax your neck, arm and shoulder muscles. Smile slightly to reduce the tension in your jaw.

★ Focus on the movement of your abdominal muscles. Notice your stomach muscles tightening and relaxing.

★ Take a slow, deep breath using the diaphragm. Notice you are extending your stomach.

★ Consciously maintain the relaxation in your chest and shoulders. There should be minimal chest movement and absolutely no hunching or raising of the shoulders.

★ Exhale slowly. Let yourself go. Feel yourself get heavier as all your muscles relax.

★ Focus on the job that you have to do right now. Use your game focus plan or coping plan to find the correct focus point. 'All I've got to do now is . . .'

Progressive muscular relaxation (PMR)

PMR is a physical relaxation exercise that may be necessary if you are unable to effectively control your activation levels with centring alone. PMR allows you to relax to a much 'deeper' level than centring; this depth is useful for controlling insomnia (sleeping problems) and can also be useful as a lead-in to an imagery practice session.[6] There are four phases needed to learn PMR effectively so that you can progress to using centring before or during a practice or game. Use the PMR Relaxation Training Log sheets on pages 167–70 to record your PMR practice.

Phase 1: Tense-relax cycle.

This learning phase relies on the overshoot principle — when a muscle is tensed it will then relax below the initial level of tension. Allow 15–20 minutes to do this exercise. You may wish to record the following script onto an audiotape to use with a Walkman. See the PMR Relaxation Phase 1: Training Log sheet on page 167.

★ Lie down and relax your entire body. If you hear noises don't try to block them out, but focus on your breathing: inhaling, then exhaling slowly. If you want to move slightly, that's okay. Close your eyes, take it easy and relax. Focus on your breathing. Breathe in through your nose and out through your mouth.

★ Tense the muscles of your right lower leg and foot by pointing your toe. You'll tense for 5–6 seconds and then relax. You should be able to feel the tension in the foot and the calf and then totally relax. When you relax feel the warmth in the muscles as the tension drains away. Focus on the differences between tension and relaxation. Repeat this procedure again on the right leg and then repeat it twice for the left leg.

★ Think to yourself 'loose' and 'relax' every time you release the tension. Focus on your breathing again as you do so.

★ After tensing and relaxing the lower leg and foot, tense (for 5 seconds) and relax the thigh and buttocks region (twice for each leg). Tense the buttocks and thighs by pushing down with your butt.

★ Tense and relax the forearm and hand by making a fist. Do this twice for each arm.

★ Tense and relax the biceps of each arm by bending at the elbow and pretending you are doing a chin up. Repeat twice for each arm.

★ Tense (for 5 seconds) and relax the back muscles by arching the back up. Tense and relax the back twice.

★ Tense the stomach and chest muscles by breathing in deeply and releasing/relaxing. Do this twice.

★ Tense the neck and shoulders by shrugging your shoulders (pulling them upwards) and then releasing them and relaxing. Repeat this twice.

★ Tense the face and forehead by gritting your teeth and pulling your eyebrows together, then relax. Do this twice.

★ When the above progressive sequence is completed mentally check your body for any tension. Release it if you find any. By now (after about 15–20 minutes of tense/relax) you should be completely relaxed. Focus on the feelings of ease and looseness in your muscles, the deep breathing cycle you are in, and the calm, focused thoughts of your mindset. To a degree your peak level of activation should also represent a calm, semi-relaxed state.

The above 'script' is a general example of a PMR sequence. Modify the sequence of muscle relaxation to suit your personal needs and preferences.

Phase 2: Relax-only cycle.

Relax the same muscle groups without tensing. Begin to use a cue word or phrase (such as 'loose and easy', 'calm and ready') to signal relaxation. Allow 10–15 minutes each time you practise this phase. Progress to sitting, then to a standing position, and finally to a position that is relevant to your playing position. See the PMR Relaxation Phase 2: Training Log on page 168.

Phase 3: Full-speed relaxation.

Begin to add speed by learning to relax the muscle groups more quickly. You can start by dividing the body into fewer parts. The ultimate goal is to learn to relax deeply in the time it requires to take a deep breath and use your cue word or phrase (the centring procedure). Practice this about 10 times a day. See the PMR Relaxation Phase 3: Training Log on page 169.

Phase 4: Utilisation stage.

Begin to use PMR relaxation in anxiety-provoking situations. Practise first in low stress conditions (such as during training), then under moderately stressful conditions and finally in highly stressful situations. See the PMR Relaxation Phase 4: Training Log on page 170.

The time frame for moving through these four phases depends on your ability to master each phase and the time that you have available to practise.

Further techniques for lowering activation levels

Physical stretching, relaxing music, and the use of schedules or routines (such as mental preparation; see chapter 12), imagery and self-talk are other techniques that can be used to relax yourself before and, in some cases, during a game. There are also a number of other methods that you might be able to use to help you stay relaxed during a game. These techniques also require practice and modification to suit your personal needs and style, and should not be attempted during games until you have developed them to a level where you trust your ability to use them effectively.

★ Smile when you feel you are becoming too tense.[7] It is hard to become upset or mad if you are smiling, and may also distract your opponents if they see you smiling in a tense situation!

★ Focus on enjoying the game.[8] After all, one of the main reasons to play rugby in the first place is because it is enjoyable! By focusing on enjoying the experience of playing, without being too concerned about the outcome of the game, you will go a long way towards reducing the anxiety that many players feel during a performance. Most players experience a great deal of satisfaction and enjoyment when they successfully perform a particular move, pull off a great tackle, make a good run with the ball in hand, or set up a try for one of their teammates. So why not focus on these aspects of the game — the enjoyable aspects — and let the outcome of the match take care of itself? Of course it's enjoyable to win, but winning happens when you perform these different aspects of the game well. Doing these things well is enjoyable, can give you and the rest of the team confidence, and can therefore reduce the anxiety that you may have been feeling. Focusing on enjoying the various aspects of the game that make up a complete performance can be seen as an effective relaxation strategy.

★ Set up pressure situations in practice.[9] By practising your responses to simulated pressure situations, you can become accustomed to playing under pressure and will be less likely to become too anxious or uptight when these situations occur in a game. For example, during a team run, your coach or captain could tell you that there are two minutes left in the game, you have been stuck in your own 22 metres for the past five minutes and you are three points down, but have a penalty in centre field. What are your options? How will you approach this situation? Once a decision is made, practise that response. The idea is that if that situation arises in a game, the team will not get too anxious — they have experienced it before (even though it was in practice), and know that they have a strategy in place to deal with it.

★ Slow down and take your time.[10] Players often rush things when they are anxious and uptight, because they think that the easiest way to cope with the pressure is to get it over with. As a consequence their execution of the particular move or skill is often poor, which makes them even more uptight. They'll drop a pass, knock the ball on, kick the ball off the side of their boot, get offside, run ahead of the ball carrier, or get into a poor position in a ruck or maul. One of the ways to prevent these things from happening is to have an established and consistent pre-performance routine before each set piece and other game situations which incorporates some form of relaxation procedure. See the CARS plans in chapter 15.

★ Stay focused on the present.[11] What do you have to do right now? You will become even more uptight and anxious if you dwell on a mistake that you have just made, how it will feel if you lose the game, or what the opposition might try to do in the second half. These types of thoughts can only distract you from your immediate job, and often lead to mistakes because you weren't totally focused (see also chapter 7, Concentration). This can make you even more uptight, and a vicious cycle begins. Remaining focused on the present will prevent these distracting thoughts from increasing your anxiety — your attention will be taken up by what you have to do at that moment. One way to remain focused on the present is to use the referee's whistle to stop play as a cue to ask yourself, 'What do I have to do now?'. You might like to think about each stoppage in play as a chance to regroup, to analyse the last play, and to plan for the next play (see also chapter 15,

CARS plan). The whistle to restart play should be considered as an opportunity for you to perform well. For example, a flanker who has missed a number of tackles should use the whistle that signals the end of a passage of play as a cue to mark the end of a poor performance. Rather than use the time between plays to dwell upon how many tackles he has missed, he should analyse why those tackles were missed, and treat the whistle to start play again as an opportunity to perform better. This can help to keep the player focused on the present.

★ Make sure that you and the team have a well-prepared game plan, and that you know what that plan is in terms of the overall strategy of the team (for instance, keeping it tight in the first fifteen minutes, or making use of the blindside from scrums), and exactly what you have to do as a player in your particular position to make sure that the game plan is followed. If you are not exactly sure what to do, you are more likely to become uptight and anxious. In a rugby game you will be faced with hundreds of situations requiring you to make decisions (what line should I run, should I stay on my feet or go to ground, which man should I be marking, should I hold on to the ball or pass it), and a well developed, specific, and well practised game plan will make the decision-making process a lot easier. As a consequence, your reactions and responses will become quicker, which will help you to perform better. This in turn will help you become more confident, and make you more likely to remain focused and relaxed (see also chapter 12, Mental preparation).

Relaxation and centring are effective PST methods for all players to learn; however, they require sustained practice. You need to create the right physical and mental environment to develop your ability to relax: a quiet setting; a comfortable position; the use of a mental cue word, phrase or trigger; and a positive attitude. The amount of time that you need to learn to relax quickly will depend on your individual ability and the time that you have available to practice. Try the techniques described, and then modify them to suit your personal needs and style.

I think that the ability to relax and keep your balance mentally could be the x-factor that lets you perform better than your opposition.

— ZINZAN BROOKE

Training Log for Centring

Use a scale from –10 to +10 (–10 = extremely tense and +10 = extremely relaxed) to show your level of relaxation before the centring exercise and afterwards.

Practise on five consecutive days. Each session should last only 10 minutes. Before training or before bedtime is a popular time. Practise in a quiet, warm environment where you will not be disturbed. Give yourself the opportunity to relax.

	Date of practice	Time of practice	Level before relaxing	Level after relaxing
e.g.	8 May	10 p.m.	–7	+5

After three days of centring training, try putting your new skill into practice at work or in social situations. When you feel yourself getting physically tense, your thinking rushed, or your emotions gaining control over your thoughts, stop and centre. Drop your shoulders, relax your facial muscles and focus on your stomach breathing. Close your eyes if you can. Remember, centring, like all the PST methods, needs consistent practice.

PMR Relaxation Phase 1: Training Log

Use a scale from –10 to +10 (–10 = extremely tense and +10 = extremely relaxed) to show your level of relaxation before and after the Phase 1 PMR relaxation exercise.

	Date of practice	Time of practice	Level before relaxing	Level after relaxing
e.g.	30 May	6 p.m.	–8	+9

1. What physical changes did you experience as you practised?

. . . .

. . . .

. . . .

2. What mental changes did you experience as you practised?

. . . .

. . . .

. . . .

3. In what situations would you use PMR?

. . . .

. . . .

PMR Relaxation Phase 2: Training Log

Use a scale from –10 to +10 (–10 = extremely tense and +10 = extremely relaxed) to show your level of relaxation before and after the Phase 2 PMR relaxation exercise.

	Date of practice	Time of practice	Level before relaxing	Level after relaxing
e.g.	9 June	6 p.m.	–8	+9

PMR Relaxation Phase 3: Training Log for Relaxing on Cue

When you discover cue words or phrases that work for you, begin to use them with centring by thinking of your cue as you breathe. Remember that it takes time to learn relaxation. The successful association of cue words with relaxation also takes time and practice.

Practice your trigger cues with centring for 10 minutes daily.

Use the scale from –10 to +10 (–10 = extremely tense and +10 = extremely relaxed) to show your level of relaxation before the centring/cue word exercise and afterward.

	Date of practice	Venue of practice	Level before relaxing	Level after relaxing
e.g.	22 June	During training; after each set of physical drills	–7	+3

When your level after centring/cue relaxation has consistently reached +7 or better, then move to Phase 4 instructions. This usually takes three to four practice sessions.

My cue word, phrase or colour is: . . . .

PMR Relaxation Phase 4:
Relaxing Before and During the Game

By the time you are ready to move on to Phase 4 you should be able to initiate PMR relaxation by centring and in places other than a quiet room without lying down or closing your eyes. You should also be able to achieve the relaxed state in well under one minute.

Pick a situation in which you feel relaxation will be useful, for example, on the way to a game, prior to beginning your warm-up, or before critical moments in the game. Goal kickers can centre before kicking for goal, props and hookers before each scrum, hookers before each line-out throw, number eights before a backrow move, and all players can centre between sets in training. Initially you may want to close your eyes for the brief centring exercise; later you may be able to centre with your eyes open but not focused on anything specific.

★ First, centre with stomach breathing.

★ Next, visualise each muscle group loosening up (like light bulbs being turned off one by one).

★ Next, use your triggering cues to relax further.

★ Next, check for any spots that are still tense.

★ Continue centred breathing to flow the relaxation to those spots.

Date of practice	Venue of practice	Level before relaxing	Level after relaxing
e.g. 10 July	Club game	–10	+7

14. Imagery

> Bruce [Deans, All Black half-back] and I would go up into the stand and visualize situations on the field. We'd talk about what the options were from a scrum on the ten metre line, a ruck near our own line, a line-out near their line, we'd work our way through the whole field, so we were mentally prepared.
>
> — WAYNE SMITH (ALL BLACK 1982–85)

Thousands of young New Zealanders have imagined themselves wearing the All Black jersey and playing alongside their heroes. After televised test matches it is not uncommon to see young kids playing in the backyards and parks of the neighbourhood, reliving the exploits of their heroes. What are they doing? They are using their imaginations to re-create the atmosphere of the game and the performances of their idols. They have used imagery to make these things come alive.

What exactly is imagery, and how can players use imagery to help them with their performance on the rugby field? Consider the following examples:

As the first five-eighth for his club team, Bob calls all of the backline moves from set pieces and second phase, and is responsible for organising the backline defensive pattern. This weekend's game will be against one of the club's traditional rivals, whose backs stand very flat and close together. In addition, Bob knows that because of his reputation as a weak tackler, the opposition will be likely to target him from set pieces, by using runners from around the back of the line-out and from backrow moves close to the scrum.

On the Tuesday night before the game, Bob's team and the coach come up with a game plan and specific moves that they believe will defend against this team. Bob and his team rehearse the moves during the practice, and for the rest of the week Bob runs through each of the moves in his mind as if he were actually playing the game, and also running them through from an outsider's perspective, as if he were watching the game on television. In addition, Bob develops a clear and vivid image of himself successfully tackling the runners who are likely to be targeting him from line-outs and scrums, and makes sure that he rehearses that image several times on each of the days leading up to the game.

At practice on Thursday night Bob and the rest of the backline quickly run through the image of the way each move should be performed before actually performing it. Bob has organised with the coach beforehand to set up some simulated situations with the reserve players, in which they act as the opposition for Saturday and try to target Bob from simulated line-out and scrum situations. Bob re-creates the image of himself tackling these players as they come towards him, and then physically practises tackling them in the simulated drill.

On the morning of the game, Bob runs through each of the images before getting out of bed, making sure that they are clear, vivid, successful, and in real time. He gets up feeling relaxed and confident that he will perform well that afternoon.

After Saturday's game, Jack (our number eight) was disappointed that the opposition had made some penetrating breaks from backrow moves, and that he had been unable to make any effective tackles in trying to defend these moves. While sitting in the changing room after the game, before having a shower, Jack tried to re-create the image of each of the backrow moves that the opposition had run, and against which he seemed ineffective in being able to stop. In imagining these situations, he payed particular attention to the lines that he ran and his body position during these moves. He ran each image through his head a number of times, and from two perspectives: externally — as if he was watching from above — and internally — from inside his own head as if he was actually playing the game again. Jack tried to run the plays first in real time and then again in slow motion in an attempt to pinpoint the problem.

He discovered that the opposition were able to penetrate past the advantage line when the ball-carrier made an inside pass back into a support player after drawing Jack and his flanker wide. Usually, the pass was made after Jack had committed himself to attacking the ball-carrier and consequently had left a gap on the inside for the support player to run through. Sometimes Jack would be able to attempt a tackle, but he was usually off-balance because he had to change direction and so the tackle was ineffectual.

Using imagery, Jack was able to work out that from his position of number eight he was too eager to tackle the first man running with the ball, rather than trusting his flanker to cover that man and hanging back to cover the player who might have been waiting for an inside pass. Jack's lines were okay; he just needed to slow down a little from the base of the scrum and be ready for that inside pass so that he could nail the support player as soon as he took the ball. Jack then imagined those moves being tried again, but this time successfully making a tackle on the player who took the inside pass from the ball-carrier and effectively stopping the move from making the advantage line. He practised this image in his head a few times to make sure that he had it right, and then made a mental note to remind himself to ask the coach to go over backrow defence from scrums at practice on Tuesday night. Jack was determined to practise the image of correctly defending these moves so that on Tuesday he could put these mental images into actual physical practice.

In these situations, imagery was being used for a number of different purposes: to create or re-create an image of something that has happened or might happen during a game; to solve a problem and correct a technical or strategic fault in a player's performance; and/or to create a positive mental state in which to perform. In each case the player conjured up a clear, vivid and controllable image of himself performing particular rugby skills. It was their ability to do this that led them to decide upon a particular strategy or technique to use, and helped them to believe that they could physically perform that skill. Their image directly influenced their thoughts, which influenced the way they felt, and then influenced their behaviour in terms of what they physically practised.

What is imagery?

Imagery is a PST method that involves a player's ability to mentally re-create objects, people, skills, experiences and situations, while not actually being physically involved in these situations. It can also be used to create new experiences in our minds.[1] Usually, a player will generate an image from a memory of an experience or situation, much like creating your own 'instant replay'. The image can then be manipulated to create a new image, or simply used as a re-creation of a past event or experience. In the example above, Jack re-created the image of his performance in his last game, and then manipulated that image to create a new image of himself performing more successfully in the same situation. You must remember, however, that imagery is not 'daydreaming' about the great player you would like to be — it is a specific psychological method that can be used to improve your performance, but requires consistent practice to be used effectively.

Imagery has also been called visualisation, mental practice or mental rehearsal. However, it is more than just visualisation ('movies in the mind'). It can and should involve all the senses: a clear and vivid image will involve the player being able to see the image, hear it, smell it, taste it and feel it. It is a mental and physical 'blueprint' of rugby performance. The emotions associated with re-creating or creating a rugby experience in the mind are an important part of the imagery process.[2] For example, a player could imagine his thoughts and feelings during a particularly poor game in an attempt to understand how his level of anxiety may have hurt his performance.

In summary, it must be remembered that imagery:

★ Involves creating or re-creating experiences and events.

★ Involves using all of the senses.

★ Can take place without any external stimuli (you don't have to be holding a ball, wearing your rugby jersey, or physically going through the movements of the image you are trying to create).

How does imagery work?

There is a great deal of evidence to show that the use of imagery can enhance performance in a variety of sports.[3] Many top athletes have reported that imagery has helped them to perform at the very elite levels of sport, and a number of rugby players have attested to the use of imagery to help them with their rugby skills. Perhaps the best known of these has been Grant Fox, New Zealand's most prolific points scorer in internationals, who was a strong advocate of the use of imagery in helping his goal-kicking performance. Indeed, studies on rugby players have shown imagery to be effective in enhancing goal-kicking[4] and tackling performance.[5]

In simple terms, imagery allows you to practice physical skills without actually having to perform them, and thus is a form of mental practice. Imagery also gives you a chance to deal with a problem or event in your mind before being physically confronted by it. In essence, imagery provides a mental blueprint of the performance, skill, or situation.

Mental rehearsal before and during the game has helped me enormously to concentrate, to focus my attention on the job at hand.

— GRANT FOX

Key issues in learning imagery

There are a number of key considerations to be taken into account when using imagery to help you with your rugby. These considerations can affect how well your imagery is able to help you with your performance:[6]

Imagery perspective. When you practice imagery, you will usually notice that your images are either external or internal. External imagery is when you see yourself playing as if you were watching yourself on video, whereas internal imagery occurs when you experience the image from inside your body, as if you were actually performing. It has been demonstrated that top-level athletes are more likely to use internal than external imagery, although many players will be able to switch between imagery perspectives depending on what they are using their imagery for! If a player wants to conjure up the 'feeling' of performing a particular skill (such as tackling), then an internal image is more useful, whereas a player who wants to replay a particular team move may use an external perspective to get an image of how the move may have looked from the sideline, or from above (to see the lines that the players involved in the move may have run). It simply depends on what type of image you want to produce.

Mental practice and physical practice. Imagery (that is, mental practice) should never take the place of physical practice, but should be used in combination with it. It can be used as a substitute for physical practice if players are injured or unable to train for any other reason (such as illness, fatigue, or when practice fields are unavailable because of bad weather!), but whenever possible, players should use physical practice as well as imagery.

Skill level of the player. Although much of the research on the effect of imagery has indicated that more experienced athletes get the greatest performance gains from using imagery,[7] both inexperienced and experienced players can improve their performance using this technique, whether they use it for rehearsing moves, building confidence, creating peak activation levels, or learning and practising specific rugby skills.

Imagery ability of the player. It makes sense that those players who can better develop clear, vivid and controllable images will gain the most benefit from using imagery to improve their performance, and research has supported this notion. However, it is important to remember that like any skill, the development of good imagery ability takes time, and you should be prepared to persist with your imagery practice. A study conducted on Olympic athletes found that even these elite level performers did not initially have good control over their ability to develop good images, but through persistent daily practice they were able to develop their imagery ability to a high level.[8]

Uses of imagery

Imagery can be used to improve both your physical and psychological skills. As well as being useful for learning and practising specific rugby skills and strategies, imagery is helpful for setting and achieving goals, for controlling your emotions and activation levels, for coping with unexpected events or problems, for developing self-awareness and self-confidence, and for coping with pain and injury.

The advantages of using imagery to improve your rugby skills are numerous. To begin with, it is a very efficient way to practise:

★ It is not physically fatiguing.

★ You can't injure (or re-injure) yourself when you are imaging (which is useful when practising many of the contact skills of rugby such as tackling, scrummaging and rucking/mauling).

★ You can practise imagery anywhere and at any time.

★ It offers a change of pace which can help to break the monotony of physical practice.

Key issues in training imagery

If you are not familiar with using imagery, then it is important to select the right setting when you begin to practise the technique. Distractions should be avoided, so you might want to practise your imagery in a quiet and relaxed setting. Just before going to sleep at night or just after waking up in the morning are often good times. Start by using the exercises included here, then create your own imagery 'script' based on the instructions in this section. You may want to record the script on an audiotape and use your Walkman. Remember to stay relaxed but alert when learning imagery. Later on you will be able to use imagery during practices and at some stages during games, but in the beginning you should practise in a relaxed state. Keep persisting with your imagery practice. Imagery works but it takes time and effort; you need to be realistic and patient.

When developing your imagery skills, focus on three basic types of imagery exercises. First, work on developing clear and vivid images in order to strengthen your ability to create the sights, sounds, smells, tastes and feelings of playing and practising rugby. Second, learn how to control your images, in order to imagine yourself performing the way you want to. Third, improve your ability to become more self-aware when practising imagery. It is important to incorporate awareness of your thoughts and feelings during good and poor performances into your imagery in order make your images as close as possible to the real experience of playing.[9]

Basic imagery practice exercises

(All exercises are adapted with permission from Roberts, et al.) [10]

1. *Focus on the ball*

   'Open your eyes and focus on every detail of this rugby ball; look at the shape and colour.'

   (pause)

   'Close your eyes and imagine you are still looking at the ball — see all of the detail, the brand name, stitching, and the colours.'

   (pause)

   'Now open your eyes and compare your image with the real ball.'

   (pause)

   'Close your eyes again and see the ball with its colour and detail.'

   (pause)

2. *Developing clear, vivid images*

   'Now imagine your house. You are standing in the front yard looking at your house — notice the colour and the detail.'

   (pause)

   'Walk to the front door — notice how the house seems to grow as you get closer.'

   (pause)

   'Open the door, walk into your house and walk to the doorway of your room.'

   (pause)

   'See the colours of the walls, the furniture, the curtains, the floor.'

   (pause)

   'Notice all of the details as you look around your room.'

   (pause)

   'Now turn around and walk back to the front door of your house.'

   (pause)

   'Open the door and walk into the back yard — turn around and look back at your house.'

   (pause)

3. *Controlling your images*

   'Make your house get larger — make it grow bigger in size.'

   (pause)

   'Now make your house get smaller and shrink back to its normal size.'

   (pause)

'Make your house shrink smaller until it is one half its regular size.'
    (pause)

'Now make your house get bigger — back to its normal size.'
    (pause)

4. *Using all the senses in your images*

'Now imagine it's a beautiful warm summer day and you are standing on an ocean beach. You feel the warm, gritty sand between your toes.'
    (pause)

'Lie down on the beach on a towel and feel the warm, soft towel you are lying on and the penetrating warmth of the sun as you lie quietly.'
    (pause)

'Hear the ocean waves as they break on the shore and feel a slight cool breeze blow over you as you lie on the sand — you feel warm and relaxed.'
    (pause)

'Imagine the blue sky with a few white clouds skidding slowly across the sky.'
    (pause)

'You feel warm and relaxed.'
    (pause)

'Stand up and walk down to the water, wading in to knee depth — feel the cool, wet water on your legs. Cup your hands and scoop up some water — taste the salt water and spit it out. Focus on the bitter, salty taste.'
    (pause)

'Walk back up the beach and lie down on your towel again. Feel the penetrating warmth of the sun. You feel light-headed, and sleepy.'
    (pause)

'Now open your eyes and sit up, slowly.'

Advanced imagery practice exercises

Vividness exercises.[11]

★ Imagine that you are in the changing room before a game, and that your coach is giving the team talk for that game. Visualise your coach as clearly as possible. What is he wearing? What type of build is he? What mannerisms, facial expressions, distinguishing features does he have? Imagine as many details of that person as possible. Imagine that the coach is walking around the changing room as he speaks, and that he has stopped in front of you and is talking to you directly. How do you feel about your coach and what he is saying? Try to imagine this scene from an internal perspective — from inside your own body.

★ Think of the ground on which you have played the most rugby, or the one that you are most familiar with. Imagine that you are standing in the middle of that ground, and that there is nobody else there. Notice how quiet and empty it is. Look around you and pick out as many details of the ground as possible. Does it have a particular smell about it? What can you see as you look around? Now imagine that you are at the same ground, but this time you are in the changing room getting ready for a game. It is 15 minutes before kick-off. Try to imagine the scene as if you were inside your own body. Your teammates are all around you getting themselves prepared. Hear the clicking of their sprigs on the floor as they jump around in nervous anticipation. Listen to the voices of those who are still in the changing room, as well as the noise of the crowd outside waiting for the game to get underway. Try to imagine the smell of the Deep Heat and Vaseline that the players are rubbing into their muscles as they warm up, and listen to the physio tearing off bits of tape to strap up the various joints and muscles of the players. Re-create that feeling of excitement and nervous anticipation as the time ticks down to kick-off. How do you feel?

★ Think about the game ball, and imagine that you are sitting in the changing room turning it over in your hands before going out onto the field. Examine every part of it — the texture, the colour, the smell of the ball, the writing on it, the feel of it in your hands. Now imagine that you have the ball and you are running towards the goal line. You have about 15 metres to go and there is only one player to beat. See yourself from behind your own eyes, and then switch to watching yourself as if you were on television. Switch back to being inside yourself performing, and continue towards the goal line. What sounds can you hear? Is anyone close in support calling for the ball? Can you hear the crowd roar? Are you holding the ball in one hand or two? Or do you have it tucked under one arm? How does it feel? Put the sights and sounds together and imagine how it feels to be that close to the line with only one person to beat.

★ Pick a fundamental rugby skill, such as catching and passing the ball, leaping to catch a line-out ball, running upfield with the ball in hand, or making a side-on tackle. Imagine yourself performing that skill over and over again in your mind, from an internal perspective. Focus on how it feels to perform that skill. How do your muscles feel as they contract? What does it feel like when you make contact with the ground, the ball, or another player? Make sure that you imagine yourself performing this skill perfectly, and concentrate on the feeling of the movement. Now combine the sounds, sights and feelings, and try to put together the total experience of performing the skill. Don't concentrate too hard on one sense, just try to re-create the whole experience as clearly and as vividly as possible.

Controllability exercises.[12]

★ Imagine that your coach is walking around the changing room as your team is getting ready for a big game. Focus specifically on his face and pay particular attention to his features. Now watch him as he walks around the room talking to the players. Imagine that he stops and talks to various players individually. Keep watching as he walks up and begins speaking to you. Imagine the conversation that you might have with your coach at that time.

★ Choose a particular skill, move or technique that you have had trouble performing. Imagine that you are practising that skill over and over, and that you are doing this from inside your own body (internal perspective). If you make a mistake, stop the image immediately and start again. Try to perform the skill successfully every time. You might want to watch yourself performing the skill from an external perspective, as if you were watching yourself on video, to see if you can pick up what you are doing wrong when you make a mistake. If you can identify where the error occurs, try to imagine yourself performing successfully, and then revert back to an internal perspective and imagine what it feels like to perform this skill well. Practise that image over and over again.

Self-awareness exercises.[13]

★ Try to remember one of your best-ever games, not necessarily a game that your team won, but one in which you played particularly well. Using all your senses, try to re-create that experience. What were you feeling while you were playing that game? Were you confident, excited, nervous, relaxed, elated? Can you remember what your body felt like as you performed that day? What could you hear, see, smell, taste? Try to identify what it was that made you perform so well. If you manage to work this out, try to figure out why those factors were present during that game. What did you do that may have caused those things to occur? Think back — how did you prepare for that game? What thoughts and feeling did you have before going out onto the field? What specific things did you do leading up to the game, during the warm-up, or during the game that may have caused you to perform so well? Sometimes imagery is helpful in gaining an insight into why a peak performance occurred. Often players over-analyse a poor performance and try to figure out what went wrong, but get too caught up in the excitement and celebration of a peak performance to bother trying to figure out what went right! If you want a peak performance to occur again, then using imagery to help you try to figure out what went right is a good idea (see also Peak Performance Profile, pages 38–39).

★ Now go through the same exercise, but this time imagine a particularly poor performance on your part. Again, it doesn't matter whether it was in a game that your team won or lost, but it should be one in which you performed badly. Try to stay relaxed as you recall this performance, but recall how you reacted to certain things that happened during that game (such as poor referee's decisions, making simple errors, the coach's comments before the game and at half-time, opponents' behaviours, the feeling before the game). Think back — how might your thoughts and feelings have interfered with your performance that day? Run the image of that game through your head and try to find some answers to these questions.

★ Think back to a situation in which you were extremely anxious. It may have been before or during a game or practice, or perhaps a team meeting before a game or practice. Recall what you were thinking and feeling at that time. Pay particular attention to those feelings of anxiety. What caused them, and how did you react to that feeling? Were your muscles tense, did you sweat, were your hands clammy, did you fidget, or did you feel like you had to go to the toilet all the time? Re-create that situation as clearly and as vividly as you can. Conjure up those thoughts and feelings again, as if you were there right now! Now try to release all of that anxiety and let your body relax. Imagine that all of the tension is being drained away by being pulled into your lungs and exhaled from your body. With each breath out you get rid of more and more of that anxiety and tension. Keep going until you feel completely relaxed.

★ Now repeat the exercise using a situation in which you recall being extremely angry.

★ Think back to a situation during a game when things were going well until you made a bad mistake. This may have happened on more than one occasion, so try to recall several of these times. Re-create the situations in your mind and try to identify what it was that caused the mistake (for instance, a distraction, focusing on the wrong cue, an opponent's remark). Once you have identified the things that may have caused this poor performance, go over the situation again in your mind. Try to figure out a strategy to deal with these factors, and then implement that strategy when you again replay the image of that situation. See and feel yourself using the strategy to prevent the negative factors from interfering with your performance, and imagine yourself performing well in that situation. Imagine also how it feels to be able to control these negative factors and to perform well. Using imagery in this way can also be incorporated into a CARS plan (see chapter 15).

Stages in developing sports imagery

Begin with guided practice. Use an instructor (sportpsych consultant, coach or teammate) to guide the imagery session. Use the imagery exercises outlined in this chapter. Have the person take you through these exercises, or record them onto your

Walkman. Remember to develop sensory awareness, and to focus on all the senses, not just the visual. Develop vivid and clear images — hear the crowd, smell the liniment, feel the ground, feel the movement, feel the contact.

Practise self-directed imagery. Develop your own imagery 'script', record it onto an audiotape and use a Walkman to practise it. Base the script on the imagery exercises in this chapter, but develop a script that is relevant to your position in the team. Use the Imagery Training Log 1 on page 185 to record your imagery practice and to evaluate your improvement. Aim to develop clear, vivid and controllable images. Eventually you should progress to practising without the use of the tape and Walkman. Practise controlling your images — start with simple skills and move to more complex ones, making sure that you can imagine yourself correctly executing these skills. Controlling your images is very important — uncontrolled imagery (such as 'seeing' yourself fail or make errors) can increase anxiety and stress.

Use imagery during training or practice. Once you have been able to develop clear, vivid and controllable images in a quiet and relaxed setting, progress to using imagery during training or during practices. Use the Imagery Training Log 2 on page 186 to record this level of imagery practice.

Begin using imagery before and during competition. Now that you have become more skilled at using imagery, include it in your pre-game mental preparation, for developing the right frame of mind to play, or for rehearsing specific skills or moves such as a pre-goal kick routine, a line-out throw, jumping and/or lifting in the line-out, a scrum backrow move, running good 'lines' in attack and defence, a backline attacking move, and backline defensive options (use the Imagery Training Log 3 on page 187).

Imagery guidelines

★ When learning imagery, use short practice sessions (about five minutes). Consistency and quality are more important than length of practice.

★ Imagine good performances and positive outcomes.

★ Image with all the senses.

★ Follow images of incorrect performance with images of correct performance.

★ Use 'triggers' (such as cue words or phrases, the colour of your playing jersey, your boots, the smell of liniment) to strengthen the vividness of imagery.

★ Practise, practise, practise . . .

When to use imagery

Although imagery can be used at almost any time and in a variety of situations, it seems that there are some specific times when it can be most useful:[14]

Before and after practice. Either before you get to practice, or in the changing room before you go out to start your warm-up, it can be useful to go over the drills, techniques and moves that you are likely to be rehearsing. After practice, it is also useful to review the session using imagery. The feel of the movements involved in the techniques and moves that you practised will be fresh in your memory, so it should be easier to re-create a clear and vivid image of the movements. This will help to cement that image in your mind so that it (and therefore the actual movement) will be easier to recall during the next practice or game.

Before and after games. Before the game, and as part of your mental preparation for the game, create a clear and vivid image of exactly what you want to achieve and how you want to play during that game. Make sure that you include an alternative move or strategy in each of the situations that you imagine, and see and feel yourself performing successfully. This pre-game imagery will help to focus your mind onto the upcoming game, and your reactions to situations that may arise during the game will be quicker because you have mentally rehearsed strategies to deal with them. Your pre-game imagery does not have to be done at any specific time. Some players like to use imagery immediately before they go out onto the field, whereas others will do it well before the game, and before they arrive at the ground. It is very much a personal choice — experiment to find the time that suits you best.

After the game you should replay the things that you did well, as well as trying to analyse why certain things may not have gone as well as you would have liked. Try to develop a strong image of your successful moves or techniques, and also of how to successfully perform the things that went wrong during the game.

During breaks in play. Every time the referee's whistle goes for a knock-on, forward pass, penalty, or to signal a line-out, there is time to create a quick, vivid image of what you should do at the next set piece. If the break in play is long enough, you may even have time to review the last passage of play in your mind, and analyse what has just happened, before creating an image of your role in the next part of the game. For example, Bob may have just kicked the ball out from a defensive scrum. He has time to quickly review his kick under pressure from the opposition flanker before creating a clear image of his defensive role at the resulting line-out. This should take no more than a few seconds if Bob has been practising his imagery and is able to develop good, clear, controllable images in the highly charged atmosphere of a game.

During personal time. You can practise your imagery at home, at work or at any other time during the day when the opportunity presents itself. Remember, imagery practice does not have to be very long; five minutes may be all that is required!

When recovering from injury. Imagery can be useful for rehearsing the skills that you are physically unable to do while you are injured (see also chapter 18, PST for rehabilitation from injury). This imagery training can help you to return more quickly to the level at which you were able to perform prior to the injury. Developing powerful positive images of the healing process (bones and muscles knitting together, damaged tissue becoming healthy) has also been shown to aid the recovery process.[15]

Methods of practising imagery[16]

Individual versus team practice. Although it is desirable to have individually designed imagery programmes, it is often useful to have team sessions when introducing the concept. The coach can introduce imagery to the team, or can enlist the services of a sportpsych consultant if he feels unwilling or uncomfortable to do it himself. It can be useful to decide, as a team, when and how imagery can be incorporated into a systematic programme or into team practices. If you then wish to set up an individualised programme, do so! Your coach or the sportpsych consultant should help you to design a programme that is specific to you and your playing position.

Cassette tapes. Many players find it useful to make their own imagery tape rather than use commercial tapes. Commercial tapes are usually not specific to any individual or any particular sport, so there is an advantage to having your own individualised tape. Include specific verbal cues that are familiar and meaningful to you as a player. Make sure that the tape includes instructions to image specific responses to the various situations that may arise during a game, rather than just describing the situation. It might even be possible to record an imagery session that is being conducted by the coach or a sport psychology consultant. It is up to you to decide what will work best, and what you will feel most comfortable using.

Highlight videotapes. If possible, make up (or have made for you) a highlight videotape of yourself playing well in particular situations during a game. Not only will it provide a good external image of yourself, and therefore help you to form your own images, it can enhance your confidence and motivation. The edited highlights of your best ever moments during games could be set to your favourite motivational music, and then used with your own imagery to boost your confidence in returning to the field after an injury, or simply to enhance the clarity and vividness of your imagery.

Imagery logs. It is useful to monitor your imagery practice and improvement, so the use of imagery logs provides a written record of your imagery experiences. The samples on the following pages are a good way to keep track of your imagery practice. Photocopy as many of them as you need and transfer them to your Training Logbook once you have filled them out (see chapter 20).

Imagery Training Log 1

Practise your imagery script regularly and record your imagery ability. Rate your imagery vividness and your imagery control.

Practise on five consecutive days with the same imagery script. Then change the script to a more difficult one. Each practice session should last only about 10 minutes. Before training or before bedtime is a popular time. Practise in a quiet, warm environment where you will not be disturbed.

Use a scale from 1–5 (1 = low vividness/control and 5 = high vividness/control) to show your level of imagery.

	Date of practice	Time of practice	Vividness level	Control level
e.g.	30 May	6 p.m.	3	2

1. What vividness changes did you experience as you practised?

. . . .

. . . .

2. What control changes did you experience as you practised?

. . . .

. . . .

Imagery Training Log 2

Practise your more difficult imagery script for ten minutes daily. Use the scale from 1–5 (1 = low vividness/control and 5 = high vividness/control) to show your level of imagery.

Date of practice	Time of practice	Vividness level	Control level
9 June	6 p.m.	4	4

e.g.

My personal imagery script is:

. . . .
. . . .
. . . .
. . . .
. . . .
. . . .
. . . .
. . . .
. . . .

Imagery Training Log 3: Imagery on Cue

When you discover imagery cue words or phrases that work for you, begin to use them with imagery by thinking of your cue as you image. Remember that imagery takes time to learn. The successful association of cue words with imagery also takes time and practice.

Practice your trigger cues with imagery for 10 minutes daily.

Use the scale from 1–5 (1 = low vividness/control and 5 = high vividness/control) to show your level of imagery.

	Date of practice	Venue of practice	Vividness level	Control level
e.g.	22 June	In the clubrooms; after training	5	4

When your level after cue-imagery has consistently reached 4 or better for both vividness and control, then move to using imagery before or during a game.

My imagery cue word, phrase or colour is: . . . .

15. CARS plan
(Critical Action Response Strategies)

All players will benefit from working on the PST method of CARS — Critical Action Response Strategies. With its focus on 'coping' this method is similar to the coping plan described on pages 151 and 155–156, but the CARS plan is much more specific and targeted to critical moments and skills that may cause pressure for players (see also chapter 6). CARS plans are designed to help players cope with the stress and pressure associated with critical actions such as defence and tackling, goal kicking, your own mistakes, mistakes by teammates, refereeing decisions, adverse weather conditions, physical or verbal intimidation by opponents, and coming on as a substitute. This stress and pressure is one of the major challenges of playing top level rugby, and successful players learn to relish and enjoy that challenge (see chapter 6).

CARS plans are also designed to help you maintain your skill level in the 8 C's of Commitment, Confidence, Controlling activation, Coping with pressure, Concentration, team Cohesion, Captaincy and Communication (see chapters 3–9).

Why you should develop a CARS plan

The CARS psych method is vital for a continuous, interactive sport like rugby where stress and pressure must be dealt with on the go.[1] There are no time-outs or lengthy breaks in play (other than half-time or the occasional injury break), so you need a quick method — 5–20 seconds — to deal with the stress and pressure you may encounter during the game. Recent law changes have increased the pace of rugby, and as the pace has increased the time available for decision-making has drastically decreased — you must be able to think fast and be mentally tough! (See chapter 7.)

The CARS PST method is actually a combination of a number of methods. In designing your own CARS plan you will need to choose a combination that best suits the way that you to like to deal or cope with the pressure that comes with playing competitive rugby.[2] One player's CARS plan might involve a combination of imagery, self-talk and centring, while another player's CARS might include self-talk, parking and mental prep (see the CARS Plan Worksheet on page 195 and the example on page 196). Your CARS plan needs to be so well practised that it becomes an automatic action-response to critical moments and skills in the game. It is absolutely essential that the CARS Plan becomes second nature, as you will have little time to think through your response during the game.[3]

Start your CARS!

Many players invent their own label to help them remember and use the CARS method — some imagine their CARS to be a 4WD truck; others imagine a sports car. Such labels are corny, but they work because they help players remember the key aspects of the CARS plan that they have planned and practised using.

You can use your CARS plan at breaks in play such as scrums, line-outs, kick-offs, 22 metre drop-outs, penalty kicks at goal, penalty kicks for touch, half-time, and injury breaks. Use it as a means to refocus attention or effort and to cope with any stress and pressure.

The nature of your CARS plan needs to vary depending upon the type of critical action that you will be dealing with. In general, you will need to deal with two types of critical actions:

★ Critical moments — a time-referenced critical stage of the game when you need to have total concentration and confidence (such as after making a mistake).

★ Critical skills — common team skills and individual skills that can happen anytime during the game and are repeated many times during a game (e.g. scrummaging, line-out throwing).

Critical moments: CARS

Moments include such critical stages in the game as:

★ Your own mistakes

★ Mistakes by teammates

★ Refereeing decisions

★ Adverse weather or ground condition changes

★ Physical or verbal intimidation by opponents

★ Coming on as a substitute or injury replacement

★ After your opponents score a try

★ The first or last five minutes of either half of the game

★ After an injury break

★ Kick-offs — receiving (after scoring)

★ Kick-offs — chasing (after being scored against)

★ 22 metre drop-outs — receiving or chasing

★ Penalties: tap and run — defending, running

Critical moments: CARS plan for dealing with mistakes

Making a mistake is one of the most common critical moments for players. Mistakes are part of the game — for you, your teammates, and referees. Humans are not perfect so we often make mistakes. Most of them are only small errors (perhaps a knock-on that results in a scrum), but there will also be some major errors that can drastically affect the course of the game (such as missing a simple tackle and letting in a try, giving away an avoidable penalty within kicking range, or not passing to an unmarked player and 'bombing' a try).

You need a CARS plan to cope with the emotions that typically come with making a mistake. How you deal or cope with a mistake is often more important than the consequences of the mistake itself.[4] You don't want to spend a lot of time thinking about making mistakes, but you do need to be prepared to handle them. Having a CARS plan for dealing with mistakes is not negative thinking — it's a positive approach for coping with an inevitable part of rugby.

Keep this in mind: provincial coaches and selectors often hope a player they are watching will make a few mistakes or face some other pressure so that they can judge the player's ability to cope with mistakes and maintain his performance level.[5]

Sometimes after you've made a mistake the game will stop for a scrum, a line-out, or a free kick or penalty — if that happens you will have a few moments to use a CARS plan. But often the referee will apply advantage and the game will continue after your mistake — if that is the case then you need a quick CARS plan that allows you to 'let go' of the mistake and the emotions surrounding it (see the sample CARS plan on page 195). You need to keep your head in the game and not get stuck thinking in the past.

Here are some suggestions for a CARS plan for coping with mistakes:

★ *Game has stopped for a few moments.* You may choose to use a combination of a number of PST methods, like centring, imagery, and self-talk (such as 'parking'). It may also help to talk to one or more teammates. Communication can help relieve the anger and pressure that come with making a mistake and can also help identify or sort out the cause of the mistake — for example, a missed tackle may have been partially due to a lack of communication amongst the defenders.

★ *Game has carried on.* You must be able to shake off the anger and frustration immediately. You might choose to use just one or two PST methods, like centring and one self-talk or parking phrase ('stay in the game'; 'do my next job').

Once you have designed your CARS plan for mistakes you will need to practise it diligently, especially during team training. Mistakes and errors are inevitable at practice as you and your teammates strive to improve various sub-unit skills (such as

---

line-out or backline passing options), attacking strategies (such as backrow moves, backline attacking moves), and defensive strategies (such as one-out defence, spot tackling). These mistakes are opportunities to learn more about the game and to practise and fine-tune a CARS plan for dealing with the emotions and pressure that result. You must get to the stage of being able to execute your CARS plan automatically, just as you do your fundamental physical and technical skills.[6]

A mistake can either be a stumbling block or a stepping stone, depending on your approach.[7] We all make mistakes, but not all of us deal with them effectively and learn from them —indeed, some of us continue to make the same mistakes over and over again. Learn from your mistakes and practise a CARS plan to cope with the pressure that comes with the error. The easiest way to be a mistake-free player is to a avoid taking risks or having a go; but the nature of rugby requires that you take calculated risks if you wish to score tries and be successful.

Grant Fox used a combination of PST methods (imagery, centring and self-talk) to help him relax and cope with the pressure associated with the critical skill of goal kicking.

Critical skills CARS

Critical skills are common team and individual skills that happen many times during a game. While they are 'common', they are no less critical and important than the critical moments.

Individual skills are individual player task demands:

★ Passing

Relaxation is the mental-physical partnership. How you achieve it is up to you. I use a technique called mental rehearsal [imagery]. I have in my mind a picture of the ball going through the posts. The deep breathing, the shaking of the hands, are to rid the body of tension so that all is crystal-clear and unperturbed in the mind [centring] — the picture is in focus. I command myself [self-talk], 'Head down, follow through'.

— GRANT FOX

* Tackling
* Goal kicking
* Kicking for touch (from a penalty or free kick)
* Line-out throwing-in
* Line-out jumping
* Drop-out kicking
* Kicking off

Team skills are team related or sub-unit related roles or jobs:
* Scrummaging
* Line-outs
* Backline/backrow defensive pattern
* Backline/backrow attacking moves
* Counterattack
* Blindside attack/defence
* 'Hurry-up' tactics: short line-outs, quick line-out throws, tap kicks, quick turnover of second phase ball . . .
* 'Slow-the-game-down' tactics: positional kicking game, box kicks, up-and-under, rolling mauls, plugging the blindside, forward runners-into-maul setup . . .

CARS plan for 'playing on the bench'

We can't all take the field in every game — someone has to take their turn as a reserve. You don't go through all the effort and sweat of training with the goal of being on the reserves bench, but you have to expect to spend your share of time as a back-up player.

Lack of playing time is one of the hardest mental toughness challenges you will face.[8] In order to cope with this challenge you need to keep your confidence up, even though the coach has picked someone else ahead of you. You need to maintain your motivation to train and play, even though you are getting limited opportunities to play. Finally, you need to maintain a peak level of concentration and activation 'on the bench' in case you go on as a substitute or an injury replacement.

If your role in the team is that of a back-up player you need to develop your motivation and commitment with that role in mind.[9] You must be ready to perform when you do take the field as a sub or an injury replacement. If you aren't able to take your chance when it comes you may not get another one — coaches want performance, not excuses about having come on from the bench. Take the approach that you will show the coaches that they can't leave you out of the starting team in the future. Develop a specific CARS plan to help you get to your peak levels of activation and concentration when you take the field as a substitute.

CARS plan for the substitute player

With the changes to the rules in 1997, rugby now has the added playing position or role of substitute. While all players on the bench are eligible to be used as a substitute, often coaches will nominate specific players as likely substitutes for a specific game. For example, the coaches may inform Jack (our number eight) that he will be going on five minutes into the second half as an 'impact player'. The mental preparation required for Jack in this situation is quite different to that of the other bench players who expect to take the field only in the event of an injury. As coaches begin to make more tactical use of the substitution rule, players will need to adjust their mental preparation, their concentration levels, and their communication levels accordingly. You may be subbed on as a fresh set of legs, or as an impact player with a particular and specific job to do in order to make an impact in some aspect of the team's game plan. According to John Hart, the substitute player needs to 'add value', increase communication levels, and increase teammates' enthusiasm.[10] Clearly your CARS plan needs to be flexible enough to cope with the different requirements of being an injury sub versus the specific demands of being an impact sub.

CARS plan example: dealing with mistakes

Mark is a right wing for a First Division NPC team. He's played for this team for the past four years, and is an exceptional attacking player and a solid defensive player. He's had a taste of higher honours as a back-up player for a Super 12 team, but hasn't progressed higher, mainly because his form is a bit inconsistent.

Mark is playing a mid-season First Division game against a traditional rival. Thirty minutes into the first half, Mark knocks-on a regulation pass from his centre — it's his third knock-on in the game. The mistake happens as his team is swinging into counterattack after weathering a period of sustained defensive pressure. If Mark had held the pass he would have had the fullback unmarked outside him with a clear path to the goal line. He shrugged the first two knock-ons off as bad luck, but now he's very frustrated because he can't work out why his normally safe hands are letting him down. He's also annoyed with himself for not putting the fullback in the clear. The ensuing scrum is set 20 metres in from the right-hand touch, on Mark's 10 metre line. Mark has lost some confidence in himself, and he's still thinking about the third knock-on and 'what might have been' as the scrum is being set.

The opposition half-back sees the negative body language as Mark slowly trudges back into position, head down, shaking his head in disbelief, and with his back turned to the play. The half-back decides to attack Mark's wing while he's distracted; he calls up the loosehead side of the scrum and makes the call for a simple 8-9 flick on the blindside to give himself room to bang up a high box kick right on top of Mark's wing. Mark is slow to react; he barely gets to the ball on the full and ends up knocking it on. He retrieves the ball, but is tied up by the opposition number eight and buried in a tight maul 15 metres in from touch, just out from his own 22 metre line. The ref calls the knock-on and sets a scrum on the 22 metre line. Mark climbs out from under the collapsed maul and quickly jogs back into position, anxious to make up for his mistake, muttering under his breath and bitching at himself for spilling a simple catch (he would have had a simple mark just inside the 22 metres). He's really pissed-off with himself and now he's also angry at his fullback and first five-eighth who are telling him to sort himself out and show some guts under the high ball. Mark is angry, anxious and distracted as he returns to his position on the right wing.

The opposition number eight, who made the tackle on Mark, sees that he is visibly angry and that he's not paying attention to his defensive responsibilities as the scrum is forming. The number eight calls out to cancel the planned backline move on the open, and makes the call for a simple 'lefto' backrow move on the blindside to attack Mark's wing once again. The backrow move ends up being run as an 8-9-11 move with the left wing cutting back behind the half-back looking like he's going to link with the blindside flanker. The half-back dummies to the left wing, but Mark doesn't 'see' the move and buys the dummy — he moves in quickly and tackles the left wing ferociously, determined to make up for his two recent knock-ons. The half-back is quick enough to be outside the loose forward defence and he now has a clear run down the left hand touch. He draws the fullback, who's across in cover, and puts the number eight in the clear on the inside. The number eight scores in the corner in the tackle of the cover defending first five. Mark is left lying on the ground in the post-tackle tangle of bodies back on the 22 metre line. Now he's not just angry, he's angry and depressed — and it's not even half-time!

Mark needed a method to help him *cope* with the frustration, anxiety and loss of concentration that occurred after the third knock-on, and the blind anger, loss of confidence and almost complete distraction that occurred after he knocked-on the high kick. Mark is a good player — he's a tough bugger, and he doesn't give in or give up — but he didn't have the right skills to be mentally tough enough to cope with the consequences of the pressure in this game. He tried hard, but didn't have the psych skills needed for an effective action-response.

Mark needed a CARS plan that he had already practised until it was second nature; and he needed supportive teammates who could have called 'start your CARS!'. See page 196 for the plan that Bob, our first five, used for dealing with mistakes as part of his psych skills training.

CARS Plan Worksheet

Name: . . . . Position: . . . . Date: . . . .

Critical Moments: (e.g. . . . .)
[*Moment* = a time-referenced critical stage of the game]

PST skills: (circle all that apply)

Commitment	Confidence	Control	Coping
Concentration	Cohesion	Captaincy	Communication

PST methods: (circle all that apply)

Goal setting　　Self-talk　　Parking　　Centring　　Imagery　　Mental preparation

CARS plan:

Critical Skills: (e.g. . . . .)
[*Individual skill* = a repetitive individual task demand. *Team skill* = a repetitive team or sub-unit role/job]

PST skills: (circle all that apply)

Commitment	Confidence	Control	Coping
Concentration	Cohesion	Captaincy	Communication

PST methods: (circle all that apply)

Goal setting　　Self-talk　　Parking　　Centring　　Imagery　　Mental preparation

CARS plan:

CARS Plan Worksheet

Name: Bob Templeton   *Position:* First five-eighth   *Date:* 16 July 98

Critical Moments: (e.g. My mistakes; Ref's decisions; After they score)
[*Moment* = a time-referenced critical stage of the game]

PST skills: (circle all that apply)

Commitment   Confidence   (Control)   (Coping)

(Concentration)   Cohesion   Captaincy   Communication

PST methods: (circle all that apply)

Goal setting   (Self-talk)   (Parking)   (Centring)   (Imagery)   Mental preparation

CARS plan:

At critical moments like these I usually get really annoyed and I often lose my cool and struggle to stay calm and concentrate on the job at hand. I need to park all my negative thoughts and plug in some positive thoughts instead. I also need to combine this with centring to calm me down (control of activation), cope with the pressure, and clear my thinking; as well as use some imagery to rehearse the correct performance of my skills in the next phase of play. If there is enough time after the critical moment I might use self-talk and imagery to quickly look at the cause of the mistake/problem and try to sort out how to do it correctly next time — if there isn't time (e.g., play has moved on as the ref plays advantage) I will need to 'park' any thinking about the mistake/critical moment and think 'in the present' about my next job on the field.

Critical Skills: (e.g. a 'Miss-2' pass on my left hand; Goal kicking; Kickstarts)
[*Individual skill* = a repetitive individual task demand. *Team skill* = a repetitive team or sub-unit role/job]

PST skills: (circle all that apply)

Commitment   (Confidence)   Control   (Coping)

(Concentration)   Cohesion   Captaincy   Communication

PST methods: (circle all that apply)

Goal setting   (Self-talk)   (Parking)   Centring   (Imagery)   (Mental preparation)

CARS plan:

I often find that my confidence is pretty shaky with attacking backline moves run to my right where I have to pass off my left hand. Also I've recently had problems with my goal kicking and kickstarts and I've lost almost all confidence in my kicking. With critical skills like these I usually get really nervous and worry about screwing it up for my teammates. Often I struggle to stay focused and concentrate on the job at hand; sometimes I get quite nervous, my heart rate and breathing races and my timing slips as I feel tight. I need to 'park' all my negative thoughts and self-doubts, and use self-talk to cope with this self-imposed pressure; then I need to plug in some positive thoughts instead about correct skill technique. I also need to combine this with a quick mental prep plan to calm me down, clear my thinking and help me prepare my thoughts for these repetitive critical skills. Finally I need to use some imagery to rehearse the correct performance of these skills — reminding myself that I've done them correctly hundreds of times before.

Part IV

'Thinking Rugby' in Action

I know mentally that I am a lot harder than I used to be and that is a big factor. I know what an All Black spot means to me, having lost it. . . . So I suppose it's more mental hardness than anything else.

— CRAIG DOWD

16. PST for players: case studies

In rugby half the battle is in the mind, no matter how talented you are — you always need mental toughness and mental agility to get through an international game.
— IEUAN EVANS (WELSH INTERNATIONAL **1988–96**)

Throughout this book we have used Jack and Bob as examples of PST for mental toughness. In this chapter we summarise the examples that Jack and Bob provided for us to show you how the whole PST programme fits together into an organised training plan.

After completing psych skills assessments for Jack and Bob (see their Peak Performance Profiles on pages 40 and 41), we designed PST programmes for them (see pages 42–43), and then we used these two players as examples for various psych skills or methods. These two real-world case studies explain the development of PST programmes for Jack and Bob.

Individualised psych skills training for Jack and Bob

As previously discussed, PST programmes must be separately designed for each individual player. In order to individualise your PST programme you first need to identify your psych strengths and psych weaknesses (that is, your psych skill needs). Jack and Bob first needed to do a psych skills assessment by completing one or more of the following:

★ A Peak Performance Profile (see pages 38–39).

★ Interview/discussion with their coach or a sportpsych consultant

★ Match or video observation.

Once Jack and Bob had completed their Peak Performance Profiles they needed to identify their key psych skill strengths and weaknesses, which were then categorised into three types of psych skills (see chapter 2):

★ Foundation skills — such as motivation, self-confidence

★ Performance skills — such as pre-game activation or psych-up

★ Facilitative skills — such as team cohesion, communication

Then Jack and Bob were in a position to select PST methods to practise for enhancing specific psych skills — matching methods with skills. (See chapter 2 for the key distinction between psych skills and psych methods and the matching of methods with skills.) For instance, to work on the psych skill need of pre-game activation, Jack chose to use the psych methods of mental preparation, imagery, centring and self-talk.

As we saw in chapter 2, Jack's Peak Performance Profile indicated that at the start of this season he needed to commit himself fully to his rugby and his training, take control of his own pre-game psych-up, sharpen up his concentration, and be a more cohesive team player by improving his tactical skills (he had to follow the team's game plan). On the other hand, Bob's Peak Performance Profile revealed that he needed to gain some self-confidence, learn how to cope with pressure, get back his concentration, improve his decision-making, and pick up his on-field communication.

Jack was able to follow a Psych Skills Training programme that allowed him to improve his skill weaknesses. The first step Jack took was to sort his skill needs into different types of training; fitness/strength training, technical skills practice, and psych skills training. He decided that it was his psych skills that were most in need of improvement, so his next step was to categorise his psych skill needs into foundation, performance and facilitative needs. These were:

   (i) commitment (foundation skill);
   (ii) pre-game psych-up = peak activation (performance skill);
   (iii) concentration (performance skill);
   (iv) team cohesion (facilitative skill).

Based on this skill categorisation he concluded that he first needed to identify some psych methods to help him improve his foundation skill need for greater commitment — he chose to use the methods of goal setting and self-talk. Once he saw some gains in commitment he was in a position to work on some PST methods to enhance his performance skills of pre-game psych-up and concentration — he chose to combine mental preparation, imagery, centring, and self-talk to work on both these performance skills together. Finally, he decided to use team goal setting, imagery and self-talk to help him stick with the team's game plan and be a more cohesive team player (the facilitative skill).

Jack's PST programme

	PST skills needs	*PST methods*
Foundation	Commitment	Goal setting, self-talk
Performance	Peak activation	Mental prep, imagery, centring, self-talk
	Peak concentration	Mental prep, imagery, self-talk
Facilitative	Team cohesion	Goal setting, imagery, self-talk

Our first step to help Bob was to separate his skill needs. We categorised his psych skill needs as follows:

  (i) self-confidence (foundation skill);

  (ii) coping with pressure (performance skill);

  (iii) concentration and decision-making (performance skill);

  (iv) communication (facilitative skill).

Based on this classification, we picked some likely PST methods to match with each psych skill. Following the logic of the PST programme, we sorted out his foundation needs first — we decided that a blend of goal setting, imagery and self-talk could be a useful way to enhance his self-confidence. This decision was discussed with Bob and his coach, then fine-tuned with his input before we started to teach him these three PST methods. For Bob's need to cope with pressure we decided to use the PST methods of centring or relaxation, self-talk, and a CARS plan. At the same time as he was working on his coping skills he also worked on his need for improved concentration and decision-making using the PST methods of mental preparation, self-talk and a modified version of a CARS plan.

Bob's PST Programme

	PST skills needs	PST methods
Foundation	Self-confidence	Goal setting, imagery, self-talk
Performance	Coping with pressure	Centering/relaxation, self-talks, CARS
	Peak concentration	Mental prep, self-talk, CARS
Facilitative	Communication	Self-talk

PST skills

Motivation. Jack's pre-game motivation had been a real problem for him for a number of seasons. Typically he had left his pre-game motivation and mental preparation to his captain and coach, assuming that it was their job to get him and the rest of the team motivated and psyched-up for each game. However, occasionally the captain and coach failed to do much to psych Jack up, so finally he decided to do it himself. Most of his coaches had emphasised winning in their pre-game motivation, but Jack felt better prepared when the captain or coach focused on the team's game plan and a 'how to win' approach to the pre-game psych-up. So he set himself goals before every game that were related to his jobs as a number eight and how they fit into the team's game plan. His goals were based on match stats such as tackle counts, forced turnovers, ball retention, effective backrow moves, and hit-up metres. He kept track of these match stats and goals by recording them in his Training Logbook (see chapter 20). He used a task orientation approach and it really paid off — he felt much more confident, motivated, and psyched-up before each game without being over-psyched or too nervous. He started playing much better and his improved play lead to his selection in the provincial rep team.

Commitment. Jack's Peak Performance Profile on page 40 revealed that at the start of this season he needed to commit himself fully to his rugby and his training, before examining other aspects of his game. His first action was to complete a Commitment Self-Assessment Worksheet (see pages 62–63). As you can see this process of self-assessment helped Jack to realise that he really loved the game and that he was determined to enjoy his rugby and start playing to his potential. In an effort to improve his commitment (a PST skill) Jack chose to use the PST methods of goal setting and self-talk. In addition, he convinced his coach and teammates to develop a team vision, team goals based on that vision, and then specific goal achievement strategies devised to accomplish those goals.

Self-confidence. Based on the classification of Bob's psych skill needs, we decided a blend of the PST methods of goal setting, imagery and self-talk could be a useful way to enhance his self-confidence. Once Bob was happy that his self-confidence was improving we made some suggestions regarding PST methods for his need to cope with pressure.

Controlling activation. In addition to taking control of his pre-game motivation, Jack also needed to control his activation levels. He decided to utilise a combination of mental preparation, imagery (of being calm and in control), and self-talk.

Coping with pressure. Bob desperately needed to learn how to cope with the pressure that he was experiencing. We recommended the PST methods of relaxation or centring, self-talk, and a CARS plan. Bob's completed worksheets for self-talk and his CARS plan for coping with pressure are shown on pages 147 and 196 respectively.

Concentration. Bob was worrying about what his teammates were thinking if he missed important kicks at goal. He was very aware of his heart rate, butterflies in his stomach, sweaty palms, and tense muscles as he prepared for a kick, and his kicking percentage had been down on previous years (internal distraction). Jack, on the other hand, had good concentration and decision-making skills. In ruck situations, Jack always seemed to know when to 'pick-and-go', when to 'blow over' the ball, and when to 'pick-and-feed' to another player on the burst. His ability to read the play had been a major factor in his selection for the rep team this season (good concentration or focus of attention). In situations such as these, the individual's concentration has a powerful influence on his performance, either positively or negatively, and it is clear that the ability to concentrate is an important feature of successful performance in rugby. Jack used mental preparation, imagery, and self-talk to improve his peak concentration skills. On the other hand, we recommended that Bob use mental preparation, self-talk, and a CARS plan to develop his poor concentration.

Team cohesion. Jack decided to use the PST methods of goal setting, imagery and self-talk to help him stick with the team's game plan and be a more cohesive team player. He decided to use a variation on goal setting that focused on team goal setting. In addition, Jack talked his teammates into having some fun with a 'what if . . .' session called the 'Mission Impossible' exercise. Jack's plan was that the act of sorting out the team's goals so specifically would help him as a player to identify his role and become committed to proving his contribution to the team's game plan. Finally, he used imagery to mentally rehearse the team's game plan and his role in it, and he practised self-talk to help keep his concentration on the correct options within the team's game plan.

Communication. Bob was struggling with his on-field communication due to the pressure he was under to keep his place in the team. He decided that he first needed to sort out his 'internal communication', so he chose some key self-talk phrases to use for coping with pressure and maintaining concentration. Then he began to use versions of these self-talk phrases to talk with his teammates. As a result he found he was much more authoritative and decisive in his communication.

PST methods

Goal setting. Both Jack and Bob used goal setting as a PST method, but for different purposes. Jack set performance goals before each game to give himself something to be committed to during the year, while Bob used a combination of process and performance goals to help with his self-confidence for goal-kicking.

Self-talk. See page 147 for the self-talk list that Bob put together as he sought to work on improving his PST skills of self-confidence, concentration and communication.

Mental preparation. Jack's pre-game plan from the start of this season is shown on page 153. This is actually Jack's third version of the pre-game plan — he found that he needed to modify it after the first two games of the season.

Relaxation: Bob used 'centring' to help him cope with the pressure of goal-kicking. He learnt to control his breathing, heart rate and muscle tension and was able to clear his mind in order to use his self-talk and CARS plan.

Imagery. In chapter 14 we described a situation in which Jack was disappointed with his performance in a club game. In particular, he was frustrated that the opposition had made some penetrating breaks from backrow moves, and that he had been unable to make any effective tackles in trying to defend these moves. While sitting in the changing room after the game, before having a shower, Jack tried to re-create the image of each of the backrow moves that the opposition had run, against which he had seemed ineffective in being able to stop. He used his imagery for a number of different purposes — to create or re-create an image of something that had happened in the game (or might happen during a game), to solve the problems and correct the technical or strategic faults in his performance, and to create a positive mental state in which to perform. In each case Jack conjured up a clear, vivid, and controllable image of himself performing particular rugby skills. It was his ability to do this that led him to decide upon particular strategies or techniques to use, and helped him to believe that he could physically perform the skills. His imagery directly influenced his thoughts, which influenced the way he felt, and subsequently influenced his behaviour in terms of what he physically practised.

Summary

Psych skills training (PST) is intended to help you deliberately switch on your autopilot, not to overcomplicate your rugby performance. You should only plan a PST programme to work on the psych skill areas that you need to kick-start your autopilot and the Ideal Performance State. Working on your thinking skills like this does not necessarily mean that you will increase the *amount* of thinking that you do. On the contrary, PST is all about limiting your thinking to the bare minimum required to help you get into your Ideal Performance State, to get into that wonderful mental rhythm and flow when you barely need to think; instead you 'just do it'!

17. PST for individual and team training

> The most important thing is just to practise. Don't accept a weakness without trying to fix it, and always work on multi-skilling yourself. The All Blacks focus on multi-skills in our training, and it's just so important for all players to achieve.
>
> — MARTIN TOOMEY (ALL BLACK FITNESS TRAINER 1992–)

Train the way you want to play: with intensity and commitment

Individual training

Psych skills are only part of the complete picture in terms of achieving your potential as a rugby player. These skills must be trained, developed and used in conjunction with all the other skills that a player needs to possess. Many top players have talked about psych skills giving them an advantage or 'edge' over their opponents, or as a reason why they have reached the top in rugby. While this may be true, they have only been able to gain this advantage because the psych skills have been developed in addition to the hours and hours of hard work that they have spent developing their physical and technical skills. Remember, developing psych skills alone will not develop you into a good player — you must be prepared to put in the hard work at practice and during your own personal training.

Those of you who have done this will also know that most psych skills need to be developed alongside your physical, technical and tactical skills. Consider the following example:

> Wayne, a loose forward, was one of several players competing for a regular place in a First Division provincial team. Wayne went to see the team's sportpsych consultant because he felt that his confidence was lacking, and that he was losing concentration and making mistakes during games as a result. This obviously worried him, and meant that his on-field anxiety levels were higher than they should have been. He spent so much energy on the field worrying about losing concentration and making mistakes that he became tired very quickly and felt that he couldn't last the whole game. He

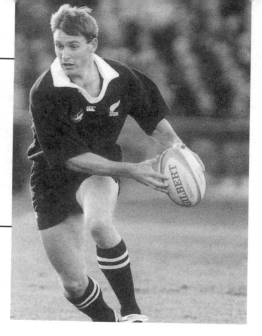

> The All Blacks work on [game simulation] by making trainings as much like game day as possible. Training under game intensity means when you take the paddock your decision-making should be second nature, without thinking too much.
>
> — ANDREW MEHRTENS (ALL BLACK 1995–)

began to 'coast' through the first half of every game because he felt the need to save himself for the last part of the game so that he was better able to contribute to the team effort and not make mistakes during this crucial phase of the game.

Wayne was expecting the sportpsych consultant to help him with some visualisation or self-talk strategies to combat his problem, but was surprised when the first question that the sportpsych consultant asked him was, 'How fit are you?' Wayne admitted that he had not been up to scratch in terms of the fitness standards set for the loose forwards. The sportpsych consultant then asked him to imagine that he was as fit, as fast, as powerful and as strong as he could possibly be when he went out onto the field to start a game. How would that affect his confidence about lasting the 80 minutes? Would he be anxious about lasting for the whole game? If he wasn't as tired during the game, would he be able to maintain his concentration? If he could maintain his concentration levels, would he make as many mistakes as he had been? If he was making fewer mistakes and performing better, what effect would that have on his confidence, concentration and anxiety levels?

Wayne was forced to admit that although his problem had a psychological effect, it was essentially a problem with his physical fitness, and so he and the sportpsych consultant worked out a goal setting programme that focused on improving his aerobic fitness, strength and power during the off-season. Using the fitness standards set for loose forwards by the provincial team's trainer as the initial goal, they established Wayne's current fitness levels, and used the goal setting guidelines in chapter 10 to work on improving Wayne's fitness. After reaching these standards, Wayne reset his goals and developed his fitness even further. He reported that during the subsequent season his confidence and concentration levels had improved, and that he was no longer as anxious as he had been during the previous season. Wayne established himself as a regular member of the provincial squad that season.

Wayne's case is a good example of how psych skills can be developed in conjunction with other types of skills. This doesn't mean that just developing your physical or technical skills will automatically develop all of the psych skills you need, but there is no doubt that improvements in one skill area can have a flow-on effect to other areas. It is not hard to understand that improving your physical fitness can improve your confidence and concentration levels, and that this can help to improve your ability to perform the technical skills of rugby. For example, if you are a number eight and you know that you have worked hard on your strength and power over the off-season, you will be more confident about being able to make the advantage line from the base of the scrum if you decide to run from this position (such as an '8-up' move). In addition, you will be likely to execute the play better from a technical perspective if you have the strength to turn in the tackle, or to stay on your feet and present the ball to your supporting flanker. If all players have greater strength, power and aerobic fitness, as well as technical ability, then the tactical options for your team become greater because each player will be able to contribute in a greater number of ways. Consequently, your coach will have the luxury of being able to develop tight or expansive game-plans to suit the conditions or the opposition, rather than sticking to a particular style because your team is not physically equipped to play an alternative! This will also make it more difficult for other teams to work out how to play against you.

Fitness comes first, and that means hard work. Do the basics in the off-season, hitting the roads, building up a good aerobic base . . . Remember, without fitness you're nowhere — you won't be in place to make the tackle if you have no aerobic base!
— JOSH KRONFELD (ALL BLACK 1995–)

PST for training. Although there is no substitute for hard work and effort during off-season physical and technical training, PST training can help you to maximise this training. For example, setting goals and developing the strategies to achieve these goals can maintain and/or improve your motivation and commitment to this type of training (see chapter 3, Motivation and commitment, and chapter 10, Goal setting), and many of the PST methods such as imagery, relaxation, self-talk and mental preparation strategies can improve the quality of your training (see chapters 11–15).

The various types of physical training lend themselves well to the technique of

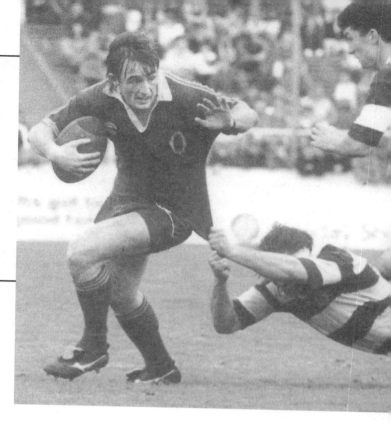

> Most players hammer themselves in fitness training in the naive belief that [fitness] alone will make them better players. Sure, fitness helps but it is only part of the complete player equation. It is then time to concentrate on improving specific skills.
>
> — PAUL HENDERSON
> (ALL BLACK 1991–95)

goal setting because the performance of these skills is easily measured (runs can be timed, distances can be measured, the amount of weight can be calculated). Your performance of these skills in training can be maximised using PST methods. You can use imagery or relaxation methods to attain the peak activation level for lifting heavy weights, and self-talk strategies can be used during hard training sessions to maintain effort, concentration, and proper technique while you are executing the various skills.

If you have worked on your physical and technical skills during the off-season, and used a number of PST methods to help you develop these skills to the fullest, then you should begin the season with some confidence. (As we know from chapter 2, self-confidence is a key foundation PST skill.) Not only will you be in the best possible shape, you will have practised using a number of PST methods that you will now be able to use, refine and further develop during practices and games. This can only help you in your efforts to develop your rugby playing ability to the fullest.

Team training

Once you have finished your off-season or pre-season training, gone through the process of trialing, and been selected for a team, you and your teammates must adjust to a new schedule of team training. There will be certain physical skills and fitness levels that you must continue to train by yourself (or at least maintain the level that you had attained during the off-season), but team practices will become an important focus.

Game simulation. The basic idea of practices is that you and your teammates rehearse what you will (you hope) be doing during a game. Initially you should develop and maintain the various rugby skills, techniques and tactics that you will use during games in a non-threatening and low pressure environment at training. Once your ability to perform these skills improves you will need to perform them in situations that are very similar to those you would experience during a game — such as defensive pressure from 'opposed' practice, little time for decision-making, making decisions when you are physically tired.

Rugby is a game that requires players to perform under pressure. You must react swiftly to developing situations, make quick and accurate decisions, and anticipate where the next play may develop while your opponents are 'pressuring' you physically and mentally. This cannot be accomplished during the game if your only exposure to pressure situations that require this ability is during the game itself! At some stage during the practices leading up to a game you should experience the pressure of having to perform under these game-like conditions. This is game simulation; the idea is to use game simulation pressure to raise the threshold of performance and increase your mental toughness.

> The emphasis is to put the players under pressure. It's only by putting yourself under pressure that you can raise the threshold of performance. Ideally your training should be more difficult than your match. So when it comes to the game you feel that you've got more time — hopefully. . . . A team session now is to have the training simulate game conditions as closely as possible.
>
> — ROBBIE DEANS

Many coaches use the 'team run' at the end of practice to simulate some of the pressure situations of a game, but pressure can also be simulated in other situations (such as sub-unit training like opposed second phase, opposed line-outs, live scrummaging). The use of PST methods can be incorporated in the practice session to help players cope with this pressure (see also chapter 6, Coping with pressure, and chapter 15, CARS plan). The higher the level of rugby you play, the greater the pressure to perform at a faster pace. This can be simulated during practices in almost any drill that you are asked to do. For example, the grids and drills that many teams use as part of their normal warm-up routines can easily be refined to place players under pressure. The coach (or the players) can demand that the grids be performed at full pace for a certain length of time (perhaps 30 seconds), or that a specific number of passes be executed accurately within a specified time. As the players improve, the conditions can be altered to better reflect the ability and performance level of the team. The coach or one of the management team can keep a record of the team's ability to perform that particular grid, and this can be used as the basis for setting goals for the team at subsequent practices.

Other forms of pressure can be created at the same time. Rather than simply setting a goal for the execution of a particular grid, the coach can place further pressure on the team by setting up a competition between two groups of players (such as forwards versus backs) in the performance of that grid or drill, and asking each group to set their own performance goals. Usually these groups have an unrealistic idea of their ability to perform under such pressure, but their performance level is easily determined after the first attempt at the grid. The coach can then ask how they might be able to better perform that grid, and the players themselves will often work out various strategies and techniques to ensure greater accuracy, timing and performance. This may include various PST methods such as the use of cue-words (that is, self-talk) during the performance of the grid, imagery of the correct performance of the grid just before doing it, or refocussing strategies to be implemented if a mistake is made (see chapter 15, CARS plan).

Whether the coach uses these techniques or not during practices, the onus is on you to set your own goals for each portion of the practice, to put yourself under pressure, and to implement the PST methods that you may have learned during your off-season training. Mentally prepare for each team practice session, perhaps setting some personal goals for the session or deciding upon a particular PST method that you may want to incorporate into the session. During each particular practice activity, whether it be the warm-up, individual skill work, small group or sub-unit skills, or the team run, you should decide what it is that you want to accomplish during that activity. Perhaps rehearse the image of yourself successfully executing that activity before physically performing it, and use whatever PST method that you find appropriate at that time to get yourself into the ideal mental and physical state for performing it. You should practise physical and technical skills at team training so that you can use them automatically during the game — if you expect to be able to use psych skills automatically you need to practise them in the same way.

Because you will have already practised these PST techniques during your off-season training, they should not be difficult to perform. They will take up very little time, and using them can often decrease the overall time it takes to successfully learn and perform any skill. For example, a new type of line-out call and type of jump can be described and discussed by the forwards before being physically practised. The jumper, the thrower, the lifters and the rest of the line-out forwards can use imagery to rehearse the successful execution of the call before being asked to put it into practice. This may only take a few seconds. Similarly, one of the backs might suggest a new attacking move from a midfield scrum. The move can be described, walked through, and then mentally rehearsed by the backs before being physically performed at greater and greater pace. The image of the move will only take a few seconds, and no time will be lost in physical performance of the move.

Summary

The use of psych skills is an important aspect of both team and individual training. Just as in a game, you must stay motivated, be able to concentrate on the right cues, control your emotions, and develop confidence in your ability to perform under the simulated pressure of an actual game, as well as being able to perform the various physical, technical and tactical skill requirements of the game. To accomplish these things, you need to implement the appropriate PST methods during training.

Goal-setting, mental preparation, relaxation techniques, mental imagery, CARS plans and self-talk can all be used to develop, maintain and improve your performance during training. Remember, none of your rugby skills exist in isolation. In order to perform to your potential, you not only have to know how to execute a rugby skill (technical ability) and possess the physical resources to perform the skill (physical ability), but also know when to execute it (tactical ability). However, in order to do all of this effectively you also must be motivated to perform the skill, be able to concentrate on the right cues in order to know when to execute the skill, be confident in your ability to successfully perform the skill, and be able to perform it in a psychological state that will maximise its effectiveness (psychological ability). All of this is a product of training! No single type of training is sufficient by itself. Although there may be flow-on effects from physical training to the development of technical, tactical and psychological skills (and sometimes vice versa), this type of training on its own is not enough. You need to train each of these skill areas in order to become the player that you want to be.

> I've never been truly fit, and I realised making the top grade that was something that I just had to do [get fit].
>
> — TANA UMAGA (ALL BLACK 1997)

18. PST for rehabilitation from injury

I'm finding it very hard just coping with having an injury. It's something I've been lucky enough to avoid for my entire career. I spoke to Michael Jones . . . and he said 'just keep thinking positive, don't make any rash decisions'. He wants to play next year and he's had more injuries than anyone.

— Sean Fitzpatrick talking about his severe knee injury in 1997,

which forced him to retire in 1998

Injury or illness is one of the biggest mental toughness challenges you will face in your rugby career. Any injury or illness serious enough to stop you playing for more than 2–3 weeks will present you with a mental challenge along with the physical challenge of rehabilitation and recovery. Sean Fitzpatrick had an amazing career of 91 test matches without serious injury until 1997; however, when he suffered an injury he demonstrated the need for discipline and mental toughness in dealing with the frustration of being out of action.

Your first discipline is to get a clear diagnosis from the doctor and then a specific rehabilitation programme from the physio. You must then approach your rehabilitation programme with the same discipline and commitment you put into your fitness and skill training.[1] Your recovery is as much a mental process as it is a physical one.[2]

You, and only you, are responsible for your rehabilitation (rehab) programme. The doctor and physio will set the programme, but you are the one who must be disciplined to follow it completely.[3] Often players are tempted to rush their rehab and try to do more exercise or physical activity than prescribed in the rehab programme. It is also common for players to lose heart when the rehab is not progressing as quickly as expected.[4] In both cases you must be disciplined to stick to the programme prescribed by the doctor and physio, and take a determined attitude to the challenge of your injury rehab.

Mental toughness and discipline are part and parcel of playing rugby, and they apply equally to succeeding in other aspects of the game. Take the view that your rehab and recovery are an opportunity to develop other skills and areas of your game.[5] Perhaps you have some technical limitations that you can work on improving while you wait for the injury to heal; alternatively, you can use the time to work with your coaches and watch match videos to enhance your tactical appreciation of the game in general and your position in particular. Of course, you can also use the time to increase your psych skills.

Above all else, regard your rehab and recovery as a challenge, just like achieving a fitness goal, playing a tough opponent, or trying to break into the provincial rep team — mentally tough players relish the opportunity to meet any challenge.

★ Use your PST methods, such as goal setting, centring, self-talk, parking, and imagery to help with the psychological aspects of recovery.[6]

★ Set yourself clear, specific and realistic goals for recovery, identify the target dates and goal achievement strategies — take immense satisfaction in achieving rehab goals during the recovery process.

★ Use centring and relaxation procedures to help relax the muscles around the injury.

★ Use self-talk to stay focused for quality training in the rehab process (for instance, during a rehab weights programme), to 'park' negative thoughts about the injury, and to maintain your confidence.

★ Use imagery to imagine the injured part of your body repairing itself.[7]

I hated being immobile, attended to and waited upon. Right from Day One I was convinced that I would work to get this thing right, whatever it took. I knew that I could do it and still had a lot to offer; I never allowed myself to get discouraged or fall into self-pity. I was soon looking forward to each step as it came, eager to get the cast off and work at re-building and re-strengthening the knee. Looking back on those weeks and months, it was one of the best things that happened to me. I really believe that those kinds of trials and tribulations build your character.

— MICHAEL JONES DESCRIBING HIS FIRST MAJOR KNEE INJURY IN 1989

I have been absolutely amazed at the mental stability and the mental hardness he has shown through all this. He has gone through an amazing growth as a person and exceeded all our expectations.

— JOHN HART TALKING ABOUT JONAH LOMU'S COMEBACK FROM KIDNEY DISEASE

It's the power of the mind and being positive. A lot of that had to do with my wife, my family, and friends.

— JONAH LOMU EXPLAINING HOW HE MADE A REMARKABLE RECOVERY FROM CHRONIC KIDNEY DISEASE IN 1997

There is some research documenting the role that imagery and positive thinking can have in helping the body to heal itself from serious illness and injury.[8] Indeed, as Jonah Lomu discovered during his recovery from serious kidney disease in 1997, the power of positive thinking can be quite remarkable — mental toughness can take many forms.

You can also use imagery to rehearse the technical and tactical skills of your playing position — when you take the field again you need to be mentally ready as well as physically ready to perform.[9] Your confidence may be shaky if you haven't 'kept your head in the game' during your time off the field. Watching videos and using imagery to rehearse and practise your technical and tactical skills can make a huge difference to your confidence when you return to play.

Use your psych skills during the physical activity prescribed for your rehab programme. You need to be disciplined enough to stick to the prescribed amount of exercise — more is not better! Focus on quality, not quantity, so that you don't re-injure yourself or stall your rehab process.

Take a 'team' approach to recovery

You have chosen to play one of the ultimate team sports, so make sure you use a 'team' approach to your injury rehab. The rehab team will include your doctor and physio, probably your coach and your teammates, and maybe family and friends. You don't have to tough it out alone to be mentally tough — seeking support and help from others is not a sign of weakness but a sign of strength. We rely on teammates at training and on the field, and they rely on us — so it is in injury rehab: you should seek help from others and then look to repay their support in the future. Something as simple as a teammate going to the gym with you for company and to provide encouragement during your weights programme can make an enormous difference to your motivation and commitment during recovery. Teammates and the coach can also help keep your head in the game by talking tactics and reviewing videos with you.

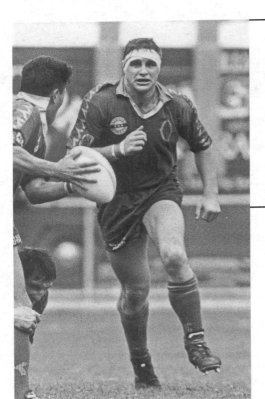

The hardest thing about coming back after a long break [due to injury] is getting back to full strength mentally. Physically I'm fine. I've done the hard work and I feel great out there. But keeping up the concentration level for 80 minutes is something I'm still having to work on . . .

— Brendan Timmins (Otago NPC player 1992–) describing his comeback in 1998

Gordon Slater's injury comeback

In 1995 Gordon Slater broke his leg playing for Taranaki. Not just bone was shattered, but also the hopes of a young player already earmarked as an All Black in the making.[10] After 18 months of painful and trying convalescence and rehabilitation he emerged in 1997 to display confirmation that the investment in him as a member of the New Zealand Colts, Divisional and Development teams had not been ill-founded, by being selected for the All Blacks.

> Yeah, there are times when I thought I'd never be doing this [playing for the All Blacks]. I just had to sit out 18 months and wait for it to come right. At the end of the day it was worth the wait.
>
> — GORDON SLATER

Slater's convalescence was tough, physically and mentally. Though he was never told his career was under threat, he was not exactly filled with optimism either. 'They did say it was one of the worst breaks you could get. I had no idea how long it would take.' The doubts crept in, too, especially at the start of this year when he attended Hurricanes training camps and came away in some pain. 'It's certainly been worth it. It's everyone's dream to play for the All Blacks and to finally be here, let alone so soon, is just great.'[11]

Gordon Slater demonstrated the need for mental toughness when faced with severe injury. If you suffer a similar fate you will need to use your mental toughness to achieve your goals and realise your dreams. Injury is an opportunity to test yourself and develop new skills, to grow as a player, to grow as a person. If you view your injury as a stepping stone rather than a stumbling block anything is possible — be a believer!

Ready to return

If you have been out of action for a month or more, or if you have recovered from a severe injury, you will likely have to face up to some fears when you return to play.[12] Common fears are of two types:

★ The injury — 'Will it stand up to a game?' , 'Will it still hurt?' , 'Will I re-injure myself?'

★ Your confidence — 'Will I be able to play as well as I used to?' , 'Am I fit enough after the layoff?' , 'Will I be good enough get back into the starting team?' .

Once again your mental toughness takes on a different form: are you tough enough to face-down these fears and play to your potential? To utilise your mental toughness for return to play, you should make good use of the same psych skills that you have developed for performance. You need to be mentally fit as well as physically fit to play again when you return from injury.

Successfully achieving the goals you set yourself during rehab will provide you with some confidence. You should also use imagery to practise and rehearse your successful return to play.[13] Mentally practise the technical and tactical skills during rehab, so that when you return to team training you will slot back into the team pattern and be 'up to speed' with the team's game plan.

The bottom line is that you should take a proactive approach to your injury rehabilitation and recovery, instead of sitting around feeling sorry for yourself. Your mental toughness will be severely tested when you get injured;[14] but, as Michael Jones observed, 'these kinds of trials and tribulations build your character' and your mental toughness.

> I think I can get up to speed physically. It's more a matter of being mentally fit. It's that side of my game that I have to fine-tune.
>
> — JOSH KRONFELD TALKING ABOUT HIS COMEBACK FROM INJURY IN 1997

19. Retirement and lifestyle management

I don't eat and drink the game. I want people to accept me as just Jonah, not Jonah the rugby player.

— JONAH LOMU

Keeping rugby in perspective

Playing rugby 'seriously' with a dedicated focus on trying to perform to your potential requires you to commit a significant amount of your time and energy. However, if you're not careful rugby can start to take over your life. You must manage your time effectively to fit rugby in with other parts of your life and to keep it in perspective.

This chapter will mainly apply to those of you who are playing (or coaching) rugby at the top level where rugby takes up a significant part of your life. Our main message here is that you need to avoid letting it take over your life completely. To succeed in rugby and lead a happy life you need to live a balanced lifestyle that includes time for your job (or education or training for your future job if you currently make a living from playing rugby), your family, and for yourself, in terms of relaxation and recreation.[1] As Canterbury Super 12 coach Wayne Smith points out, leading a balanced life is actually an important method for helping you to be successful as a player, as well as leading a happy life.

From a selfish point of view they perform better if they've got a balance, have outside interests and some sense of direction after rugby. Our most motivated players are the ones who are working fulltime because they have to plan their week really carefully. The least motivated are the ones who aren't working or studying. . . . This is a short-term career, not a dalliance. It may last one year or ten.

— WAYNE SMITH

Retirement planning

Many players and coaches seem to avoid thinking about retirement and life after rugby, falsely believing that such planning detracts from a player's motivation for his rugby career. However, our experience in consulting players about this matter suggests that such uncertainty about the future can be a major distraction in itself.[2] Moreover, research in other sports has shown that athletes who plan for life after sport perform as well as, if not better than, those who don't plan[3] — the knowledge that their future is secure gives them the peace of mind to become totally dedicated to their current sporting career.

The New Zealand Rugby Union has already recognised the need for career and retirement planning for elite players. Such a focus has been a priority of the NZRFU Rugby Academy since its inception in 1996. Aware of the need to give specialised coaching to a group of elite 'developing' players, the NZRFU also felt a strong responsibility to ensure these players were equipped for life after the game.[4] Consequently, along with the expected rugby skill coaching, the Rugby Academy provides a personal development programme that includes career planning, tertiary study, communication skills, financial planning skills, interpersonal relations and time management.

Practical recommendations for successful retirement

Since top level rugby players put a lot of time, effort, emotion and energy into their rugby, it is perhaps not surprising that a number of them find it difficult to retire. Fortunately, there are many ways in which you can help yourself to prepare for and cope with the retirement transition. The following practical recommendations have been developed from considerable work in the USA,[5] Canada,[6] Australia,[7] and New Zealand.[8]

★ Pre-retirement counselling should be available to help top players prepare for retirement.[9] Such counselling should help you to find new interests (polytechnic or university, a new career, working part-time, or seeking new physical and recreational activities), to understand why you are retiring, and to understand the effects it could have on you. This counselling might consist of team seminars and individual sessions, and would include specific career planning. Ideally this would involve the coach and a sportpsych consultant working with you.

In the special and important case of career planning there are several recommendations.[10] These recommendations are taken from the career planning programmes in the USA and Canada; the US Olympic Committee's Career Assistance Program for Athletes (CAPA)[11], and the Canadian Olympic Association's Olympic Athlete Career Centre.[12]

Recommendations.

(a) You need to understand the process of developing a career, rather than just getting a job.

(b) You need to develop job-relevant skills for your chosen career.

(c) You need to spend considerable time to identify your personal career needs.

(d) You need to identify job-related opportunities while you're still playing rugby seriously.

(e) You need to use your rugby motivation skills to help you set career goals.

(f) You need to remind yourself to transfer the many psychological and physical skills you have developed for rugby into career skills.

(g) You should seek out from coaches and administrators the opportunity for individual counselling that focuses on: improving self-awareness ; emotional and social support; enhancement of coping skills; and developing a sense of personal control.

★ It is important that you understand why you are retiring. This will be easier if it is a voluntary decision on your part.[13]

> I did accounting at Auckland University, because I wanted security for the future. Rugby is a short-term occupation, and my accounting degree will get more and more use in the future. A few lucky All Blacks earn good money, but even if they make it, there's lots of life after rugby.
> — OLO BROWN (ALL BLACK 1992–)

★ Less pressure from coaches and the player's family to retire would help — you need to feel that it is solely your own decision to retire. As with the suggestions above, this recommendation focuses on prevention rather than cure.

★ Support and understanding from coaches and teammates is needed to help you during the retirement decision and the subsequent transition to retirement. You should also develop a social support network inside and outside of the rugby context to use for help and emotional support.

★ Coaches need to be aware of the resources available to help a player if they do not feel they can help the player themselves. This includes other retired players, sportpsych consultants, financial planners and career counsellors.

★ Support and ongoing contact from your team, club, provincial union and the national union is important to counter any feelings of abandonment upon retirement.[14]

★ Ongoing consultations by rugby administrators with both current and former players and coaches regarding continual upgrading of 'planning for retirement' programmes would be useful and desirable.[15]

★ Phase out your physical training over a few months if possible. A gradual 'wind down' is better than a sudden, abrupt change in physical exercise and lifestyle.[16]

★ There is a need for nutrition and weight control advice for many retired players.

Since you will be used to consuming a large number of calories and using large amounts of energy, you may need to learn new dietary habits as your physical training is decreased.[17]

★ While still playing, ensure that you are keeping open other social networks apart from your rugby friends. You should not allow your rugby to restrict your social life and other interests.

> Professionalism means having balance in life: creating the right environment to succeed; being totally at ease with what you're doing; having a good family life, good work relationships, and knowing how to train.
>
> — SEAN FITZPATRICK

★ If possible, try to continue your involvement in rugby in some capacity. For example, you might choose to coach or participate in Golden Oldies rugby or Touch.[18]

> I guess the only fear is that when rugby finishes, you don't get what you want out of life. Because for a long time you put that side of life on hold. You live such a fantastic, sort of exuberant life, it's not really who a person is.
>
> — JOSH KRONFELD ON THE DEMANDS OF PROFESSIONAL RUGBY

★ It is vital that you regard the Psychological Skills Training (PST) you have developed for rugby as life skills training as well.[19] For example, the PST skills of self-confidence, assertiveness, motivation, concentration, stress management, and communication that you have developed through rugby can be used as coping skills in other life situations.[20]

> Anyone aiming for a rugby career without back-up is risking a lot for these reasons. Rugby is a career with no guarantees — injuries and selections can always go against you. It's also short, so if you work it out, a long-term 'normal' career will see you earn much more.
>
> — DAVID KIRK (ALL BLACK 1983–87)

20. PST training logbook

This chapter contains a number of training logsheets for you to choose from in designing your personalised training logbook. There is also a sample logsheet for you to record your PST training in your logbook.

In a number of chapters in this book we have emphasised the need to keep a training logbook for yourself on a regular basis. A training logbook is not a 'diary' in the sense of recording your general thoughts and feelings (although you may wish to do this), rather it is a written record of your Peak Performance Profiles, goals, training methods, periodised training plan, and daily practice sessions or workouts. These training logsheets have been adapted from Hodge, Sleivert, and McKenzie, *Smart Training for Peak Performance: A Complete Sports Training Guide for Athletes* (1996).[1]

These daily logsheets are vital for training motivation and commitment, and also for evaluating the overall success of your training plan. The information you record on the daily logsheets is objective evidence for you to use in modifying or adapting your ongoing training plans. We encourage you to choose a logsheet from those provided that suits your style of recording information. For example, some players prefer to write general comments about a particular training session/workout, while other players prefer to use rating scales and circle numbers or tick boxes instead of writing comments. The choice is yours, but the key point is that we regard a training logbook as absolutely vital to a successful training plan. Choose the worksheet that you prefer, or design one of your own, photocopy multiple copies of it and file them in a ring binder. Photocopy your completed Peak Performance Profile and Goal Achievement Worksheets too, and file them in your training logbook as well.

Training Log: General Workout

Weekly goal:. . . . . to . . . .

. . . .

Date: . . . .   Time: . . . .   Venue: . . . .

Resting heart rate (HR): . . . .   beats per min (BPM)

Daily goal:. . . . .

. . . .

Today's activities:. . . . .

. . . .

Activity intensity:. . . . .

Activity duration:. . . . .

Comments:. . . . .

. . . .

. . . .

. . . .

. . . .

Daily goal achievement (?):. . . . .

. . . .

. . . .

Date: | **Time:** to

Daily Log

Goal(s) for today: ....

Resting heart rate: .... bpm   Sleep: # of hrs: ....   Quality: 1   2   3   4   5
                                                                              Sound   Avg   Restless

---

PHYSICAL: (Circle appropriate energy system)

       Aerobic   *Anaerobic*

                           Lactic   *Phosphagen*

Duration (min): ....   Interval length/time: ....

Intensity: HR: .... bpm   Rest length/time: ....

1   2   3   4   5   **RPE**   Number of repetitions: ....

very easy *moderate*   *extremely difficult*   Intensity(% effort): ....

Other: ....

....

Assessment of physical training: (circle the number)

    ☺ *Excellent session*   1   2   3   4   5   *Very poor session* ☹

Why? Energy *Energised*   1   2   3   4   5   *Drained*

       Attitude *Positive*   1   2   3   4   5   *Negative*

MENTAL: PST method (circle one)

   Self-talk   *Relaxation/centring*   *Imagery*   *Mental preparation*   *CARS*

Duration(min): ....   Type/content: ....

Assessment of mental training: (circle the number)

    ☺ *Excellent session*   1   2   3   4   5   *Very poor session* ☹

Why? Focus *Totally focused*   1   2   3   4   5   *Poor*

       Attitude *Positive*   1   2   3   4   5   *Negative*

TECHNICAL: Skill #1 ....   Skill #2 ....   Skill #3 ....

Assessment of technical training: (circle the number)

    ☺ *Excellent session*   1   2   3   4   5   *Very poor session* ☹

Why?   *Physical*   *Mental*   *Other*

Explain: ....

NUTRITION: (No. of servings) Fluids ..... Carbohydrates ..... Fats ..... Proteins .....

GENERAL COMMENTS: Success/Hassles/Distractions/Injuries/Illness/Medications?

....

....

Date: | **Time:** to

Daily PST Log

Goal(s) for today: ....
....
....

PST method	Planned PST training		
	Duration (mins)	Purpose

Assessment: (circle the number)

☺	*Excellent session*	1	2	3	4	5	*Very poor session*	☹
Why? Focus	*Totally focused*	1	2	3	4	5	*Poor*	
Attitude	*Positive*	1	2	3	4	5	*Negative*	

COMMENTS:
....
....
....
....

Recommended reading and resources

Reading for players and coaches

Dugdale, J., & Hodge, K. (1997). *Psychological Skills Training: Practical Guidelines for Athletes, Coaches, & Officials.* Wellington, NZ: Sport Science NZ.

Hodge, K. (1994). *Sport Motivation: Training Your Mind for Peak Performance.* Auckland, NZ: Reed.

Hodge, K., Sleivert, G., & McKenzie, A. (1996). *Smart Training for Peak Performance: A Complete Sports Training Guide for Athletes.* Auckland, NZ: Reed.

Orlick, T. (1986). *Psyching for Sport: Mental Training for Athletes.* Champaign, IL, USA: Human Kinetics.

NZ Sport Psychology Association. (1996). *NZ Sport Psychology Association Directory of Members.* Available from NZSPA Executive, c/o Gary Hermansson, Department of Human Development Studies, Massey University, Private Bag 11-222, Palmerston North, New Zealand.

Sportpsych videos for players and coaches

Hamshire, R., Iverson, I., & Catell, R. (1994). *Winning With Sport Psychology* [Video]. Available from Fundamental Communications, PO Box 35-230, Browns Bay, Auckland.

Biesterfeld, P. (1987). *Visualisation: What You See Is What You Get* [Video]. Available from Coaching Association of Canada, 1600 Naismith Drive, Gloucester, ON, Canada, K1B 5N4.

Advanced reading for sportpsych consultants

Hardy, L., Jones, G., & Gould, D. (1996). *Understanding Psychological Preparation for Sport: Theory and Practice of Elite Performers.* Chichester, UK: John Wiley & Sons.

Williams, J. (1998). *Applied Sport Psychology: Personal growth to peak performance.* Third Edition. Mountain View, CA, USA: Mayfield.

References

Preface

1. Gallaher, D., & Stead, W. (1906) *The Complete Rugby Footballer of the New Zealand System*. London: Methuen's Colonial Library.

1. The Basis of 'Thinking Rugby'

1. McKenzie, A. (1991) 'The Effect of Imagery on Tackling Performance in Rugby.' *Journal of Human Movement Studies* 20, 163–76.
   Pickford, S. (1994) 'The Effects of Mental Imagery on Rugby Goal Kicking Performance.' Honours dissertation, University of Otago, NZ.
   Hardy, L., Jones, G. & Gould, D. (1996) *Understanding Psychological Preparation for Sport: Theory and Practice of Elite Performers*. Chichester: John Wiley & Sons.

2. Howitt, B., & McConnell, R. (1996). *Laurie Mains*. Auckland, NZ: Rugby Publishing.

3. Ibid

4. Ibid

5. Saxton, C. (1960). *The ABC of Rugby*. Wellington, NZ: NZRFU.

6. Howitt, B., & McConnell, R. (1996). op cit.
   Veysey, A., Caffell, G., & Palenski, R. (1996). *Lochore: An Authorised Biography*. Auckland, NZ: Hodder Moa Beckett.

7. Veysey, A., Caffell, G., & Palenski, R. (1996). op cit.

8. Mahoney, M., Gabriel, T., & Perkins, T. (1987). 'Psychological skills and exceptional performance.' *The Sport Psychologist, 1*, 181–99.
   Orlick, T., & Partington, J. (1988). 'Mental links to excellence.' *The Sport Psychologist, 2*, 105–30.
   Williams, J., & Krane, V. (1993). 'Psychological characteristics of peak performance.' In J. Williams (ed.), *Applied Sport Psychology: Personal growth to peak performance* (137–47). Second edition. Palo Alto, CA, USA: Mayfield.

9. Dugdale, J. (1996). *An Exploratory Investigation into the Relationship between Focused Attention and Peak Performance*. Unpublished Masters thesis, University of Otago, NZ.

10. Gould, D., Eklund, , R., & Jackson, S. (1992). '1988 U.S. Olympic Wrestling Excellence: II. Thoughts and Affect Occurring During Competition.' *The Sport Psychologist, 6*, 383–402.
    Jackson, S. (1992). 'Athletes in Flow: A Qualitative Investigation of Flow States in Elite Figure Skaters.' *Journal of Applied Sport Psychology, 4*, 161–80.
    Jackson, S., & Roberts, G. (1992). 'Positive performance states of athletes: Toward a conceptual understanding of peak performance.' *The Sport Psychologist, 6*, 156–71.
    McInman, A., & Grove, J. R., (1991). 'Peak Moments in Sport: A Literature Review.' *Quest, 43*, 333–51.

11. Jackson, S. (1992). 'Athletes in Flow: A Qualitative Investigation of Flow States in Elite Figure Skaters.' *Journal of Applied Sport Psychology, 4*, 161–80.
    Jackson, S., & Roberts, G. (1992). 'Positive performance states of athletes: Toward a conceptual understanding of peak performance.' *The Sport Psychologist, 6*, 156–71.

12. Jackson, S., & Roberts, G. (1992). op. cit.

13. Gould, D., Eklund, , R., & Jackson, S. (1992). op. cit.
    Jackson, S. (1992). op. cit.

14. Jackson, S., & Roberts, G. (1992). op. cit.
    McInman, A., & Grove, J. R., (1991). 'Peak Moments in Sport: A Literature Review. ' *Quest, 43*, 333–51.
    Csikszentmihalyi, M., & Csikszentmihalyi, I. (1988). *Optimal Experience: Psychological Studies in Flow of Consciousness*. New York, USA: Cambridge University Press.

15. Jackson, S., & Roberts, G. (1992). op. cit.

2. Psychological Skills Training (PST)

1. Dugdale, J., & Hodge, K. (1997). *Psychological Skills Training: Practical Guidelines for Athletes, Coaches, & Officials*. Wellington, NZ: Sport Science NZ.
2. Hodge, K. (1994) *Sport Motivation: Training Your Mind for Peak Performance*. Auckland, NZ: Reed.
   Vealey, R. (1988) 'Future Directions in Psychological Skills Training.' *The Sport Psychologist* 5, 318–36.
3. Hodge, K., Sleivert, G. & McKenzie, A. (1996). *Smart Training for Peak Performance*. Auckland, NZ: Reed.
4. Hodge, K. (1990). 'Sport Psychology: Psychological Skills Training (PST) for Rugby.' In NZRFU, *Level III Coaching Accreditation Manual*. (39–60). Wellington: New Zealand Rugby Football Union Coaching Publications.
   Hodge, K. (1994). op cit.
   Butler, R., & Hardy, L. (1992) 'The performance profile: theory and application.' *The Sport Psychologist* 6, 253–64.
5. Butler, R., & Hardy, L. (1992). op cit.
6. Weinberg, R., & Williams, J. (1993). 'Integrating and implementing a psychological skills training programme.' In J. Williams, (ed.), *Applied Sport Psychology: Personal Growth to Peak Performance* (274–98). Palo Alto, CA, USA: Mayfield. .

3. Motivation and commitment

1. Wilson, K., & Hodge, K. (1998). *Intrinsic Motivation in Rugby: Professional vs. Club Players*. Unpublished manuscript, University of Otago.
   Hodge, K., & Zaharopoulos, E. (1993). 'Dropouts in Rugby.' *NZ Coach* 2, 7–8.
   Hodge, K., & Petlichkoff, L. (1998). *Goal Profiles in Sport Motivation: A Cluster Analysis*. Manuscript submitted for publication. University of Otago.
2. Duda, J. (1992). 'Motivation in Sport Settings: A Goal Perspective Approach.' In G.C. Roberts (ed.). *Motivation in Sport and Exercise* (57–91). Champaign, IL: Human Kinetics.
   Maehr, M., & Nicholls, J. (1980). 'Culture and Achievement Motivation: A Second Look.' In N. Warren (ed.). *Studies in Cross-Cultural Psychology*. New York: Academic.
   Nicholls, J. (1992). 'The general and the specific in the development and expression of achievement motivation.' In G. Roberts (ed.). *Motivation in Sport and Exercise* (31–56). Champaign, IL, USA: Human Kinetics.
3. Nicholls, J. (1992). op cit.
4. Roberts, G. (1984) 'Toward a new theory of motivation in sport: the role of perceived ability.' In J. Silva & R. Wienberg (eds.). *Psychological Foundations of Sport* (214–40). Champaign, IL, USA: Human Kinetics.
5. Duda, J. (1992). op cit.
6. Wilson, K., & Hodge, K. (1998). op cit.
7. Howitt, B., & McConnell, R. (1996). *Laurie Mains*. Auckland, NZ: Rugby Publishing.
8. Scanlon, T., et al. (1993). 'An Introduction to the Sport Commitment Model.' *Journal of Sport and Exercise Psychology* 15, 1–15.
9. Scanlan, T., & Russell, D. (1992). *The Peak Project*. Dunedin, NZ: University of Otago.
10. Pinel, B. (1997). 'Enjoyment and Fun: Implications for Youth Sport Coaches.' *New Zealand Coach* 6, 10–11.
    Pinel, B. (1998). *Enjoyment-Profiling: A Practical Look at Enjoyment*. Proceedings of the Children's Issues Centre Child and Family Conference, July, 1997 (231–36). Dunedin, NZ: University of Otago.
11. Scanlan, T., Stein, G., & Ravizza, K. (1989). 'An In-depth Study of Former Elite Figure Skaters: 2. Sources of Enjoyment.' *Journal of Sport and Exercise Psychology* 11, 65–83.
12. Howitt, B., & McConnell, R. (1996). op cit.
13. Ibid.
14. Mazany, P. (1995). *TeamThink — Team New Zealand: The 'Black Magic' of Management Behind the 1995 America's Cup Success*. Auckland, NZ: VisionPlus Developments.
15. Schnackenberg, T. (1995). Cited in P. Mazany. *TeamThink — Team New Zealand*. Auckland, NZ: VisionPlus Developments.

4. Self-confidence

1. Horsley, C. (1995). 'Confidence and sporting performance.' In T. Morris & J. Summers (eds.), *Sport Psychology: Theory, Application, and Current Issues*, (311–38). Sydney, Aust.: Jacaranda Wiley.
2. Weinberg, R., & Gould, D. (1995). *Foundations of Sport and Exercise Psychology*. Champaign, IL, USA: Human Kinetics.
3. Ibid.

4. Bunker, L., Williams, J., & Zinsser, N. (1993). 'Cognitive Techniques for Improving Performance and Building Confidence.' In J. Williams (ed.), *Applied Sport Psychology* (225–42). Palo Alto, CA, USA: Mayfield.

5. Hardy, L., Jones, G., & Gould, D. (1996). *Understanding Psychological Preparation for Sport: Theory and Practice of Elite Performers.* Chichester, UK: John Wiley & Sons.

6. Bandura, A. (1977). 'Self-efficacy: Toward a unifying theory of behaviour change.' *Psychological Review* 8, 191–215. (1986). Bandura, A. (1986). *Social Foundations of Thought and Actions: A Social Cognitive Theory.* Englewood Cliffs, NJ, USA: Prentice Hall.

7. Weinberg, R., & Gould, D. (1995). op. cit.

8. Ibid.

5. Controlling activation

1. Hodge, K. (1988). 'Sport Psychology: Mental Training for Rugby.' In *Level II Coaching Accreditation Manual*, (pp. 31–44). Wellington: NZ Rugby Football Union Coaching Publications.

2. Weinberg, R., & Gould, D. (1995). *Foundations of Sport and Exercise Psychology*. Champaign, IL, USA: Human Kinetics.
Hardy, L., Jones, G., & Gould, D. (1996). *Understanding Psychological Preparation for Sport: Theory and Practice of Elite Performers.* Chichester, UK: John Wiley & Sons.

3. Weinberg, R., & Gould, D. (1995). op. cit.

4. Landers, D., & Boutcher, S. (1993). 'Arousal-Performance Relationships.' In J. Williams (ed.), *Applied Sport Psychology* (170–84). Palo Alto, CA, USA: Mayfield.

5. Ibid.

6. Hardy, L., Jones, G., & Gould, D. (1996). op. cit.

7. Weinberg, R., & Gould, D. (1995). op. cit.

8. Ibid.

9. Harris, D., & Harris, B. (1984). *The Athlete's Guide to Sport Psychology.* New York: Leisure Press.

10. Weinberg, R., & Gould, D. (1995). op. cit.

11. Ibid.

12. Ibid.

6. Coping with pressure

1. Hardy, L., Jones, G., & Gould, D. (1996). *Understanding Psychological Preparation for Sport: Theory and Practice of Elite Performers.* Chichester, UK: John Wiley & Sons.

2. Anderson, M., & Williams, J. (1988). 'A model of stress and athletic injury: Prediction and prevention.' *Journal of Sport & Exercise Psychology* 10, 294–306.
Smith, R. E. (1986). 'Toward a cognitive-affective model of athletic burnout.' *Journal of Sport Psychology* 8, 36–50.

3. Smith, R. E. (1986). op. cit.
Lazarus, R.S., & Folkman, S. (1984). *Stress, appraisal, and coping.* New York, USA: Springer Verlag.

4. Smith, R. E. (1986). op. cit.
Carver, C. S., & Scheier, M. F. (1981). *Attention and self-regulation: A control theory approach to human behaviour.* New York, USA: Springer Verlag.

5. Smith, R. E. (1986). op. cit.
Gould, D. (1996). 'Personal Motivation Gone Awry: Burnout in Competitive Athletes.' *Quest* 48, 275–89.

6. Anshel, M., Williams, L., & Hodge, K. (1997). 'Cross-cultural and gender differences in coping style in sport.' *International Journal of Sport Psychology, 28,* 141–56.

7. Jones, G., & Swain, A. (1992). 'Intensity and direction as dimensions of competitive anxiety and relationships with competitiveness.' *Perceptual and Motor Skills* 74, 67–72.

8. Lazarus, R.S., & Folkman, S. (1984). op. cit.

9. Hardy, L., Jones, G., & Gould, D. (1996). op. cit.
Lazarus, R.S., & Folkman, S. (1984). op. cit.

10. Roth, S., & Cohen, L.J. (1986). 'Approach, avoidance, and coping with stress.' *American Psychologist* 41, 813–19.

11. Hardy, L., Jones, G., & Gould, D. (1996). op cit.

12. Lane, A., Rodger, J., & Karageorghis, C. (1997). 'Antecedents of state anxiety in Rugby.' *Perceptual and Motor Skills* 84, 427–33.

13. Hardy, L., Jones, G., & Gould, D. (1996). op cit.
Roth, S., & Cohen, L.J. (1986). op. cit.

14. Krohne, H., & Hindel, C. (1988). 'Trait anxiety, state anxiety, and coping behavior as predictors of athletic performance.' *Anxiety Research, 1,* 225–234.

15. Roth, S., & Cohen, L.J. (1986). op. cit.

16. Ibid.

17. Ibid.

18. Bramson, R. (1981). *Coping with difficult people*. New York, USA: Doubleday.
19. Hardy, L., Jones, G., & Gould, D. (1996). op. cit.
20. Hanson, T., & Gould, D. (1988). 'Factors affecting the ability of coaches to estimate their athletes' trait and state anxiety levels.' *The Sport Psychologist* 2 (4), 298–313.
21. Hanson, T. (1992). 'The Mental Aspects of Hitting in Baseball: A Case Study of Hank Aaron.' *Contemporary Thought on Performance Enhancement*, 1, (1), 49–70.

7. Concentration and decision-making

1. Nideffer, R. (1993). 'Concentration and attention control training.' In J. Williams (ed.), *Applied sport psychology: Personal growth to peak performance*. Second edition: 243 – 261. Mountain View, CA, USA: Mayfield.
2. Nideffer, R. (1976). *The Inner Athlete*. New York, USA: Crowell..
3. Maynard, I., & Howe, B. (1989). 'Attentional Styles in Rugby players.' *Perceptual and Motor Skills* 69, 283–89.
4. Weinberg, R., & Gould, D. (1995). *Foundations of Sport and Exercise Psychology*. Champaign, IL, USA: Human Kinetics.
5. Nideffer, R. (1993). op. cit. (1976) op. cit.
6. Bull, S., Albinson, J., & Shambrook, C. (1996). *The Mental Game Plan: Getting Psyched for Sport*. Eastbourne, UK: Sports Dynamics.
7. Ibid.
8. Nideffer, R. (1993). op. cit. (1976) op. cit.
9. Nideffer, R. (1993). op. cit. (1976) op. cit. Weinberg, R., & Gould, D. (1995) op. cit.
10. Bull, S., Albinson, J., & Shambrook, C. (1996). op. cit.
11. Brewer, M. (1991). *Dominion Sunday Times* 18/8/91, 33.
12. Bull, S., Albinson, J., & Shambrook, C. (1996). op. cit.
13. Bull, S., Albinson, J., & Shambrook, C. (1996). op. cit. Hardy, L., Jones, G., & Gould, D. (1996) *Understanding Psychological Preparation for Sport: Theory and Practice of Elite Performers*. Chichester, UK: John Wiley & Sons.
14. Howe, B. (1991). 'Notes on "Mental Preparation": Canadian Rugby Union.' Unpublished manuscript. University of Victoria, B.C., Can.

8. Team cohesion

1. Hart, J. (1997). 'Coaching in the professional environment.' *New Zealand Coach* 5, 16–19.
2. Cartwright, D., & Zander, A. (1968). *Group Dynamics: Research and Theory*. New York, USA: Harper & Row.
3. Hodge, K. (1995). 'Team dynamics.' In T. Morris & J. Summers (eds.), *Sport Psychology: Theory, Application, and Current Issues*, (190–212). Sydney.: Jacaranda Wiley. Carron, A. V. (1993). 'The sport team as an effective group.' In J. Williams (ed.), *Applied Sport Psychology: Personal Growth to Peak Performance*, Second edition. (110–21). Mountain View, CA, USA: Mayfield.
4. Zander, A. (1982). *Making Groups Effective*. San Francisco, CA: Jossey-Bass.
5. McGrath, J. (1984). *Groups: Interaction and Performance*. Englewood Cliffs, NJ: Prentice-Hall.
6. Hodge, K. (1995). op. cit.
7. Ibid.
8. Steiner, I. (1972). *Group Processes and Group Productivity*. New York, USA: Academic.
9. Hodge, K. (1995). op. cit.
10. Steiner, I. (1972). op. cit.
11. Hardy, C. J. (1990). 'Social Loafing: Motivational Losses in Collective Performance.' *International Journal of Sport Psychology* 21, 305–27.
12. Hardy, C. J., & Latene, B. (1988). 'Social loafing in cheerleaders: Effects of team membership and competition.' *Journal of Sport & Exercise Psychology* 10, 109–114. Harkins, S. G. (1987). 'Social loafing and social facilitation.' *Journal of Experimental Social Psychology* 23, 1–18.
13. Harkins, S. G., & Szymanski, K. (1987). 'Social loafing and social facilitation: New wine in old bottles.' In C. Hendrick (ed.), *Review of Personality and Social Psychology* vol 9, (167–88). Beverly Hills, CA, USA: Sage. Williams, K., Harkins, S., & Latene, B. (1981). 'Identifiability as a deterrent to social loafing: Two cheering experiments.' *Journal of Experimental Social Psychology* 40, 303–11.
14. Latene, B., Williams, K., & Harkins, S. (1979). 'Many hands make light work: The cause and consequences of social loafing'. *Journal of Experimental Social Psychology* 37, 822– 32.
15. Yukelson, D. (1984). 'Group motivation in

sport teams.' In J. Silva & Weinberg, R. (eds.). *Psychological Foundations of Sport* (229–40). Champaign, IL: Human Kinetics.

16. Zander, A. (1975). 'Motivation and performance of sports groups.' In D. M. Landers (ed.), *Psychology of Sport and Motor Behaviour II*. University Park, PA, USA: Pennsylvania State University Press.
Yukelson, D. (1984). op. cit.

17. Zander, A. (1982). op. cit.
Winter, G. (1995). 'Goal Setting.' In J. Summers & T. Morris (eds.). *Sport Psychology: Theory, Applications, and Current Issues* (259–70). Sydney, Aust.: Jacandra Wiley.

18. Larson, C., & LaFasto, F. (1989). *Teamwork: What Must Go Right / What Can Go Wrong*. Newbury Park, CA, USA: Sage.

19. Zander, A. (1975). op. cit.

20. Ibid.

21. Carron, A. (1988). *Group Dynamics in Sport*. London, Ontario, Can.: Spodym.
Westre, K. R., & Weiss, M. R. (1991). 'The Relationship Between Perceived Coaching Behaviours and Group Cohesion in a High School Football Team.' *The Sport Psychologist* 5, 41–54.

22. Zander, A. (1975). op. cit.

23. Yukelson, D. (1993). 'Communicating effectively.' In J. Williams (ed.), *Applied Sport Psychology: Personal Growth to Peak Performance*, Second edition (122–36). Mountain View, CA, USA: Mayfield.

24. Carron, A. (1988). op. cit.

25. Brawley, L. R.; Carron, A. V., & Widmeyer, W. N. (1988). 'Exploring the Relationship Between Cohesion and Group Resistance to Disruption.' *Journal of Sport & Exercise Psychology* 10, 199–213.

26. Carron, A. (1988). op. cit. 23.
Brawley, L. R. (1990). 'Group Cohesion: Status, Problems and Future Directions.' *International Journal of Sport Psychology* 21, 355–79.

27. Ibid.

28. Brown, N. (1997). 'The Cohesion-Performance Relationship in Professional Rugby.' Unpublished Honours Dissertation. University of Otago, NZ.

9. Captaincy and communication

1. Gibson, J. (1994). *When All Is Said And Done*. Sydney, Aust.: Pan Macmillan.

2. Hart, J. (1997). 'Coaching in the professional environment.' *New Zealand Coach* 5, 16–19.

3. Murray, M. C. & Mann, B. L. (1993). 'Leadership effectiveness.' In J. M. Williams (ed.). *Applied Sport Psychology: Personal Growth for Peak Performance*. Second edition. Mountain View, CA, USA: Mayfield.
Weinberg, R. & Gould, D. (1995). *Foundations of Sport and Exercise Psychology*. Champaign, IL, USA: Human Kinetics.

4. Massimo, J. (1973). cited in Murray, M. C. & Mann, B. L. (1993).
Massimo, J. 'Leadership effectiveness.' In J. M. Williams (ed.). *Applied Sport Psychology: Personal Growth for Peak Performance*. Second edition. Mountain View, CA, USA: Mayfield.

5. Ibid.

6. Massimo, J. (1973). op. cit.
Winter, G. (1992). *The Psychology of Cricket: How to Play the Inner Game of Cricket*. Sydney, Aust.: Pan Macmillan.

7. Massimo, J. (1973). op. cit.

8. Murray, M. C. & Mann, B. L. (1993). op. cit.

9. Ibid.

10. Murray, M. C. & Mann, B. L. (1993). op. cit.
Winter, G. (1992). op. cit.

11. Hart, J. (1997). op. cit.

12. Hart, J. (1997). op. cit.
Winter, G. (1992). op. cit.

13. Martens, R. (1990). *Successful Coaching*. Champaign, IL, USA: Human Kinetics.

14. Orlick, T. (1986). *Psyching For Sport: Mental Training For Sport*. Champaign, IL, USA: Human Kinetics.

15. Martens, R. (1990). op. cit.

16. Orlick, T. (1986). op. cit.

17. Ibid.

18. Ibid.

19. Martens, R. (1990). op. cit.

20. Ibid.

21. Orlick, T. (1986). op. cit.

22. Martens, R. (1990). op. cit.
Orlick, T. (1986). op. cit.

23. Orlick, T. (1986). op. cit.

10. Goal setting

1. Gould, D. (1993). 'Goal setting for peak performance.' In J. Williams (ed.), *Applied sport psychology: Personal growth to peak performance*. Second edition. (158–69). Mountain View, CA, USA: Mayfield.

2. Hardy, L. (1986). 'How can we help performers?' *Coaching Focus, 4,* Autumn: 2–3.
3. Gould, D. (1993). op. cit.
4. Kingston, K., & Hardy, L. (1997). 'Effects of different types of goals on processes that support performance.' *The Sport Psychologist* 11, 277–93.
5. See also Hodge, K., Sleivert, G., & McKenzie, A. (1996). *Smart Training for Peak Performance: A Complete Sports Training Guide for Athletes.* Auckland, NZ: Reed.

11. Self-talk

1. Bunker, L., Williams, J., & Zinsser, N. (1993). 'Cognitive Techniques for Improving Performance and Building Confidence.' In J. Williams (ed.), *Applied Sport Psychology* (225–42). Palo Alto, CA, USA: Mayfield.
2. Ibid.
3. Orlick, T. (1986). *Psyching For Sport: Mental Training For Sport.* Champaign, IL, USA: Human Kinetics.

12. Mental preparation

1. Hodge, K. (1994). *Sport Motivation: Training Your Mind for Peak Performance.* Auckland, NZ: Reed.
   Orlick, T. (1986). *Psyching for Sport.* Champaign, IL, USA: Human Kinetics.
2. Brooke, Z. In L. Parore (1997). *Zinzan Brooke's Competitive Edge.* Auckland, NZ: Celebrity Books.
3. International Rugby Board (1998). *IRB WebSite.* http://www.irfb.com/

13. Relaxation techniques

1. Weinberg, R., & Gould, D. (1995). *Foundations of Sport and Exercise Psychology.* Champaign, IL, USA: Human Kinetics.
2. Ibid.
3. Nideffer, R. (1985). *Athlete's Guide to Mental Training.* Champaign IL, USA: Human Kinetics.
4. Nideffer, R. (1985). op. cit.
   Harris, D., & Harris, B. (1984). *The Athlete's Guide to Sport Psychology: Mental Skills for Physical People.* New York, USA: Leisure Press.
5. Nideffer, R. (1985). op. cit.
   Harris, D., & Harris, B. (1984). op. cit.
6. Weinberg, R., & Gould, D. (1995). op. cit.
7. Ibid.

8. Ibid.
9. Ibid.
10. Ibid.
11. Ibid.

14. Imagery

1. Vealey, R.S., & Greenleaf, C.A. (1998). 'Seeing is believing: Understanding and using imagery in sport.' In J.M. Williams (ed.), *Applied sport psychology: Personal growth to peak performance.* Third edition. (237–69). Mountain View, CA, USA: Mayfield.
2. Ibid.
3. Ibid.
4. Pickford, S. (1994). 'The effect of mental imagery on rugby goal-kicking performance.' Unpublished honours dissertation, University of Otago.
5. McKenzie, A.D., & Howe, B.L. (1991). 'The effect of imagery on tackling performance in rugby.' *Journal of Human Movement Studies 20,* 163–76.
6. Vealey, R.S., & Greenleaf, C.A. (1998). op. cit.
7. Feltz, D., & Landers, D. (1983). 'The effects of mental practice on motor skill learning and performance: A meta-analysis.' *Journal of Sport Psychology 5,* 25–57.
8. Orlick, T., & Partington, J. (1988). 'Mental links to excellence.' *The Sport Psychologist 2,* 105–30.
9. Vealey, R.S., & Greenleaf, C.A. (1998). op. cit.
10. Roberts, G.C., Spink, K.S., & Pemberton, C.L. (1986). *Learning Experiences in Sport Psychology.* Champaign, IL, USA: Human Kinetics.
11. Vealey, R.S., & Greenleaf, C.A. (1998). op. cit.
12. Ibid.
13. Ibid.
13. Weinberg, R., & Gould, D. (1995). *Foundations of Sport and Exercise Psychology.* Champaign, IL, USA: Human Kinetics.
14. Orlick, T., & Partington, J. (1988). op cit.
15. Iveleva, L., & Orlick, T. (1991). 'Mental links to enhanced healing: An exploratory study.' *The Sport Psychologist 5,* 25–40.
16. Vealey, R.S., & Greenleaf, C.A. (1998). op. cit.

15. CARS plan

1. Hardy, L., Jones, G., & Gould, D. (1996). *Understanding Psychological Preparation for Sport: Theory and Practice of Elite Performers.* Chichester, UK: John Wiley & Sons.

2. Gould, D., Finch, L., & Jackson, S. (1993). 'Coping strategies used by National champion Figure Skaters' *Research Quarterly for Exercise and Sport* 64, 453–68.'

3. Gould, D., Eklund, R., & Jackson, S. (1993). 'Coping strategies used by U.S. Olympic wrestlers'. *Research Quarterly for Exercise and Sport* 64, 83–93.

4. Hardy, L., Jones, G., & Gould, D. (1996). op. cit.
   Ravizza, K., & Hanson, T. (1995). *Heads-Up Baseball: Playing the Game One Pitch at a Time*. Indianapolis, IN, USA: Masters Press.

5. Ravizza, K., & Hanson, T. (1995). op. cit.

6. Hardy, L., Jones, G., & Gould, D. (1996). op. cit.
   Gould, D., Eklund, R., & Jackson, S. (1993). op. cit.

7. Ravizza, K., & Hanson, T. (1995). op. cit.

8. Ibid.

9. Ibid.

10. Hart, J. (1997). 'Coaching in the professional environment.' *New Zealand Coach* 5, 16–19.

18. PST for rehabilitation from injury

1. Hodge, K., & McNair, P. (1990). 'Psychological Rehabilitation of Sports Injuries.' *New Zealand Journal of Sports Medicine* 18, 64–67.
   Ravizza, K., & Hanson, T. (1995). *Heads-Up Baseball: Playing the Game One Pitch at a Time*. Indianapolis, IN, USA: Masters Press.

2. Sullivan, J. (1998). 'Psychological Rehabilitation of Injured Athletes: A Prospective Study.' Unpublished manuscript, University of Otago, NZ.
   Iveleva, L., & Orlick, T. (1991). 'Mental links to enhanced healing: An exploratory study.' *The Sport Psychologist* 5, 25–40.

3. Hodge, K., & McNair, P. (1990). op. cit.
   Sullivan, J. (1998). op. cit.

4. Sullivan, J. (1998). op. cit.

5. Ravizza, K., & Hanson, T. (1995). op. cit.

6. Sullivan, J. (1998). op. cit.
   Iveleva, L., & Orlick, T. (1991). op. cit.

7. Iveleva, L., & Orlick, T. (1991). op. cit.

8. Ibid.

9. Ravizza, K., & Hanson, T. (1995). op. cit.

10. (1997). 'Gordon Slater's Injury Comeback.' *Sunday Star-Times*, 30/11/97, B4.

11. Ibid.

12. Ravizza, K., & Hanson, T. (1995). op. cit.

13. Ibid.

14. Gould, D., Udry, E., Bridges, D., & Beck, L. (1997). 'Coping with Season-Ending Injuries.' *The Sport Psychologist* 11, 379–99.

19. Retirement and lifestyle management

1. Petitpas, A., Champagne, D., Chartrand, J., Danish, S., & Murphy, S. (1997). *Athlete's Guide to Career Planning: Keys to Success from the Playing Field to Professional Life.* Champaign, IL, USA: Human Kinetics.
   Sinclair, D., & Orlick, T. (1993). 'Positive transitions from high-performance sport.' *The Sport Psychologist* 7. 138–50.

2. Petitpas, A., et al (1997). op. cit.

3. Sinclair, D., & Orlick, T. (1993). op. cit.

4. Johnstone, D. (1998). 'Kiwis to fore in life-after-the-game'. *Sunday Star-Times*, 29/3/98; p. Sport2.

5. Petitpas, A., et al (1997). op. cit.
   Baillie, P. (1993). 'Understanding retirement from sports: Therapeutic ideas for helping athletes in transition.' *The Counselling Psychologist* 21, 399–410.
   Coakley, J. J. (1983). 'Leaving competitive sport: Retirement or rebirth?' *Quest* 35, 1–11.
   Greendorfer, S., & Blinde, E. (1985). 'Retirement from intercollegiate sports: Theoretical and empirical considerations.' *Sociology of Sport Journal* 2, 101–10.
   Murphy, S. (1995). 'Transitions in competitive sport: Maximizing individual potential.' In S. M. Murphy (ed.), *Sport psychology interventions* (331–46). Champaign, IL, USA: Human Kinetics.
   Ogilvie, B. C. (1987). 'Counselling for sports career termination.' In J. R. May, & M. J. Asken (eds.), *Sport psychology: The psychological health of the athlete* (365–82), New York: PMA.

6. Sinclair, D., & Orlick, T. (1993). op. cit.
   Werthner, P., & Orlick, T. (1986). Retirement experiences of successful Olympic athletes. *International Journal of Sport Psychology* 17, 337–63.

7. Gordon, S. (1995). 'Career transitions in competitive sport.' In T. Morris & J. Summers (eds.), *Sport Psychology: Theory, Applications, and Current Issues* (pp. 474–501). Sydney, Aust.: Jacaranda Wiley.

8. Hodge, K. P. (1993). '1992 Olympic report: Sport psychology at the Barcelona Olympics.' *New Zealand Journal of Health, Physical Education, and Recreation* 26, 8–11.
Hodge, K. (1997). 'Retirement from competitive sport: Psychological issues and practical recommendations.' *New Zealand Coach* 5, 5–8.
Strang, F., & Hodge, K. (1996). 'Retirement from competitive swimming: Psychological issues.' Unpublished manuscript, University of Otago, NZ.
9. Johnstone, D. (1998). op. cit.
10. Petitpas, A., et al (1997). op. cit.
Murphy, S. (1995). op. cit.
Orlick, T., & Werthner, P. (1992). *New beginnings: Transitions from high performance sport workbook.* Ottawa: Olympic Athlete Career Centre, Canadian Olympic Association.
11. Petitpas, A., Danish, S., McKelvain, R., & Murphy, S. (1992). 'A career assistance programme for elite athletes.' *Journal of Counselling & Development* 70, 383–86.
12. Orlick, T., & Werthner, P. (1992). op. cit.
13. Blinde, E., & Stratta, T. (1991). 'The "sport career death" of college athletes: Involuntary and unanticipated exits.' *Journal of Sport Behaviour* 15, 3–20.
14. Sinclair, D., & Orlick, T. (1993). op. cit.
Parker, K. (1994). ' "Has-beens" and "Wanna-bes": Transition experiences of former major college football players.' *The Sport Psychologist* 8, 287–304.
Thomas, C., & Ermler, K. (1988). 'Institutional obligations in the athlete retirement process.' *Quest* 40, 137–150.
15. Australian Institute of Sport (1991). *LEAP: Life Skills for Elite Athletes Programme.* Canberra, Australia: Australian Institute of Sport.

NZOCGA (1994). 'Athletes' Olympic Job Opportunity Programme (OJOP).' *NZOCGA 84th Annual Report, December 31, 1994.* Wellington, NZ: New Zealand Olympic and Commonwealth Games Association.
16. Hodge, K., Sleivert, G., & McKenzie, A. (1996). *Smart Training for Peak Performance: A Complete Sports Training Guide for Athletes.* Auckland, NZ: Reed.
17. Pearce, J. (1990). *Eat to Compete: Sports Excellence though Good Nutrition.* Auckland, NZ: Reed.
18. Hodge, K. (1997). 'Retirement from competitive sport: Psychological issues and practical recommendations.' *New Zealand Coach* 5, 5–8.
19. Baillie, P. (1993). op. cit.
Danish, S., Petitpas, A., & Hale, B. (1993). 'Life development intervention for athletes: Life skills through sports.' *The Counselling Psychologist* 21, 352–85.
Hodge, K., & Danish, S. (1998). 'Promoting life skills for adolescent males through sport.' In A. Horne & M. Kiselica. (eds.). *Handbook of counselling boys and adolescent males.* Thousand Oaks, CA: Sage.
20. Hodge, K., & Danish, S. (1998, in press). op. cit.
Hodge, K. P. (1994). 'Mental toughness in sport: Lessons for life.' *Journal of Physical Education New Zealand* 27, 12–16.

20. PST training logbook

1. For more on the use of training logbooks, see: Hodge, K., Sleivert, G., & McKenzie, A. (1996). *Smart Training for Peak Performance: A Complete Sports Training Guide for Athletes.* Auckland, NZ: Reed.

Quote references

The authors gratefully acknowledge the support of authors and publishers of the following works, from which they sourced quotes in the text (page numbers refer to location of quotes in *Thinking Rugby*):

Fox, G., (1992). *The Game, the Goal: The Grant Fox Story.* Auckland, NZ: Rugby Press. 35, 53, 140, 148, 175, 191.

Gifford, P. (1991). *Grizz: The Legend.* Auckland, NZ: Rugby Press. 150.

Howitt, B. & McConnell, R. (1996). *Laurie Mains.* Auckland, NZ: Rugby Press. 16, 55, 58, 112.

Kirwan, J. (1992). *Kirwan: Running on Instinct.* Auckland, NZ: Moa. 52, 78, 128.

Knight, L. (1986). *Knight, Dalton, Ashworth: The Geriatrics.* Auckland, NZ: Moa. 80, 81, 118.

McConnell, R. (1994). *Iceman: The Michael Jones Story.* Auckland, NZ; Rugby Press. 103, 149, 212.

Mourie, G. (1982). *Graham Mourie: Captain.* Auckland, NZ: Moa. 11, 49, 82, 111, 122, 123, 130, 158.

Parore, L. (1997). *Zinzan Brooke's Competitive Edge.* Auckland, NZ: Celebrity Books. 15, 30, 82, 132, 142, 165.

Thomas, P. (1993). *Straight from the Hart.* Auckland, NZ: Moa Beckett. 107.

Veysey, A., Caffell, G., &; Palenski, R (1996). *Lochore: An Authorised Biography.* Auckland, NZ: Moa Beckett. 18, 20, 108, 123.

Inside Sport 136.
New Zealand Coach 23.
NZ Rugby Monthly 53, 214.
NZ Sport Monthly 84, 89, 99.
Nike TV Advertisement 64.
North & South 120, 220.
Otago Daily Times 20, 52, 55, 64, 121, 128, 132, 148, 157, 159, 171, 216.
Pacific Wave 119.
Rugby News 26, 54, 129.
Rugby Rave 19, 47, 56, 67, 72, 124, 204, 205, 206, 210, 219, 220, 221.
Southland Times 74, 101, 207.
Sunday News 174.
Sunday Star-Times 14, 17, 48, 49, 51, 83, 86, 88, 89, 92, 110, 131, 197, 208, 211, 213, 215.
The Evening Post 213.
The Guardian 21, 198.
The Independent 217.
The Listener 217.